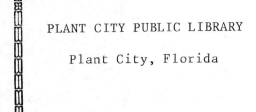

The
California Dante,
in addition to the intro-
duction, facing text, and verse
translation volume dedicated to
each *cantica* of *The Divine Comedy*,
will present, under the General Edi-
torship of Allen Mandelbaum, a separate volume of commentary for each of the
*cantiche*. These three commentary volumes
will constitute the California Lectura Dantis;
in these volumes, which will call on American, Italian, English, German, and other in-
ternational scholar-critics, each contributor
will present his or her reading, in essay
form, of one or of several cantos. The
thirty-three—or in the case of *Inferno*,
thirty-four—canto readings in each
volume will be supplemented
by a comprehensive index-
glossary and synoptic
appendices.

OTHER BOOKS BY ALLEN MANDELBAUM

POETRY

*Journeyman*, 1967
*Leaves of Absence*, 1976
*Chelmaxioms: The Maxims, Axioms, Maxioms of Chelm*, 1978
*A Lied of Letterpress*, 1980
*The Savantasse of Montparnasse* (forthcoming)

VERSE TRANSLATIONS/EDITIONS

*Life of a Man* by Giuseppe Ungaretti, 1958
*Selected Writings of Salvatore Quasimodo*, 1960
*The Aeneid of Virgil*, 1972 (National Book Award, 1973), 1981
*Selected Poems of Giuseppe Ungaretti*, 1975
*Inferno of Dante*, 1980
*Purgatorio of Dante*, 1982
*Mediterranean: Selected Poems of Eugenio Montale* (forthcoming)

DANTE ALIGHIERI

1983

*The Divine Comedy of*

# Dante Alighieri

A Verse Translation

with Introductions & Commentary by

*Allen Mandelbaum*

Drawings by Barry Moser

*University of California Press*

Berkeley · Los Angeles · London

*This translation of the* PARADISO *is inscribed to*
*Toni Burbank and Stanley Holwitz,*
*whose* DOPPIO LUME S'ADDUA

UNIVERSITY OF CALIFORNIA PRESS
Berkeley and Los Angeles, California
University of California Press, Ltd.
London, England

ISBN 0-520-04517-3
Library of Congress Catalogue Number 73-94441

PRINTED IN THE UNITED STATES OF AMERICA

# PARADISO

Part One: Introduction,

Italian Text & Translation,

and Nineteen Drawings

# INTRODUCTION

*Paradiso* is a poem of spectacle, of wheeling shapes that enter and exit, form, re-form, and dis-form; of voices that discourse out of their faceless flames; of letters and words spelled out across the heavens by living lights in flight; of flames that shape the remarkable Eagle; of the vast amphitheater of the Celestial Rose in the tenth and final heaven, the Empyrean, where the blessed range in carefully orchestrated ranks.

That expanse is such that when, some two-thirds of the way through Paradise, the voyager turns his gaze back and downward toward the earth, he sees (XXII, 134–135 and 148–152):

> *. . . this globe in such a way that I*
> *smiled at its meager image . . .*
> . . . . . . . . . . . . . . .
> *And all the seven heavens showed to me*
> *their magnitudes, their speeds, the distances*
> *of each from each. The little threshing floor*
> *that so incites our savagery was all—*
> *from hills to river mouths—revealed to me . . .*

Such cosmic expanse and order does admit of likeness to spacious waters (I, 112–117):

> *Therefore, these natures move to different ports*
> *across the mighty sea of being, each*
> *given the impulse that will bear it on.*
> *This impulse carries fire to the moon;*
> *this is the motive force in mortal creatures;*
> *this binds the earth together, makes it one.*

But that expanse does not allow us solitude or intimacy— with one exception: our intimate entry into the making of the poem, into the atelier, forge, foundry, workshop, mind and heart, of the maker-orchestrator.

Here we find the exilic despair that was so imperative a source of the energies and exhilaration of a work unlike anything Dante had completed before. That despair forms the bitter part of the burden of the prophecy he hears from his ancestor, Cacciaguida, at the center of *Paradiso* (XVII, 55–60):

> *"You shall leave everything you love most dearly:*
> *this is the arrow that the bow of exile*
> *shoots first. You are to know the bitter taste*
> *of others' bread, how salt it is, and know*
> *how hard a path it is for one who goes*
> *descending and ascending others' stairs."*

And here we find the pride that this terminal *cantica* engenders, Dante's sense of the uniqueness of this work as against any wrought prior to him (II, 7–9 and XIX, 7–9):

> *The waves I take were never sailed before;*
> *Minerva breathes, Apollo pilots me,*
> *and the nine Muses show to me the Bears.*
>
> *And what I now must tell has never been*
> *reported by a voice, inscribed by ink,*
> *never conceived by the imagination . . .*

There is pride—and there is the nakedly buoyant, joyous presumption, and even fleeting complacency, of one who contemplates not only from the heights (as in XXII, 148–152, above) but also savors the height itself (XI, 1–12):

> *O senseless cares of mortals, how deceiving*
> *are syllogistic reasonings that bring*
> *your wings to flight so low, to earthly things!*
> *One studied law and one the Aphorisms*
> *of the physicians; one was set on priesthood*
> *and one, through force or fraud, on rulership;*
> *one meant to plunder, one to politick;*
> *one labored, tangled in delights of flesh,*
> *and one was fully bent on indolence;*
> *while I, delivered from our servitude*

*to all these things, was in the height of heaven*
*with Beatrice, so gloriously welcomed.*

And in Dante's envisioning of this ever-widening expanse
—so unlike the ever-narrowing hellish voyage to the deepest
pit, and the hopeful, ever-narrowing voyage to the Mount of
Purgatory's summit—we are asked to share the travail of the
writer, the constraints and limits of speech and memory, as
he struggles with magnitudes. Time and time again, the very
scribe who tells us (x, 22–27):

> *Now, reader, do not leave your bench, but stay*
> *to think on that of which you have foretaste;*
> *you will have much delight before you tire.*
> *I have prepared your fare; now feed yourself,*
> *because that matter of which I am made*
> *the scribe calls all my care unto itself.*

also asks us to enter—intimately—into his cares and concerns
at his own bench. But each of the chimings on obstacles and
barriers, on the immensity of the task, on its impossibility,
only serves to magnify the dimensions and intensity of the
vision—whether it be the vision of the smile of Beatrice, or
of the happiness of St. Peter coming to greet Beatrice, or of
the mystery of the Incarnation.

The full force of these visions rests in and rises from the
temporal shapes and duration of fabulation in the *Comedy*, a
long poem, long in the time of its making ("this work so
shared by heaven and by earth/ that it has made me lean
through these long years," xxv, 2–3). But Dante's leaps and
lapses in the making of *Paradiso*, the gyres and wheelings of
his dervishing desk, do offer, in themselves, another "strange
sight" (xxxiii, 136), an extraordinary spectacle, a vision of the
cunning yet transparent place of Dante's own incarnating
(i, 4–9; xxiii, 55–63; xxiv, 25–27; xxx, 22–33; xxxiii, 55–57,
58–63, 106–108, 121–123):

> *I was within the heaven that receives*
> *more of His light; and I saw things that he*
> *who from that height descends, forgets or can*

not speak; for nearing its desired end,
our intellect sinks into an abyss
so deep that memory fails to follow it.

If all the tongues that Polyhymnia
together with her sisters made most rich
with sweetest milk, should come now to assist
   my singing of the holy smile that lit
the holy face of Beatrice, the truth
would not be reached—not its one-thousandth part.
   And thus, in representing Paradise,
the sacred poem has to leap across,
as does a man who finds his path cut off.

My pen leaps over it; I do not write:
our fantasy and, all the more so, speech
are far too gross for painting folds so deep.

I yield: I am defeated at this passage
more than a comic or a tragic poet
has ever been by a barrier in his theme;
   for like the sun that strikes the frailest eyes,
so does the memory of her sweet smile
deprive me of the use of my own mind.
   From that first day when, in this life, I saw
her face, until I had this vision, no
thing ever cut the sequence of my song,
   but now I must desist from this pursuit,
in verses, of her loveliness, just as
each artist who has reached his limit must.

From that point on, what I could see was greater
than speech can show: at such a sight, it fails—
and memory fails when faced with such excess.

As one who sees within a dream, and, later,
the passion that had been imprinted stays,
but nothing of the rest returns to mind,
   such am I, for my vision almost fades
completely, yet it still distills within
my heart the sweetness that was born of it.

> *What little I recall is to be told,*
> *from this point on, in words more weak than those*
> *of one whose infant tongue still bathes at the breast.*

> *How incomplete is speech, how weak, when set*
> *against my thought! And this, to what I saw*
> *is such—to call it little is too much.*

Much, of course, is tellable, is chartable. We, seated at our benches, intent on Dante's dervishing, may have at hand both the *Paradiso* and a gazetteer for sedentaries therefor, a gazetteer with seven entries for the seven heavenly bodies that were considered planets (and Dante will also call the planets stars)—Moon, Mercury, Venus, Sun, Mars, Jupiter, Saturn. Three additional entries would cover the Eighth Heaven or Sphere of the Fixed Stars, those stars that are invariant in their position in relation to each other; the Ninth Heaven, the "swiftest of the spheres" (I, 123) and "matter's largest sphere" (xxx, 38), the Primum Mobile, the primal source of motion for all the eight spheres that lie below and within it; and the Tenth Heaven, the Empyrean, a Christian addition to the gazetteer, a heaven not envisioned by Ptolemy, Alfraganus, or Alpetragius. This gazetteer—except for the entry under the Empyrean—may well be subject to the cavil muttered by another exile, Osip Mandelstam: "The Middle Ages . . . did not fit into the Ptolemaic system: they took refuge there."

But Dante's refuge is also ours: a way to scan his journey in space, riprap or calculated scaffold, a frame of composition in which he and we can rest, as he labors at the fundamental, experimental, scribal trial and task: invention. We can see the invented becoming memory as it is made, and we can also see Dante outreading readers, conjuring his being remembered in a future. The energy of his invention informs the words of Mandelstam:

> Dante is an antimodernist. His contemporaneity is inexhaustible, measureless, and unending. . . . It is unthinkable to read the cantos of Dante without aiming them in the direction of the present day. They were made for that. They are missiles for capturing the future. They demand the commentary of the *futurum*.

We, bruised by this incredibly cruel century, are part, a small part of that future, and Dante is concerned for his place among us. That concern and desire are momentarily shadowed by his fear that too much truth may offend the readers of his own age. But that shadow is quickly dispelled; for Dante to compromise his words would lose, for him, fame, honor, audience, in the future (xvii, 118–120):

> "Yet if I am a timid friend of truth,
> I fear that I may lose my life among
> those who will call this present, ancient times."

Thus, he holds fast to Cacciaguida's injunction (xvii, 127–134):

> "Nevertheless, all falsehood set aside,
> let all that you have seen be manifest,
> and let them scratch wherever it may itch.
>     For if, at the first taste, your words molest,
> they will, when they have been digested, end
> as living nourishment. As does the wind,
>     so shall your outcry do—the wind that sends
> its roughest blows against the highest peaks . . ."

We, too, as part of the future, are asked by Dante to measure our fitness as readers, to measure our hungering for the fare that he calls the "bread of angels" (ii, 1–6 and 10–15):

> O you who are within your little bark,
> eager to listen, following behind
> my ship that, singing, crosses to deep seas,
>     turn back to see your shores again: do not
> attempt to sail the seas I sail; you may,
> by losing sight of me, be left astray.
>
> . . . . . . . . . . . . . . . . .
>
>     You other few who turned your minds in time
> unto the bread of angels, which provides
> men here with life—but hungering for more—
>     you may indeed commit your vessel to
> the deep salt-sea, keeping your course within
> my wake, ahead of where waves smooth again.

In a literal sense, we may fall short. For to have turned to the "bread of angels" means, in the most probable "translation" of Dante's metaphorical use of biblical manna, to have begun the study of speculative theology. Such study is less than frequent today, such disciplined recognition and schooling of a hungering that can only be fully appeased with the enlightenment found in the beatific vision proper to the angels—and perhaps not even to them.

But the "bread of angels" as object of the hungering of the mind for meaning involves "a reachless goal," a search that must for us, here—and even for the Seraphim there—collide with mystery (XXI, 91–99):

> *"But even Heaven's most enlightened soul,*
> *that Seraph with his eye most set on God,*
> *could not provide the* why, *not satisfy*
>     *what you have asked; for deep in the abyss*
> *of the Eternal Ordinance, it is*
> *cut off from all created beings' vision.*
>     *And to the mortal world, when you return,*
> *tell this, lest men continue to trespass*
> *and set their steps toward such a reachless goal."*

And if "we cannot satisfy/ our mind unless it is enlightened by/ the truth beyond whose boundary no truth lies" (IV, 124–126), then Dante would accord with Stevens's assessment of our earthly situation: "It can never be satisfied, the mind, never."

That collision with mystery, that dissatisfaction of the mind—we do know. It is from this earth that we turn to the "bread of angels," and upon this earth that Dante envisions. That "bread" is also the bread of desire and of the forms that longing engenders. It is the manna that all of us receive in act and memory, the manna of days and nights of grace that lies beyond any algebra of merits.

Now we can set aside the gazetteer. Now we can share the hungering. We, in this future, may lack the resolution and independence of Dante, but we certainly share his metamorphic vicissitudes, the mutabilities of a man who defines himself as one "who by my very nature am/ given to every sort of change" (V, 98–99). And when the changing Dante

appropriates, it is not only the mediators of antiquity, the
gods and muses of his invocations, whom he calls upon; he
also appropriates our age, the future angels of Rilke and of
Stevens; and he even appropriates the still nameless poets of
the future (I, 34–36):

> Great fire can follow a small spark: there may
> be better voices after me to pray
> to Cyrrha's god for aid—that he may answer.

That future also includes the future of the poet after the
completion of the poem. For though Dante's *Paradiso* is completed near the end of his life, his poem is not equatable with
his life. And in the opening of the final canto we are to share
the sense of poetry as prayer—as vocative that pleads not
only for the present need to reach, to see, but also for help in
persevering, in living after the envisioning. The prayer of
Bernard of Clairvaux to Mary, "Virgin mother, daughter of
your Son," after fixing her place as centerpoint in universal
time, turns to the needs of "*this* man," Dante (XXXIII, 19–36):

> "In you compassion is, in you is pity,
> in you is generosity, in you
> is every goodness found in any creature.
>     This man—who from the deepest hollow in
> the universe, up to this height, has seen
> the lives of spirits, one by one—now pleads
>     with you, through grace, to grant him so much virtue
> that he may lift his vision higher still—
> may lift it toward the ultimate salvation.
>     And I, who never burned for my own vision
> more than I burn for his, do offer you
> all of my prayers—and pray that they may not
>     fall short—that, with your prayers, you may disperse
> all of the clouds of his mortality
> so that the Highest Joy be his to see.
>     This, too, o Queen, who can do what you would,
> I ask of you: that after such a vision,
> his sentiments preserve their perseverance."

That Saint Bernard should be the speaker here, and that
this prayer should occupy so privileged a place in *Paradiso*—

these attest to the complex conjoining in Dante of two often diverging paths: the path of intellect and the path of love.

Dante inhabits and inherits the extraordinary intellectual edifice, foreshadowed a century earlier by Abelard, that finds its culmination in the university life and institutions of thirteenth-century Paris. His Ulysses in the *Inferno* may indeed represent Dante's recoiling from the very limits that the ultimate exaltation of intellect may reach, extend, transgress.

Against Abelard and that nascent reason-able tradition stood his ferocious adversary Bernard, emblem of the rich expansion of the language of God-directed love, in which the theologians outdo all poets before—and often including—Dante. That line exalts affection, the ardor of God-seeking.

Aquinas had already charted the erotics of knowing with enduring precision; he had already wed intellect and affect. But in Aquinas, Dante could never have found so central a place for the feminine protagonist of affect: Mary. And in Aquinas, he could certainly not have found his incarnate Beatrice. Beatrice, of course, also shares the modes of argumentation, the instruments of the "other"—intellectual—tradition. If not Theology or Sacred Science itself, she is a confident theologian. But she is, too, a feminine apparition—yet not an icon or idol. She is the living daughter of Memory and Affection.

Mary herself, before Bernard's prayer, had been evoked by Dante in the present tense of the writer writing of his life on our earth, outside the poem of Paradise, in lines that are no less memorable than Bernard's prayer to Mary: "The name of that fair flower which I always/ invoke, at morning and at evening . . ." (XXIII, 88–89), where that fair flower is Mary, the Rosa Mystica, the Mary of the Rosary and "the Rose in which the Word of God became/ flesh" (XXIII, 73–74).

And when Dante evokes Beatrice in Canto XXIII, he finally brings to bear on her two earthly likenesses most dear to him, the maternal and the ornithological, here joined to his stupendous string of dawn and pre-dawn scenes (XXIII, 1–15):

*As does the bird, among beloved branches,*
*when, through the night that hides things from us, she*
*has rested near the nest of her sweet fledglings*
    *and, on an open branch, anticipates*
*the time when she can see their longed-for faces*
*and find the food with which to feed them—chore*
    *that pleases her, however hard her labors—*
*as she awaits the sun with warm affection,*
*steadfastly watching for the dawn to break:*
    *so did my lady stand, erect, intent,*
*turned toward that part of heaven under which*
*the sun is given to less haste; so that,*
    *as I saw her in longing and suspense,*
*I grew to be as one who, while he wants*
*what is not his, is satisfied with hope.*

Along the way to Beatrice as bird among "beloved branches," along the way to Bernard's prayer, we are asked to share the work of a maker who is ever conscious that the praise and enactment of music or dance are auto-celebrations of the movement of verse itself (even as Milton was in praising Harry Lawes, or Hopkins in praising the "colossal smile" of Henry Purcell, or Fray Luis in praising Salinas). A maker conscious, too, that verse can mime the movement of the soul in joyous love (XIV, 19–24):

*As dancers in a ring, when drawn and driven*
*by greater gladness, lift at times their voices*
*and dance their dance with more exuberance,*
    *so, when they heard that prompt, devout request,*
*the blessed circles showed new joyousness*
*in wheeling dance and in amazing song.*

That "amazing song" is sung in a poem that, may, in program, claim to be a timeless poem. *Paradiso* may be intent on the vision of the everlasting, a poem that sees—apparently —what are the simultaneous presences of the blessed in the Empyrean stretched out over time and space only to accommodate Dante's earthly eyes (IV, 37–45):

*"They showed themselves to you here not because*
*this is their sphere, but as a sign for you*

*that in the Empyrean their place is lowest.*
*Such signs are suited to your mind, since from*
*the senses only can it apprehend*
*what then becomes fit for the intellect.*
*And this is why the Bible condescends*
*to human powers, assigning feet and hands*
*to God, but meaning something else instead.''*

Yet Dante does not hesitate to glory in the timing mechanism of the clock and in seeing in its machinery the movement of music, of dance, of the time-borne verse line itself, and of the spirit's growth in love (x, 139–148 and xxiv, 13–18):

*Then, like a clock that calls us at the hour*
*in which the bride of God, on waking, sings*
*matins to her Bridegroom, encouraging*
*His love (when each clock-part both drives and draws),*
*chiming the sounds with notes so sweet that those*
*with spirit well-disposed feel their love grow;*
*so did I see the wheel that moved in glory*
*go round and render voice to voice with such*
*sweetness and such accord that they can not*
*be known except where joy is everlasting.*

*And just as, in a clock's machinery,*
*to one who watches them, the wheels turn so*
*that, while the first wheel seems to rest, the last*
*wheel flies; so did those circling dancers—as*
*they danced to different measures, swift and slow—*
*make me a judge of what their riches were.*

And on the way to Bernard's prayer we will also find that our sympathy with Dante's metamorphic nature has been instructed in one specific way of change within his book of changes: the use of multiple possibilities as instruments and way stations in the conversion of the self to an integral presence (not unakin to Saint Augustine's: "Love made me what I am, that I may be what I was not before"). Variety and vicissitude—even exile—may be the apprenticeship and bondage needed before the freedom of oneness can be reached. (And perhaps this mode of metamorphosis is not that un-Ovidian. Did not Ovid himself beseech a "seamless" way in his incipit?

*My soul would sing of metamorphoses,*
*but since, o gods, you were the source of these*
*bodies becoming other bodies, breathe*
*your breath into my book of changes: may*
*the song I sing be seamless as its way*
*weaves from the world's beginning to our day.)*

To that end, the "*io sol uno*," "I myself/ alone," of *Inferno* (II, 3–4) extends through "I crown and miter you over yourself" of *Purgatorio* (XXVII, 142) to—now in a political context—Dante's best party as his own "self" at the end of the prophecy by Cacciaguida, Dante's ancestor (XVII, 61–69):

*"And what will be most hard for you to bear*
*will be the scheming, senseless company*
*that is to share your fall into this valley;*
*against you they will be insane, completely*
*ungrateful and profane; and yet, soon after,*
*not you but they will have their brows bloodred.*
*Of their insensate acts, the proof will be*
*in the effects; and thus, your honor will*
*be best kept if your party is your self."*

That self finds an almost obsessively narcissistic model in the image of the Three-in-One of the Trinity toward the end of Canto XXXIII (124–126):

*Eternal Light, You only dwell within*
*Yourself, and only You know You; Self-knowing,*
*Self-known, You love and smile upon Yourself!*

But the vast population of the *Comedy* is proof against the claustrophobia of that model, as is Dante's gratefulness in the *Paradiso* to the otherness of Beatrice. Her otherness made possible his engendering the *Paradiso*, even as the otherness of Virgil nurtured the making of *Inferno* and *Purgatorio*. The Paradisiac gratitude of Dante to Beatrice stands in a diptych with his valediction to Virgil (*Purg.* XXX, 43–54), even as her silent smile complements the silent smile of Virgil in the Earthly Paradise, in *Purgatorio*, XXVIII, 147 (*Par.* XXXI, 79–93):

*"O lady, you in whom my hope gains strength,*
*you who, for my salvation, have allowed*

*your footsteps to be left in Hell, in all*
*    the things that I have seen, I recognize*
*the grace and benefit that I, depending*
*upon your power and goodness, have received.*
*    You drew me out from slavery to freedom*
*by all those paths, by all those means that were*
*within your power. Do, in me, preserve*
*    your generosity, so that my soul,*
*which you have healed, when it is set loose from*
*my body, be a soul that you will welcome."*
*    So did I pray. And she, however far*
*away she seemed, smiled, and she looked at me.*
*Then she turned back to the eternal fountain.*

Even as the smile of Beatrice and Dante's gratitude were—earlier—condensed in one of the rare passages in *Paradiso* where Dante is likened to a dreamer (XXIII, 49–54):

*I was as one who, waking from a dream*
*he has forgotten, tries in vain to bring*
*that vision back into his memory,*
*    when I heard what she offered me, deserving*
*of so much gratitude that it can never*
*be canceled from the book that tells the past.*

---

I am no less indebted now, completing this translation of the *Comedy*, to those already acknowledged in the *Inferno* and *Purgatorio* volumes, not least to Laury Magnus, whose "*anima . . . più di me degna*" overlooked one who was "drawn and driven" from the "*selva oscura*" through to "new trees . . . renewed when they bring forth new boughs."

But the *Paradiso* translation was completed under somewhat charred circumstances. In this time, those who have "[i]mparadisa[to] *la mia mente*" and my gazetteer were: Gigliola and Donatella Nocera and their parents in Siracusa, where their Ortygia offered me a blessed stay; Pieraldo Vola in Rome; and Olga and Vittore Branca in Venice. West of the Mississippi, there were the Zwickers and Stangs of St. Louis, the Bassoffs of Boulder, the Richardsons and Feldmans of Denver, the Estesses and Bernards of Houston, and Nanette

Heiman of San Francisco. Eastward of the Mississippi: the Alcalays; Leonard and Rayma Feldman; Leon and Peggy Gold; Gale Sigal and Walter Stiller; K. S. Rust; the Austers; Henry Weinfield and Joyce Block; Thomas Harrison; Leon Gottfried; Anthony Oldcorn, Charles Ross, Teodolinda Barolini, and Giuseppe Di Scipio, colleagues whose work on the *Lectura Dantis* volumes freed me for these ten spheres; the Hanses; the Marianis; and Joseph Marbach, a truly Hippocratic physician *"che natura/ a li animali fé ch'ell' ha più cari."*

After the death of my mother, Leah Gordon Mandelbaum, at the completion of this work, Ely Pilchik provided unexpected Paradisiac consolation, as did shared readings with my seminar at the Graduate Center.

The visit of Mario Luzi to the States—so warmly abetted by Jon Snyder and Francesca Valente—focused much for us both in mulling on magma and metamorphosis. Anne Greenberg, Cecilia Hunt, and Daniel Feldman nurtured editorially beyond anything my *ruminare* and *vanare* could conjure. For Barry Moser, Michael Bixler, Czeslaw Jan Grycz, and myself, the road of this bookmaking has indeed been such that *dicer*, *cor*, and labor "shared one way." The most tenacious tutelary spirits, whose "double lights" gave me the strength to see The End, share the dedication of this book; New York to Los Angeles spans much less than their *magnificenza* does.

In Valbonne and Mougins, Elisa and Nicholas, grandchildren whose "differing voices join to sound sweet music," were joined in turn by Margherita, Jonathan, and Anne in amply providing the "bread of angels."

*The Graduate Center*                      Allen Mandelbaum
*of the City University of New York*
*May, 1984*

# PARADISO

PARADISO

# CANTO I

The glory of the One who moves all things
permeates the universe but glows
in one part more and in another less.
    I was within the heaven that receives      4
more of His light; and I saw things that he
who from that height descends, forgets or can
    not speak; for nearing its desired end,      7
our intellect sinks into an abyss
so deep that memory fails to follow it.
    Nevertheless, as much as I, within      10
my mind, could treasure of the holy kingdom
shall now become the matter of my song.
    O good Apollo, for this final task      13
make me the vessel of your excellence,
what you, to merit your loved laurel, ask.
    Until this point, one of Parnassus' peaks      16
sufficed for me; but now I face the test,
the agon that is left; I need both crests.
    Enter into my breast; within me breathe      19
the very power you made manifest
when you drew Marsyas out from his limbs' sheath.
    O godly force, if you so lend yourself      22
to me, that I might show the shadow of
the blessed realm inscribed within my mind,
    then you would see me underneath the tree      25
you love; there I shall take as crown the leaves
of which my theme and you shall make me worthy.
    So seldom, father, are those garlands gathered      28
for triumph of a ruler or a poet—
a sign of fault or shame in human wills—
    that when Peneian branches can incite      31
someone to long and thirst for them, delight
must fill the happy Delphic deity.

*Proem and Invocation to Apollo. Dante's passing beyond the human, beyond the earth, in heavenward ascent with Beatrice. His wonder. Beatrice on the Empyrean and the order of the universe.*

La gloria di colui che tutto move
per l'universo penetra, e risplende
in una parte più e meno altrove.

Nel ciel che più de la sua luce prende     4
fu' io, e vidi cose che ridire
né sa né può chi di là sù discende;

perché appressando sé al suo disire,     7
nostro intelletto si profonda tanto,
che dietro la memoria non può ire.

Veramente quant' io del regno santo     10
ne la mia mente potei far tesoro,
sarà ora materia del mio canto.

O buono Appollo, a l'ultimo lavoro     13
fammi del tuo valor sì fatto vaso,
come dimandi a dar l'amato alloro.

Infino a qui l'un giogo di Parnaso     16
assai mi fu; ma or con amendue
m'è uopo intrar ne l'aringo rimaso.

Entra nel petto mio, e spira tue     19
sì come quando Marsïa traesti
de la vagina de le membra sue.

O divina virtù, se mi ti presti     22
tanto che l'ombra del beato regno
segnata nel mio capo io manifesti,

vedra'mi al piè del tuo diletto legno     25
venire, e coronarmi de le foglie
che la materia e tu mi farai degno.

Sì rade volte, padre, se ne coglie     28
per trïunfare o cesare o poeta,
colpa e vergogna de l'umane voglie,

che parturir letizia in su la lieta     31
delfica deïtà dovria la fronda
peneia, quando alcun di sé asseta.

Great fire can follow a small spark: there may          34
be better voices after me to pray
to Cyrrha's god for aid—that he may answer.

The lantern of the world approaches mortals          37
by varied paths; but on that way which links
four circles with three crosses, it emerges

joined to a better constellation and          40
along a better course, and it can temper
and stamp the world's wax more in its own manner.

Its entry from that point of the horizon          43
brought morning there and evening here; almost
all of that hemisphere was white—while ours

was dark—when I saw Beatrice turn round          46
and left, that she might see the sun; no eagle
has ever stared so steadily at it.

And as a second ray will issue from          49
the first and reascend, much like a pilgrim
who seeks his home again, so on her action,

fed by my eyes to my imagination,          52
my action drew, and on the sun I set
my sight more than we usually do.

More is permitted to our powers there          55
than is permitted here, by virtue of
that place, made for mankind as its true home.

I did not bear it long, but not so briefly          58
as not to see it sparkling round about,
like molten iron emerging from the fire;

and suddenly it seemed that day had been          61
added to day, as if the One who can
had graced the heavens with a second sun.

The eyes of Beatrice were all intent          64
on the eternal circles; from the sun,
I turned aside; I set my eyes on her.

In watching her, within me I was changed          67
as Glaucus changed, tasting the herb that made
him a companion of the other sea gods.

Passing beyond the human cannot be          70
worded; let Glaucus serve as simile—
until grace grant you the experience.

Whether I only was the part of me          73
that You created last, You—governing
the heavens—know: it was Your light that raised me.

Poca favilla gran fiamma seconda:      34
forse di retro a me con miglior voci
si pregherà perché Cirra risponda.

    Surge ai mortali per diverse foci      37
la lucerna del mondo; ma da quella
che quattro cerchi giugne con tre croci,

    con miglior corso e con migliore stella      40
esce congiunta, e la mondana cera
più a suo modo tempera e suggella.

    Fatto avea di là mane e di qua sera      43
tal foce, e quasi tutto era là bianco
quello emisperio, e l'altra parte nera,

    quando Beatrice in sul sinistro fianco      46
vidi rivolta e riguardar nel sole:
aguglia sì non li s'affisse unquanco.

    E sì come secondo raggio suole      49
uscir del primo e risalire in suso,
pur come pelegrin che tornar vuole,

    così de l'atto suo, per li occhi infuso      52
ne l'imagine mia, il mio si fece,
e fissi li occhi al sole oltre nostr' uso.

    Molto è licito là, che qui non lece      55
a le nostre virtù, mercé del loco
fatto per proprio de l'umana spece.

    Io nol soffersi molto, né sì poco,      58
ch'io nol vedessi sfavillar dintorno,
com' ferro che bogliente esce del foco;

    e di sùbito parve giorno a giorno      61
essere aggiunto, come quei che puote
avesse il ciel d'un altro sole addorno.

    Beatrice tutta ne l'etterne rote      64
fissa con li occhi stava; e io in lei
le luci fissi, di là sù rimote.

    Nel suo aspetto tal dentro mi fei,      67
qual si fé Glauco nel gustar de l'erba
che 'l fé consorto in mar de li altri dèi.

    Trasumanar significar *per verba*      70
non si poria; però l'essemplo basti
a cui esperïenza grazia serba.

    S'i' era sol di me quel che creasti      73
novellamente, amor che 'l ciel governi,
tu 'l sai, che col tuo lume mi levasti.

When that wheel which You make eternal through   76
the heavens' longing for You drew me with
the harmony You temper and distinguish,

   the fire of the sun then seemed to me   79
to kindle so much of the sky, that rain
or river never formed so broad a lake.

   The newness of the sound and the great light   82
incited me to learn their cause—I was
more keen than I had ever been before.

   And she who read me as I read myself,   85
to quiet the commotion in my mind,
opened her lips before I opened mine

   to ask, and she began: "You make yourself   88
obtuse with false imagining; you can
not see what you would see if you dispelled it.

   You are not on the earth as you believe;   91
but lightning, flying from its own abode,
is less swift than you are, returning home."

   While I was freed from my first doubt by these   94
brief words she smiled to me, I was yet caught
in new perplexity. I said: "I was

   content already; after such great wonder,   97
I rested. But again I wonder how
my body rises past these lighter bodies."

   At which, after a sigh of pity, she   100
settled her eyes on me with the same look
a mother casts upon a raving child,

   and she began: "All things, among themselves,   103
possess an order; and this order is
the form that makes the universe like God.

   Here do the higher beings see the imprint   106
of the Eternal Worth, which is the end
to which the pattern I have mentioned tends.

   Within that order, every nature has   109
its bent, according to a different station,
nearer or less near to its origin.

   Therefore, these natures move to different ports   112
across the mighty sea of being, each
given the impulse that will bear it on.

   This impulse carries fire to the moon;   115
this is the motive force in mortal creatures;
this binds the earth together, makes it one.

Quando la rota che tu sempiterni          76
desiderato, a sé mi fece atteso
con l'armonia che temperi e discerni,

    parvemi tanto allor del cielo acceso          79
de la fiamma del sol, che pioggia o fiume
lago non fece alcun tanto disteso.

    La novità del suono e 'l grande lume          82
di lor cagion m'accesero un disio
mai non sentito di cotanto acume.

    Ond' ella, che vedea me sì com' io,          85
a quïetarmi l'animo commosso,
pria ch'io a dimandar, la bocca aprio

    e cominciò: "Tu stesso ti fai grosso          88
col falso imaginar, sì che non vedi
ciò che vedresti se l'avessi scosso.

    Tu non se' in terra, sì come tu credi;          91
ma folgore, fuggendo il proprio sito,
non corse come tu ch'ad esso riedi."

    S'io fui del primo dubbio disvestito          94
per le sorrise parolette brevi,
dentro ad un nuovo più fu' inretito

    e dissi: "Già contento *requievi*          97
di grande ammirazion; ma ora ammiro
com' io trascenda questi corpi levi."

    Ond' ella, appresso d'un pïo sospiro,          100
li occhi drizzò ver' me con quel sembiante
che madre fa sovra figlio deliro,

    e cominciò: "Le cose tutte quante          103
hanno ordine tra loro, e questo è forma
che l'universo a Dio fa simigliante.

    Qui veggion l'alte creature l'orma          106
de l'etterno valore, il qual è fine
al quale è fatta la toccata norma.

    Ne l'ordine ch'io dico sono accline          109
tutte nature, per diverse sorti,
più al principio loro e men vicine;

    onde si muovono a diversi porti          112
per lo gran mar de l'essere, e ciascuna
con istinto a lei dato che la porti.

    Questi ne porta il foco inver' la luna;          115
questi ne' cor mortali è permotore;
questi la terra in sé stringe e aduna;

Not only does the shaft shot from this bow                  118
strike creatures lacking intellect, but those
who have intelligence, and who can love.

   The Providence that has arrayed all this                 121
forever quiets—with Its light—that heaven
in which the swiftest of the spheres revolves;

   to there, as toward a destined place, we now             124
are carried by the power of the bow
that always aims its shaft at a glad mark.

   Yet it is true that, even as a shape                     127
may, often, not accord with art's intent,
since matter may be unresponsive, deaf,

   so, from this course, the creature strays at times       130
because he has the power, once impelled,
to swerve elsewhere; as lightning from a cloud

   is seen to fall, so does the first impulse,              133
when man has been diverted by false pleasure,
turn him toward earth. You should—if I am right—

   not feel more marvel at your climbing than               136
you would were you considering a stream
that from a mountain's height falls to its base.

   It would be cause for wonder in you if,                  139
no longer hindered, you remained below,
as if, on earth, a living flame stood still.''

   Then she again turned her gaze heavenward.               142

né pur le creature che son fore 118
d'intelligenza quest' arco saetta,
ma quelle c'hanno intelletto e amore.

La provedenza, che cotanto assetta, 121
del suo lume fa 'l ciel sempre quïeto
nel qual si volge quel c'ha maggior fretta;

e ora lì, come a sito decreto, 124
cen porta la virtù di quella corda
che ciò che scocca drizza in segno lieto.

Vero è che, come forma non s'accorda 127
molte fïate a l'intenzion de l'arte,
perch' a risponder la materia è sorda,

così da questo corso si diparte 130
talor la creatura, c'ha podere
di piegar, così pinta, in altra parte;

e sì come veder si può cadere 133
foco di nube, sì l'impeto primo
l'atterra torto da falso piacere.

Non dei più ammirar, se bene stimo, 136
lo tuo salir, se non come d'un rivo
se d'alto monte scende giuso ad imo.

Maraviglia sarebbe in te se, privo 139
d'impedimento, giù ti fossi assiso,
com' a terra quïete in foco vivo."

Quinci rivolse inver' lo cielo il viso. 142

OVERLEAF:
*Beatrice*
*The Sun*

# CANTO II

O you who are within your little bark,
eager to listen, following behind
my ship that, singing, crosses to deep seas,
    turn back to see your shores again: do not          4
attempt to sail the seas I sail; you may,
by losing sight of me, be left astray.
    The waves I take were never sailed before;         7
Minerva breathes, Apollo pilots me,
and the nine Muses show to me the Bears.
    You other few who turned your minds in time    10
unto the bread of angels, which provides
men here with life—but hungering for more—
    you may indeed commit your vessel to         13
the deep salt-sea, keeping your course within
my wake, ahead of where waves smooth again.
    Those men of glory, those who crossed to Colchis,  16
when they saw Jason turn into a ploughman
were less amazed than you will be amazed.
    The thirst that is innate and everlasting—    19
thirst for the godly realm—bore us away
as swiftly as the heavens that you see.
    Beatrice gazed upward. I watched her.        22
But in a span perhaps no longer than
an arrow takes to strike, to fly, to leave
    the bow, I reached a place where I could see    25
that something wonderful drew me; and she
from whom my need could not be hidden, turned
    to me (her gladness matched her loveliness):    28
"Direct your mind to God in gratefulness,"
she said; "He has brought us to the first star."
    It seemed to me that we were covered by      31
a brilliant, solid, dense, and stainless cloud,
much like a diamond that the sun has struck.

*Address to the reader. Arrival in the First Heaven, the Sphere of the Moon. Beatrice's vigorous confutation of Dante, who thinks that rarity and density are the causes of the spots we see on the body of the Moon.*

O voi che siete in piccioletta barca,
desiderosi d'ascoltar, seguiti
dietro al mio legno che cantando varca,

    tornate a riveder li vostri liti:            4
non vi mettete in pelago, ché forse,
perdendo me, rimarreste smarriti.

    L'acqua ch'io prendo già mai non si corse;    7
Minerva spira, e conducemi Appollo,
e nove Muse mi dimostran l'Orse.

    Voialtri pochi che drizzaste il collo        10
per tempo al pan de li angeli, del quale
vivesi qui ma non sen vien satollo,

    metter potete ben per l'alto sale         13
vostro navigio, servando mio solco
dinanzi a l'acqua che ritorna equale.

    Que' glorïosi che passaro al Colco        16
non s'ammiraron come voi farete,
quando Iasón vider fatto bifolco.

    La concreata e perpetüa sete           19
del deïforme regno cen portava
veloci quasi come 'l ciel vedete.

    Beatrice in suso, e io in lei guardava;    22
e forse in tanto in quanto un quadrel posa
e vola e da la noce si dischiava,

    giunto mi vidi ove mirabil cosa        25
mi torse il viso a sé; e però quella
cui non potea mia cura essere ascosa,

    volta ver' me, sì lieta come bella,        28
"Drizza la mente in Dio grata," mi disse,
"che n'ha congiunti con la prima stella."

    Parev' a me che nube ne coprisse        31
lucida, spessa, solida e pulita,
quasi adamante che lo sol ferisse.

Into itself, the everlasting pearl                                                      34
received us, just as water will accept
a ray of light and yet remain intact.

    If I was body (and on earth we can                                                  37
not see how things material can share
one space—the case, when body enters body),

    then should our longing be still more inflamed                                      40
to see that Essence in which we discern
how God and human nature were made one.

    What we hold here by faith, shall there be seen,                                    43
not demonstrated but directly known,
even as the first truth that man believes.

    I answered: "With the most devotion I                                               46
can summon, I thank Him who has brought me
far from the mortal world. But now tell me:

    what are the dark marks on this planet's body                                       49
that there below, on earth, have made men tell
the tale of Cain?" She smiled somewhat, and then

    she said: "If the opinion mortals hold                                              52
falls into error when the senses' key
cannot unlock the truth, you should not be

    struck by the arrows of amazement once                                              55
you recognize that reason, even when
supported by the senses, has short wings.

    But tell me what you think of it yourself."                                         58
And I: "What seems to us diverse up here
is caused—I think—by matter dense and rare."

    And she: "You certainly will see that your                                          61
belief is deeply sunk in error if
you listen carefully as I rebut it.

    The eighth sphere offers many lights to you,                                        64
and you can tell that they, in quality
and size, are stars with different visages.

    If rarity and density alone                                                         67
caused this, then all the stars would share one power
distributed in lesser, greater, or

    in equal force. But different powers must                                           70
be fruits of different formal principles;
were you correct, one only would be left,

    the rest, destroyed. And more, were rarity                                          73
the cause of the dim spots you question, then
in part this planet would lack matter through

Per entro sé l'etterna margarita 34
ne ricevette, com' acqua recepe
raggio di luce permanendo unita.

S'io era corpo, e qui non si concepe 37
com' una dimensione altra patìo,
ch'esser convien se corpo in corpo repe,

accender ne dovria più il disio 40
di veder quella essenza in che si vede
come nostra natura e Dio s'unio.

Lì si vedrà ciò che tenem per fede, 43
non dimostrato, ma fia per sé noto
a guisa del ver primo che l'uom crede.

Io rispuosi: "Madonna, sì devoto 46
com' esser posso più, ringrazio lui
lo qual dal mortal mondo m'ha remoto.

Ma ditemi: che son li segni bui 49
di questo corpo, che là giuso in terra
fan di Cain favoleggiare altrui?"

Ella sorrise alquanto, e poi "S'elli erra 52
l'oppinïon," mi disse, "d'i mortali
dove chiave di senso non diserra,

certo non ti dovrien punger li strali 55
d'ammirazione omai, poi dietro ai sensi
vedi che la ragione ha corte l'ali.

Ma dimmi quel che tu da te ne pensi." 58
E io: "Ciò che n'appar qua sù diverso
credo che fanno i corpi rari e densi."

Ed ella: "Certo assai vedrai sommerso 61
nel falso il creder tuo, se bene ascolti
l'argomentar ch'io li farò avverso.

La spera ottava vi dimostra molti 64
lumi, li quali e nel quale e nel quanto
notar si posson di diversi volti.

Se raro e denso ciò facesser tanto, 67
una sola virtù sarebbe in tutti,
più e men distributa e altrettanto.

Virtù diverse esser convegnon frutti 70
di princìpi formali, e quei, for ch'uno,
seguiterieno a tua ragion distrutti.

Ancor, se raro fosse di quel bruno 73
cagion che tu dimandi, o d'oltre in parte
fora di sua materia sì digiuno

and through, or else as, in a body, lean                76
and fat can alternate, so would this planet
alternate the pages in its volume.

    To validate the first case, in the sun's           79
eclipse, the light would have to show through, just
as when it crosses matter that is slender.

    This is not so; therefore we must consider          82
the latter case—if I annul that too,
then your opinion surely is confuted.

    If rarity does not run through and through          85
the moon, then there must be a limit where
thickness does not allow the light to pass;

    from there, the rays of sun would be thrown back,    88
just as, from glass that hides lead at its back,
a ray of colored light returns, reflected.

    Now you will say that where a ray has been          91
reflected from a section farther back,
that ray will show itself to be more dim.

    Yet an experiment, were you to try it,              94
could free you from your cavil—and the source
of your arts' course springs from experiment.

    Taking three mirrors, place a pair of them          97
at equal distance from you; set the third
midway between those two, but farther back.

    Then, turning toward them, at your back have placed  100
a light that kindles those three mirrors and
returns to you, reflected by them all.

    Although the image in the farthest glass            103
will be of lesser size, there you will see
that it must match the brightness of the rest.

    Now, just as the sub-matter of the snow,            106
beneath the blows of the warm rays, is stripped
of both its former color and its cold,

    so is your mind left bare of error; I               109
would offer now to you a new form, light
so living that it trembles in your sight.

    Within the heaven of the godly peace                112
revolves a body in whose power lies
the being of all things that it enfolds.

    The sphere that follows, where so much is shown,    115
to varied essences bestows that being,
to stars distinct and yet contained in it.

esto pianeto, o, sì come comparte 76
lo grasso e 'l magro un corpo, così questo
nel suo volume cangerebbe carte.

Se 'l primo fosse, fora manifesto 79
ne l'eclissi del sol, per trasparere
lo lume come in altro raro ingesto.

Questo non è: però è da vedere 82
de l'altro; e s'elli avvien ch'io l'altro cassi,
falsificato fia lo tuo parere.

S'elli è che questo raro non trapassi, 85
esser conviene un termine da onde
lo suo contrario più passar non lassi;

e indi l'altrui raggio si rifonde 88
così come color torna per vetro
lo qual di retro a sé piombo nasconde.

Or dirai tu ch'el si dimostra tetro 91
ivi lo raggio più che in altre parti,
per esser lì refratto più a retro.

Da questa instanza può deliberarti 94
esperïenza, se già mai la provi,
ch'esser suol fonte ai rivi di vostr' arti.

Tre specchi prenderai; e i due rimovi 97
da te d'un modo, e l'altro, più rimosso,
tr'ambo li primi li occhi tuoi ritrovi.

Rivolto ad essi, fa che dopo il dosso 100
ti stea un lume che i tre specchi accenda
e torni a te da tutti ripercosso.

Ben che nel quanto tanto non si stenda 103
la vista più lontana, lì vedrai
come convien ch'igualmente risplenda.

Or, come ai colpi de li caldi rai 106
de la neve riman nudo il suggetto
e dal colore e dal freddo primai,

così rimaso te ne l'intelletto 109
voglio informar di luce sì vivace,
che ti tremolerà nel suo aspetto.

Dentro dal ciel de la divina pace 112
si gira un corpo ne la cui virtute
l'esser di tutto suo contento giace.

Lo ciel seguente, c'ha tante vedute, 115
quell' esser parte per diverse essenze,
da lui distratte e da lui contenute.

The other spheres, in ways diverse, direct 118
the diverse powers they possess, so that
these forces can bear fruit, attain their aims.

So do these organs of the universe 121
proceed, as you now see, from stage to stage,
receiving from above and acting downward.

Now do attend to how I pass by way 124
of reason to the truth you want that—then—
you may learn how to cross the ford alone.

The force and motion of the holy spheres 127
must be inspired by the blessed movers,
just as the smith imparts the hammer's art;

and so, from the deep Mind that makes it wheel, 130
the sphere that many lights adorn receives
that stamp of which it then becomes the seal.

And as the soul within your dust is shared 133
by different organs, each most suited to
a different potency, so does that Mind

unfold and multiply its bounty through 136
the varied heavens, though that Intellect
itself revolves upon its unity.

With the dear body that it quickens and 139
with which, as life in you, it too is bound,
each different power forms a different compound.

Because of the glad nature of its source, 142
the power mingled with a sphere shines forth,
as gladness, through the living pupil, shines.

From this, and not from matter rare or dense, 145
derive the differences from light to light;
this is the forming principle, producing,

conforming with its worth, the dark, the bright." 148

Li altri giron per varie differenze 118
le distinzion che dentro da sé hanno
dispongono a lor fini e lor semenze.

Questi organi del mondo così vanno, 121
come tu vedi omai, di grado in grado,
che di sù prendono e di sotto fanno.

Riguarda bene omai sì com' io vado 124
per questo loco al vero che disiri,
sì che poi sappi sol tener lo guado.

Lo moto e la virtù d'i santi giri, 127
come dal fabbro l'arte del martello,
da' beati motor convien che spiri;

e 'l ciel cui tanti lumi fanno bello, 130
de la mente profonda che lui volve
prende l'image e fassene suggello.

E come l'alma dentro a vostra polve 133
per differenti membra e conformate
a diverse potenze si risolve,

così l'intelligenza sua bontate 136
multiplicata per le stelle spiega,
girando sé sovra sua unitate.

Virtù diverso fa diversa lega 139
col prezïoso corpo ch'ella avviva,
nel qual, sì come vita in voi, si lega.

Per la natura lieta onde deriva, 142
la virtù mista per lo corpo luce
come letizia per pupilla viva.

Da essa vien ciò che da luce a luce 145
par differente, non da denso e raro;
essa è formal principio che produce,

conforme a sua bontà, lo turbo e 'l chiaro." 148

# CANTO III

That sun which first had warmed my breast with love
had now revealed to me, confuting, proving,
the gentle face of truth, its loveliness;
    and I, in order to declare myself            4
corrected and convinced, lifted my head
as high as my confessional required.
    But a new vision showed itself to me;             7
the grip in which it held me was so fast
that I did not remember to confess.
    Just as, returning through transparent, clean    10
glass, or through waters calm and crystalline
(so shallow that they scarcely can reflect),
    the mirrored image of our faces meets          13
our pupils with no greater force than that
a pearl has when displayed on a white forehead—
    so faint, the many faces I saw keen           16
to speak; thus, my mistake was contrary
to that which led the man to love the fountain.
    As soon as I had noticed them, thinking       19
that what I saw were merely mirrorings,
I turned around to see who they might be;
    and I saw nothing; and I let my sight         22
turn back to meet the light of my dear guide,
who, as she smiled, glowed in her holy eyes.
    "There is no need to wonder if I smile,"     25
she said, "because you reason like a child;
your steps do not yet rest upon the truth;
    your mind misguides you into emptiness:    28
what you are seeing are true substances,
placed here because their vows were not fulfilled.
    Thus, speak and listen; trust what they will say:  31
the truthful light in which they find their peace
will not allow their steps to turn astray."

*The First Heaven: the Sphere of the Moon. Dante's first vision*
*of the blessed. Piccarda Donati. Her explanation of the souls'*
*place in the sphere assigned to them by God. The Moon as site*
*of those whose vows gave way before violence. The empress*
*Constance. Disappearance of the souls.*

Quel sol che pria d'amor mi scaldò 'l petto,
di bella verità m'avea scoverto,
provando e riprovando, il dolce aspetto;

e io, per confessar corretto e certo     4
me stesso, tanto quanto si convenne
leva' il capo a proferer più erto;

ma visïone apparve che ritenne     7
a sé me tanto stretto, per vedersi,
che di mia confession non mi sovvenne.

Quali per vetri trasparenti e tersi,     10
o ver per acque nitide e tranquille,
non sì profonde che i fondi sien persi.

tornan d'i nostri visi le postille     13
debili sì, che perla in bianca fronte
non vien men forte a le nostre pupille;

tali vid' io più facce a parlar pronte;     16
per ch'io dentro a l'error contrario corsi
a quel ch'accese amor tra l'omo e 'l fonte.

Sùbito sì com' io di lor m'accorsi,     19
quelle stimando specchiati sembianti,
per veder di cui fosser, li occhi torsi;

e nulla vidi, e ritorsili avanti     22
dritti nel lume de la dolce guida,
che, sorridendo, ardea ne li occhi santi.

"Non ti maravigliar perch' io sorrida,"     25
mi disse, "appresso il tuo püeril coto,
poi sopra 'l vero ancor lo piè non fida,

ma te rivolve, come suole, a vòto:     28
vere sustanze son ciò che tu vedi,
qui rilegate per manco di voto.

Però parla con esse e odi e credi;     31
ché la verace luce che le appaga
da sé non lascia lor torcer li piedi."

Then I turned to the shade that seemed most anxious   34
to speak, and I began as would a man
bewildered by desire too intense:

   "O spirit born to goodness, you who feel,   37
beneath the rays of the eternal life,
that sweetness which cannot be known unless

   it is experienced, it would be gracious   40
of you to let me know your name and fate."
At this, unhesitant, with smiling eyes:

   "Our charity will never lock its gates   43
against just will; our love is like the Love
that would have all Its court be like Itself.

   Within the world I was a nun, a virgin;   46
and if your mind attends and recollects,
my greater beauty here will not conceal me,

   and you will recognize me as Piccarda,   49
who, placed here with the other blessed ones,
am blessed within the slowest of the spheres.

   Our sentiments, which only serve the flame   52
that is the pleasure of the Holy Ghost,
delight in their conforming to His order.

   And we are to be found within a sphere   55
this low, because we have neglected vows,
so that in some respect we were deficient."

   And I to her: "Within your wonderful   58
semblance there is something divine that glows,
transforming the appearance you once showed:

   therefore, my recognizing you was slow;   61
but what you now have told me is of help;
I can identify you much more clearly.

   But tell me: though you're happy here, do you   64
desire a higher place in order to
see more and to be still more close to Him?"

   Together with her fellow shades she smiled   67
at first; then she replied to me with such
gladness, like one who burns with love's first flame:

   "Brother, the power of love appeases our   70
will so—we only long for what we have;
our yearning calls upon no other thing.

   Should we desire a higher sphere than ours,   73
then our desires would be discordant with
the will of Him who has assigned us here,

E io a l'ombra che parea più vaga      34
di ragionar, drizza'mi, e cominciai,
quasi com' uom cui troppa voglia smaga:
   "O ben creato spirito, che a' rai      37
di vita etterna la dolcezza senti
che, non gustata, non s'intende mai.
   grazïoso mi fia se mi contenti      40
del nome tuo e de la vostra sorte."
Ond' ella, pronta e con occhi ridenti:
   "La nostra carità non serra porte      43
a giusta voglia, se non come quella
che vuol simile a sé tutta sua corte.
   I' fui nel mondo vergine sorella;      46
e se la mente tua ben sé riguarda,
non mi ti celerà l'esser più bella.
   ma riconoscerai ch'i' son Piccarda,      49
che, posta qui con questi altri beati,
beata sono in la spera più tarda.
   Li nostri affetti, che solo infiammati      52
son nel piacer de lo Spirito Santo,
letizian del suo ordine formati.
   E questa sorte che par giù cotanto,      55
però n'è data, perché fuor negletti
li nostri voti, e vòti in alcun canto."
   Ond' io a lei: "Ne' mirabili aspetti      58
vostri risplende non so che divino
che vi trasmuta da' primi concetti:
   però non fui a rimembrar festino;      61
ma or m'aiuta ciò che tu mi dici,
sì che raffigurar m'è più latino.
   Ma dimmi: voi che siete qui felici,      64
disiderate voi più alto loco
per più vedere e per più farvi amici?"
   Con quelle altr' ombre pria sorrise un poco;      67
da indi mi rispuose tanto lieta,
ch'arder parea d'amor nel primo foco:
   "Frate, la nostra volontà quïeta      70
virtù di carità, che fa volerne
sol quel ch'avemo, e d'altro non ci asseta.
   Se disïassimo esser più superne,      73
foran discordi li nostri disiri
dal voler di colui che ne cerne;

but you'll see no such discord in these spheres; 76
to live in love is—here—necessity,
if you think on love's nature carefully.
   The essence of this blessed life consists 79
in keeping to the boundaries of God's will,
through which our wills become one single will;
   so that, as we are ranged from step to step 82
throughout this kingdom, all this kingdom wills
that which will please the King whose will is rule.
   And in His will there is our peace: that sea 85
to which all beings move—the beings He
creates or nature makes—such is His will."
   Then it was clear to me how every place 88
in Heaven is in Paradise, though grace
does not rain equally from the High Good.
   But just as, when our hunger has been sated 91
with one food, we still long to taste the other—
while thankful for the first, we crave the latter—
   so was I in my words and in my gestures, 94
asking to learn from her what was the web
of which her shuttle had not reached the end.
   "A perfect life," she said, "and her high merit 97
enheaven, up above, a woman whose
rule governs those who, in your world, would wear
   nuns' dress and veil, so that, until their death, 100
they wake and sleep with that Spouse who accepts
all vows that love conforms unto His pleasure.
   Still young, I fled the world to follow her; 103
and, in her order's habit, I enclosed
myself and promised my life to her rule.
   Then men more used to malice than to good 106
took me—violently—from my sweet cloister:
God knows what, after that, my life became.
   This other radiance that shows itself 109
to you at my right hand, a brightness kindled
by all the light that fills our heaven—she
   has understood what I have said: she was 112
a sister, and from her head, too, by force,
the shadow of the sacred veil was taken.
   But though she had been turned back to the world 115
against her will, against all honest practice,
the veil upon her heart was never loosed.

che vedrai non capere in questi giri,                                                              76
s'essere in carità è qui *necesse*,
e se la sua natura ben rimiri.

　　Anzi è formale ad esto beato *esse*                                                              79
tenersi dentro a la divina voglia,
per ch'una fansi nostre voglie stesse;

　　sì che, some noi sem di soglia in soglia                                                        82
per questo regno, a tutto il regno piace
com' a lo re che 'n suo voler ne 'nvoglia.

　　E 'n la sua volontade è nostra pace:                                                            85
ell' è quel mare al qual tutto si move
ciò ch'ella crïa o che natura face."

　　Chiaro mi fu allor come ogne dove                                                              88
in cielo è paradiso, *etsi* la grazia
del sommo ben d'un modo non vi piove.

　　Ma sì com' elli avvien, s'un cibo sazia                                                         91
e d'un altro rimane ancor la gola,
che quel si chere e di quel si ringrazia,

　　così fec' io con atto e con parola,                                                             94
per apprender da lei qual fu la tela
onde non trasse infino a co la spuola.

　　"Perfetta vita e alto merto inciela                                                            97
donna più sù," mi disse, "a la cui norma
nel vostro mondo giù si veste e vela,

　　perché fino al morir si vegghi e dorma                                                        100
con quello sposo ch'ogne voto accetta
che caritate a suo piacer conforma.

　　Dal mondo, per seguirla, giovinetta                                                            103
fuggi'mi, e nel suo abito mi chiusi
e promisi la via de la sua setta.

　　Uomini poi, a mal più ch'a bene usi,                                                           106
fuor mi rapiron de la dolce chiostra:
Iddio si sa qual poi mia vita fusi.

　　E quest' altro splendor che ti si mostra                                                       109
da la mia destra parte e che s'accende
di tutto il lume de la spera nostra,

　　ciò ch'io dico di me, di sé intende;                                                           112
sorella fu, e così le fu tolta
di capo l'ombra de le sacre bende.

　　Ma poi che pur al mondo fu rivolta                                                             115
contra suo grado e contra buona usanza,
non fu dal vel del cor già mai disciolta.

This is the splendor of the great Costanza,      118
who from the Swabians' second gust engendered
the one who was their third and final power."

    This said, she then began to sing "*Ave*      121
*Maria*" and, while singing, vanished as
a weighty thing will vanish in deep water.

    My sight, which followed her as long as it      124
was able to, once she was out of view,
returned to where its greater longing lay,

    and it was wholly bent on Beatrice;      127
but she then struck my eyes with so much brightness
that I, at first, could not withstand her force;

    and that made me delay my questioning.      130

Quest' è la luce de la gran Costanza     118
che del secondo vento di Soave
generò 'l terzo e l'ultima possanza."

    Così parlommi, e poi cominciò "*Ave,*     121
*Maria*" cantando, e cantando vanio
come per acqua cupa cosa grave.

    La vista mia, che tanto lei seguio     124
quanto possibil fu, poi che la perse,
volsesi al segno di maggior disio,

    e a Beatrice tutta si converse;     127
ma quella folgorò nel mïo sguardo
si che da prima il viso non sofferse;

    e ciò mi fece a dimandar più tardo.     130

OVERLEAF:
*The First Star*

# CANTO IV

Before a man bit into one of two
foods equally removed and tempting, he
would die of hunger if his choice were free;
 so would a lamb stand motionless between     4
the cravings of two savage wolves, in fear
of both; so would a dog between two deer;
 thus, I need neither blame nor praise myself     7
when both my doubts compelled me equally:
what kept me silent was necessity.
 I did not speak, but in my face were seen     10
longing and questioning, more ardent than
if spoken words had made them evident.
 Then Beatrice did just as Daniel did,     13
when he appeased Nebuchadnezzar's anger,
the rage that made the king unjustly fierce.
 She said: "I see how both desires draw you,     16
so that your anxiousness to know is self-
entangled and cannot express itself.
 You reason: 'If my will to good persists,     19
why should the violence of others cause
the measure of my merit to be less?'
 And you are also led to doubt because     22
the doctrine Plato taught would find support
by souls' appearing to return to the stars.
 These are the questions that, within your will,     25
press equally for answers; therefore, I
shall treat the most insidious question first.
 Neither the Seraph closest unto God,     28
nor Moses, Samuel, nor either John—
whichever one you will—nor Mary has,
 I say, their place in any other heaven     31
than that which houses those souls you just saw,
nor will their blessedness last any longer.

*Still the First Heaven: the Sphere of the Moon. Dante's two*
*questions. Beatrice's first answer: the true place of the souls in*
*the Empyrean; how their appearance in lower spheres is suited*
*to Dante's limited apprehension. Her second answer: violence*
*and unfulfilled vows, absolute and relative will. Dante's further*
*query. Beatrice's dazzling gaze.*

Intra due cibi, distanti e moventi
d'un modo, prima si morria di fame,
che liber' omo l'un recasse ai denti;

    sì si starebbe un agno intra due brame        4
di fieri lupi, igualmente temendo;
sì si starebbe un cane intra due dame:

    per che, s'i' mi tacea, me non riprendo,        7
da li miei dubbi d'un modo sospinto,
poi ch'era necessario, né commendo.

    Io mi tacea, ma 'l mio disir dipinto        10
m'era nel viso, e 'l dimandar con ello,
più caldo assai che per parlar distinto.

    Fé sì Beatrice qual fé Danïello,        13
Nabuccodonosor levando d'ira,
che l'avea fatto ingiustamente fello;

    e disse: "Io veggio ben come ti tira        16
uno e altro disio, sì che tua cura
sé stessa lega sì che fuor non spira.

    Tu argomenti: 'Se 'l buon voler dura,        19
la vïolenza altrui per qual ragione
di meritar mi scema la misura?'

    Ancor di dubitar ti dà cagione        22
parer tornarsi l'anime a le stelle,
secondo la sentenza di Platone.

    Queste son le question che nel tuo *velle*        25
pontano igualmente; e però pria
tratterò quella che più ha di felle.

    D'i Serafin colui che più s'india,        28
Moïsè, Samuel, e quel Giovanni
che prender vuoli, io dico, non Maria,

    non hanno in altro cielo i loro scanni        31
che questi spirti che mo t'appariro,
né hanno a l'esser lor più o meno anni;

But all those souls grace the Empyrean;          34
and each of them has gentle life—though some
sense the Eternal Spirit more, some less.

They showed themselves to you here not because   37
this is their sphere, but as a sign for you
that in the Empyrean their place is lowest.

Such signs are suited to your mind, since from   40
the senses only can it apprehend
what then becomes fit for the intellect.

And this is why the Bible condescends            43
to human powers, assigning feet and hands
to God, but meaning something else instead.

And Gabriel and Michael and the angel            46
who healed the eyes of Tobit are portrayed
by Holy Church with human visages.

That which Timaeus said in reasoning             49
of souls does not describe what you have seen,
since it would seem that as he speaks he thinks.

He says the soul returns to that same star       52
from which—so he believes—it had been taken
when nature sent that soul as form to body;

but his opinion is, perhaps, to be               55
taken in other guise than his words speak,
intending something not to be derided.

If to these spheres he wanted to attribute       58
honor and blame for what they influence,
perhaps his arrow reaches something true.

This principle, ill-understood, misled           61
almost all of the world once, so that Jove
and Mercury and Mars gave names to stars.

The other doubt that agitates you is             64
less poisonous; for its insidiousness
is not such as to lead you far from me.

To mortal eyes our justice seems unjust;         67
that this is so, should serve as evidence
for faith—not heresy's depravity.

But that your intellect may penetrate            70
more carefully into your other query,
I shall—as you desire—explain it clearly.

If violence means that the one who suffers       73
has not abetted force in any way,
then there is no excuse these souls can claim:

ma tutti fanno bello il primo giro,                    34
e differentemente han dolce vita
per sentir più e men l'etterno spiro.

  Qui si mostraro, non perché sortita         37
sia questa spera lor, ma per far segno
de la celestïal c'ha men salita.

  Cosi parlar conviensi al vostro ingegno,     40
però che solo da sensato apprende
ciò che fa poscia d'intelletto degno.

  Per questo la Scrittura condescende          43
a vostra facultate, e piedi e mano
attribuisce a Dio e altro intende;

  e Santa Chiesa con aspetto umano             46
Gabrïel e Michel vi rappresenta,
e l'altro che Tobia rifece sano.

  Quel che Timeo de l'anime argomenta          49
non è simile a ciò che qui si vede,
però che, come dice, par che senta.

  Dice che l'alma a la sua stella riede,       52
credendo quella quindi esser decisa
quando natura per forma la diede;

  e forse sua sentenza è d'altra guisa         55
che la voce non suona, ed esser puote
con intenzion da non esser derisa.

  S'elli intende tornare a queste ruote        58
l'onor de la influenza e 'l biasmo, forse
in alcun vero suo arco percuote.

  Questo principio, male inteso, torse         61
già tutto il mondo quasi, sì che Giove,
Mercurio e Marte a nominar trascorse.

  L'altra dubitazion che ti commove            64
ha men velen, però che sua malizia
non ti poria menar da me altrove.

  Parere ingiusta la nostra giustizia          67
ne li occhi d'i mortali, è argomento
di fede e non d'eretica nequizia.

  Ma perché puote vostro accorgimento          70
ben penetrare a questa veritate,
come disiri, ti farò contento.

  Se vïolenza è quando quel che pate           73
nïente conferisce a quel che sforza,
non fuor quest' alme per essa scusate:

for will, if it resists, is never spent,                                    76
but acts as nature acts when fire ascends,
though force—a thousand times—tries to compel.

So that, when will has yielded much or little,                              79
it has abetted force—as these souls did:
they could have fled back to their holy shelter.

Had their will been as whole as that which held                             82
Lawrence fast to the grate and that which made
of Mucius one who judged his own hand, then

once freed, they would have willed to find the faith                        85
from which they had been dragged; but it is all
too seldom that a will is so intact.

And through these words, if you have grasped their bent, 88
you can eliminate the argument
that would have troubled you again—and often.

But now another obstacle obstructs                                          91
your sight; you cannot overcome it by
yourself—it is too wearying to try.

I've set it in your mind as something certain                               94
that souls in blessedness can never lie,
since they are always near the Primal Truth.

But from Piccarda you were also able                                        97
to hear how Constance kept her love of the veil:
and here Piccarda seems to contradict me.

Before this—brother—it has often happened                                   100
that, to flee menace, men unwillingly
did what should not be done; so did Alcmaeon,

to meet the wishes of his father, kill                                      103
his mother—not to fail in filial
piety, he acted ruthlessly.

At that point—I would have you see—the force                                106
to which one yielded mingles with one's will;
and no excuse can pardon their joint act.

Absolute will does not concur in wrong;                                     109
but the contingent will, through fear that its
resistance might bring greater harm, consents.

Therefore, Piccarda means the absolute                                      112
will when she speaks, and I the relative;
so that the two of us have spoken truth."

Such was the rippling of the holy stream                                    115
issuing from the fountain from which springs
all truth: it set to rest both of my longings.

ché volontà, se non vuol, non s'ammorza,       76
ma fa come natura face in foco,
se mille volte vïolenza il torza.

Per che, s'ella si piega assai o poco,       79
segue la forza; e così queste fero
possendo rifuggir nel santo loco.

Se fosse stato lor volere intero,       82
come tenne Lorenzo in su la grada,
e fece Muzio a la sua man severo,

così l'avria ripinte per la strada       85
ond' eran tratte, come fuoro sciolte;
ma così salda voglia è troppo rada.

E per queste parole, se ricolte       88
l'hai come dei, è l'argomento casso
che t'avria fatto noia ancor più volte.

Ma or ti s'attraversa un altro passo       91
dinanzi a li occhi, tal che per te stesso
non usciresti: pria saresti lasso.

Io t'ho per certo ne la mente messo       94
ch'alma beata non poria mentire,
però ch'è sempre al primo vero appresso;

e poi potesti da Piccarda udire       97
che l'affezion del vel Costanza tenne;
sì ch'ella par qui meco contradire.

Molte fïate già, frate, addivenne       100
che, per fuggir periglio, contra grato
si fé di quel che far non si convenne;

come Almeone, che, di ciò pregato       103
dal padre suo, la propria madre spense,
per non perder pietà si fé spietato.

A questo punto voglio che tu pense       106
che la forza al voler si mischia, e fanno
sì che scusar non si posson l'offense.

Voglia assoluta non consente al danno;       109
ma consentevi in tanto in quanto teme,
se si ritrae, cadere in più affanno.

Però, quando Piccarda quello spreme,       112
de la voglia assoluta intende, e io
de l'altra; sì che ver diciamo insieme."

Cotal fu l'ondeggiar del santo rio       115
ch'uscì del fonte ond' ogne ver deriva;
tal puose in pace uno e altro disio.

Then I said: "O beloved of the First    118
Lover, o you—divine—whose speech so floods
and warms me that I feel more and more life,

however deep my gratefulness, it can    121
not match your grace with grace enough; but He
who sees and can—may He grant recompense.

I now see well: we cannot satisfy    124
our mind unless it is enlightened by
the truth beyond whose boundary no truth lies.

Mind, reaching that truth, rests within it as    127
a beast within its lair; mind can attain
that truth—if not, all our desires were vain.

Therefore, our doubting blossoms like a shoot    130
out from the root of truth; this natural
urge spurs us toward the peak, from height to height.

Lady, my knowing why we doubt, invites,    133
sustains, my reverent asking you about
another truth that is obscure to me.

I want to know if, in your eyes, one can    136
amend for unkept vows with other acts—
good works your balance will not find too scant."

Then Beatrice looked at me with eyes so full    139
of sparks of love, eyes so divine that my
own force of sight was overcome, took flight,

and, eyes downcast, I almost lost my senses.    142

"O amanza del primo amante, o diva," 118
diss' io appresso, "il cui parlar m'inonda
e scalda sì, che più e più m'avviva,

non è l'affezion mia tanto profonda, 121
che basti a render voi grazia per grazia;
ma quei che vede e puote a ciò risponda.

Io veggio ben che già mai non si sazia 124
nostro intelletto, se 'l ver non lo illustra
di fuor dal qual nessun vero si spazia.

Posasi in esso, come fera in lustra, 127
tosto che giunto l'ha; e giugner puollo:
se non, ciascun disio sarebbe *frustra*.

Nasce per quello, a guisa di rampollo, 130
a piè del vero il dubbio; ed è natura
ch'al sommo pinge noi di collo in collo.

Questo m'invita, questo m'assicura 133
con reverenza, donna, a dimandarvi
d'un'altra verità che m'è oscura.

Io vo' saper se l'uom può sodisfarvi 136
ai voti manchi sì con altri beni,
ch'a la vostra statera non sien parvi."

Beatrice mi guardò con li occhi pieni 139
di faville d'amor così divini,
che, vinta, mia virtute diè le reni,

e quasi mi perdei con li occhi chini. 142

# CANTO V

"If in the fire of love I seem to flame
beyond the measure visible on earth,
so that I overcome your vision's force,

you need not wonder; I am so because                    4
of my perfected vision—as I grasp
the good, so I approach the good in act.

Indeed I see that in your intellect                     7
now shines the never-ending light; once seen,
that light, alone and always, kindles love;

and if a lesser thing allure your love,                 10
it is a vestige of that light which—though
imperfectly—gleams through that lesser thing.

You wish to know if, through a righteous act,           13
one can repair a promise unfulfilled,
so that the soul and God are reconciled."

So Beatrice began this canto, and                       16
as one who does not interrupt her speech,
so did her holy reasoning proceed:

"The greatest gift the magnanimity                      19
of God, as He created, gave, the gift
most suited to His goodness, gift that He

most prizes, was the freedom of the will;               22
those beings that have intellect—all these
and none but these—received and do receive

this gift: thus you may draw, as consequence,           25
the high worth of a vow, when what is pledged
with your consent encounters God's consent;

for when a pact is drawn between a man                  28
and God, then through free will, a man gives up
what I have called his treasure, his free will.

What, then, can be a fitting compensation?              31
To use again what you had offered, would
mean seeking to do good with ill-got gains.

*Still the First Heaven: the Sphere of the Moon. Beatrice on the*
*cause of her own radiance, and then on the possibility of rec-*
*ompensing for unfulfilled vows. Ascent to the Second Heaven,*
*the Sphere of Mercury. Encounter with the shades there. The*
*nameless holy form whose discourse will constitute the next*
*canto and reveal him to be Justinian.*

"S'io ti fiammeggio nel caldo d'amore
di là dal modo che 'n terra si vede,
sì che del viso tuo vinco il valore,

non ti maravigliar, ché ciò procede                    4
da perfetto veder, che, come apprende,
così nel bene appreso move il piede.

Io veggio ben sì come già resplende                    7
ne l'intelletto tuo l'etterna luce,
che, vista, sola e sempre amore accende;

e s'altra cosa vostro amor seduce,                    10
non è se non di quella alcun vestigio,
mal conosciuto, che quivi traluce.

Tu vuo' saper se con altro servigio,                  13
per manco voto, si può render tanto
che l'anima sicuri di letigio."

Sì cominciò Beatrice questo canto;                    16
e sì com' uom che suo parlar non spezza,
continüò così 'l processo santo:

"Lo maggior don che Dio per sua larghezza             19
fesse creando, e a la sua bontate
più conformato, e quel ch'e' più apprezza,

fu de la volontà la libertate;                        22
di che le creature intelligenti,
e tutte e sole, fuore e son dotate.

Or ti parrà, se tu quinci argomenti,                  25
l'alto valor del voto, s'è sì fatto
che Dio consenta quando tu consenti;

ché, nel fermar tra Dio e l'omo il patto,             28
vittima fassi di questo tesoro,
tal quale io dico; e fassi col suo atto.

Dunque che render puossi per ristoro?                 31
Se credi bene usar quel c'hai offerto,
di maltolletto vuo' far buon lavoro.

By now you understand the major point;    34
but since the Holy Church gives dispensations—
which seems in contrast with the truth I stated—
    you need to sit at table somewhat longer:    37
the food that you have taken was tough food—
it still needs help, if you are to digest it.
    Open your mind to what I shall disclose,    40
and hold it fast within you; he who hears,
but does not hold what he has heard, learns nothing.
    Two things are of the essence when one vows    43
a sacrifice: the matter of the pledge
and then the formal compact one accepts.
    This last can never be annulled until    46
the compact is fulfilled: it is of this
that I have spoken to you so precisely.
    Therefore, the Hebrews found it necessary    49
to bring their offerings, although—as you
must know—some of their offerings might be altered.
    As for the matter of the vow—discussed    52
above—it may be such that if one shifts
to other matter, one commits no sin.
    But let none shift the burden on his shoulder    55
through his own judgment, without waiting for
the turning of the white and yellow keys;
    and let him see that any change is senseless,    58
unless the thing one sets aside is not
contained in one's new weight, as four in six.
    Thus, when the matter of a vow has so    61
much weight and worth that it tips every scale,
no other weight can serve as substitute.
    Let mortals never take a vow in jest;    64
be faithful and yet circumspect, not rash
as Jephthah was, in offering his first gift;
    he should have said, 'I did amiss,' and not    67
done worse by keeping faith. And you can find
that same stupidity in the Greeks' chief—
    when her fair face made Iphigenia grieve    70
and made the wise and made the foolish weep
for her when they heard tell of such a rite.
    Christians, proceed with greater gravity:    73
do not be like a feather at each wind,
nor think that all immersions wash you clean.

Tu se' omai del maggior punto certo;        34
ma perché Santa Chiesa in ciò dispensa,
che par contra lo ver ch'i' t'ho scoverto,

   convienti ancor sedere un poco a mensa,      37
però che 'l cibo rigido c'hai preso,
richiede ancora aiuto a tua dispensa.

   Apri la mente a quel ch'io ti paleso        40
e fermalvi entro; ché non fa scïenza,
sanza lo ritenere, avere inteso.

   Due cose si convegnono a l'essenza        43
di questo sacrificio: l'una è quella
di che si fa; l'altr' è la convenenza.

   Quest' ultima già mai non si cancella      46
se non servata; e intorno di lei
sì preciso di sopra si favella:

   però necessitato fu a li Ebrei          49
pur l'offerere, ancor ch'alcuna offerta
si permutasse, come saver dei.

   L'altra, che per materia t'è aperta,       52
puote ben esser tal, che non si falla
se con altra materia si converta.

   Ma non trasmuti carco a la sua spalla     55
per suo arbitrio alcun, sanza la volta
e de la chiave bianca e de la gialla;

   e ogne permutanza credi stolta,        58
se la cosa dimessa in la sorpresa
come 'l quattro nel sei non è raccolta.

   Però qualunque cosa tanto pesa        61
per suo valor che tragga ogne bilancia,
sodisfar non si può con altra spesa.

   Non prendan li mortali il voto a ciancia;   64
siate fedeli, e a ciò far non bieci,
come Ieptè a la sua prima mancia;

   cui più si convenia dicer 'Mal feci,'     67
che, servando, far peggio; e così stolto
ritrovar puoi il gran duca de' Greci,

   onde pianse Efigènia il suo bel volto,    70
e fé pianger di sé i folli e i savi
ch'udir parlar di così fatto cólto.

   Siate, Cristiani, a muovervi più gravi:   73
non siate come penna ad ogne vento,
e non crediate ch'ogne acqua vi lavi.

You have both Testaments, the Old and New,                    76
you have the shepherd of the Church to guide you;
you need no more than this for your salvation.

   If evil greed would summon you elsewhere,                  79
be men, and not like sheep gone mad, so that
the Jew who lives among you not deride you!

   Do not act like the foolish, wanton lamb                   82
that leaves its mother's milk and, heedless, wants
to war against—and harm—its very self!"

   These words of Beatrice I here transcribe;                 85
and then she turned—her longing at the full—
to where the world is more alive with light.

   Her silence and the change in her appearance               88
imposed a silence on my avid mind,
which now was ready to address new questions;

   and even as an arrow that has struck                       91
the mark before the bow-cord comes to rest,
so did we race to reach the second realm.

   When she had passed into that heaven's light,              94
I saw my lady filled with so much gladness
that, at her joy, the planet grew more bright.

   And if the planet changed and smiled, what then            97
did I—who by my very nature am
given to every sort of change—become?

   As in a fish-pool that is calm and clear,                  100
the fish draw close to anything that nears
from outside, if it seems to be their fare,

   such were the far more than a thousand splendors           103
I saw approaching us, and each declared:
"Here now is one who will increase our loves."

   And even as each shade approached, one saw,                106
because of the bright radiance it sent forth,
the joyousness with which that shade was filled.

   Consider, reader, what your misery                         109
and need to know still more would be if, at
this point, what I began did not go on;

   and you will—unassisted—feel how I                         112
longed so to hear those shades narrate their state
as soon as they appeared before my eyes.

   "O you born unto gladness, whom God's grace                115
allows to see the thrones of the eternal
triumph before your war of life is ended,

Avete il novo e 'l vecchio Testamento,      76
e 'l pastor de la Chiesa che vi guida;
questo vi basti a vostro salvamento.

    Se mala cupidigia altro vi grida,      79
uomini siate, e non pecore matte,
sì che 'l Giudeo di voi tra voi non rida!

    Non fate com' agnel che lascia il latte      82
de la sua madre, e semplice e lascivo
seco medesmo a suo piacer combatte!"

    Così Beatrice a me com' ïo scrivo;      85
poi si rivolse tutta disïante
a quella parte ove 'l mondo è più vivo.

    Lo suo tacere e 'l trasmutar sembiante      88
puoser silenzio al mio cupido ingegno,
che già nuove questioni avea davante;

    e sì come saetta che nel segno      91
percuote pria che sia la corda queta,
così corremmo nel secondo regno.

    Quivi la donna mia vid' io sì lieta,      94
come nel lume di quel ciel si mise,
che più lucente se ne fé 'l pianeta.

    E se la stella si cambiò e rise,      97
qual mi fec'io che pur da mia natura
trasmutabile son per tutte guise!

    Come 'n peschiera ch'è tranquilla e pura      100
traggonsi i pesci a ciò che vien di fori
per modo che lo stimin lor pastura,

    sì vid' io ben più di mille splendori      103
trarsi ver' noi, e in ciascun s'udia:
"Ecco chi crescerà li nostri amori."

    E sì come ciascuno a noi venìa,      106
vedeasi l'ombra piena di letizia
nel folgór chiaro che di lei uscia.

    Pensa, lettor, se quel che qui s'inizia      109
non procedesse, come tu avresti
di più savere angosciosa carizia;

    e per te vederai come da questi      112
m'era in disio d'udir lor condizioni,
sì come a li occhi mi fur manifesti.

    "O bene nato a cui veder li troni      115
del trïunfo etternal concede grazia
prima che la milizia s'abbandoni,

the light that kindles us is that same light                    118
which spreads through all of heaven; thus, if you
would know us, sate yourself as you may please."

So did one of those pious spirits speak                         121
to me. And Beatrice then urged: "Speak, speak
confidently; trust them as you trust gods."

"I see—plainly—how you have nested in                           124
your own light; see—you draw it from your eyes—
because it glistens even as you smile;

but I do not know who you are or why,                           127
good soul, your rank is in a sphere concealed
from mortals by another planet's rays."

I said this as I stood turned toward the light                  130
that first addressed me; and at this, it glowed
more radiantly than it had before.

Just as the sun, when heat has worn away                        133
thick mists that moderate its rays, conceals
itself from sight through an excess of light,

so did that holy form, through excess gladness,                 136
conceal himself from me within his rays;
and so concealed, concealed, he answered me

even as the next canto is to sing.                              139

del lume che per tutto il ciel si spazia — 118
noi semo accesi; e però, se disii
di noi chiarirti, a tuo piacer ti sazia."

Così da un di quelli spirti pii — 121
detto mi fu; e da Beatrice: "Dì, dì
sicuramente, e credi come a dii."

"Io veggio ben sì come tu t'annidi — 124
nel proprio lume, e che de li occhi il traggi,
perch' e' corusca sì come tu ridi;

ma non so chi tu se', né perché aggi, — 127
anima degna, il grado de la spera
che si vela a' mortai con altrui raggi."

Questo diss' io diritto a la lumera — 130
che pria m'avea parlato; ond' ella fessi
lucente più assai di quel ch'ell' era.

Sì come il sol che si cela elli stessi — 133
per troppa luce, come 'l caldo ha róse
le temperanze d'i vapori spessi,

per più letizia sì mi si nascose — 136
dentro al suo raggio la figura santa;
e così chiusa chiusa mi rispuose

nel modo che 'l seguente canto canta. — 139

OVERLEAF:
*The Never-Ending Light*

# CANTO VI

---

"After Constantine had turned the Eagle
counter to heaven's course, the course it took
behind the ancient one who wed Lavinia,
    one hundred and one hundred years and more,       4
the bird of God remained near Europe's borders,
close to the peaks from which it first emerged;
    beneath the shadow of the sacred wings,       7
it ruled the world, from hand to hand, until
that governing—changing—became my task.
    Caesar I was and am Justinian,       10
who, through the will of Primal Love I feel,
removed the vain and needless from the laws.
    Before I grew attentive to this labor,       13
I held that but one nature—and no more—
was Christ's—and in that faith, I was content;
    but then the blessed Agapetus, he       16
who was chief shepherd, with his words turned me
to that faith which has truth and purity.
    I did believe him, and now clearly see       19
his faith, as you with contradictories
can see that one is true and one is false.
    As soon as my steps shared the Church's path,       22
God, of His grace, inspired my high task
as pleased Him. I was fully drawn to that.
    Entrusting to my Belisarius       25
my arms, I found a sign for me to rest
from war: Heaven's right hand so favored him.
    My answer to the question you first asked       28
ends here, and yet the nature of this answer
leads me to add a sequel, so that you
    may see with how much reason they attack       31
the sacred standard—those who seem to act
on its behalf and those opposing it.

*The Second Heaven: the Sphere of Mercury. Justinian's canto-*
*long discourse on the destiny and career of the Roman Eagle*
*and on the souls, in Mercury, of those whose acts were right-*
*eous but motivated by the desire for honor and fame. His praise*
*of Romeo of Villeneuve.*

"Poscia che Costantin l'aquila volse
contr' al corso del ciel, ch'ella seguio
dietro a l'antico che Lavina tolse,

   cento e cent' anni e più l'uccel di Dio       4
ne lo stremo d'Europa si ritenne,
vicino a' monti de' quai prima uscìo;

   e sotto l'ombra de le sacre penne       7
governò 'l mondo lì di mano in mano,
e, sì cangiando, in su la mia pervenne.

   Cesare fui e son Iustinïano,       10
che, per voler del primo amor ch'i' sento,
d'entro le leggi trassi il troppo e 'l vano.

   E prima ch'io a l'ovra fossi attento,       13
una natura in Cristo esser, non piùe,
credea, e di tal fede era contento;

   ma 'l benedetto Agapito, che fue       16
sommo pastore, a la fede sincera
mi dirizzò con le parole sue.

   Io li credetti; e ciò che 'n sua fede era,       19
vegg' io or chiaro sì, come tu vedi
ogne contradizione e falsa e vera.

   Tosto che con la Chiesa mossi i piedi,       22
a Dio per grazia piacque di spirarmi
l'alto lavoro, e tutto 'n lui mi diedi;

   e al mio Belisar commendai l'armi,       25
cui la destra del ciel fu sì congiunta,
che segno fu ch'i' dovessi posarmi.

   Or qui a la question prima s'appunta       28
la mia risposta; ma sua condizione
mi stringe a seguitare alcuna giunta,

   perché tu veggi con quanta ragione       31
si move contr' al sacrosanto segno
e chi 'l s'appropria e chi a lui s'oppone.

See what great virtue made that Eagle worthy     34
of reverence, beginning from that hour
when Pallas died that it might gain a kingdom.

    You know that for three hundred years and more,     37
it lived in Alba, until, at the end,
three still fought three, contending for that standard.

    You know how, under seven kings, it conquered     40
its neighbors—in the era reaching from
wronged Sabine women to Lucrece's grief—

    and what it did when carried by courageous     43
Romans, who hurried to encounter Brennus,
Pyrrhus, and other principates and cities.

    Through this, Torquatus, Quinctius (who is named     46
for his disheveled hair), the Decii,
and Fabii gained the fame I gladly honor.

    That standard brought the pride of Arabs low     49
when they had followed Hannibal across
those Alpine rocks from which, Po, you descend.

    Beneath that standard, Scipio, Pompey—     52
though young—triumphed; and to that hill beneath
which you were born, that standard seemed most harsh.

    Then, near the time when Heaven wished to bring     55
all of the world to Heaven's way—serene—
Caesar, as Rome had willed, took up that standard.

    And what it did from Var to Rhine was seen     58
by the Isère, Savone, and Seine and all
the valley-floors whose rivers feed the Rhone.

    And what it did, once it had left Ravenna     61
and leaped the Rubicon, was such a flight
as neither tongue nor writing can describe.

    That standard led the legions on to Spain,     64
then toward Durazzo, and it struck Pharsalia
so hard that the warm Nile could feel that hurt.

    It saw again its source, Antandros and     67
Simois, and the place where Hector lies;
then roused itself—the worse for Ptolemy.

    From Egypt, lightning-like, it fell on Juba;     70
and then it hurried to the west of you,
where it could hear the trumpet of Pompey.

    Because of what that standard did, with him     73
who bore it next, Brutus and Cassius howl
in Hell, and grief seized Modena, Perugia.

Vedi quanta virtù l'ha fatto degno                34
di reverenza; e cominciò da l'ora
che Pallante morì per darli regno.

  Tu sai ch'el fece in Alba sua dimora            37
per trecento anni e oltre, infino al fine
che i tre a' tre pugnar per lui ancora.

  E sai ch'el fé dal mal de le Sabine            40
al dolor di Lucrezia in sette regi,
vincendo intorno le genti vicine.

  Sai quel ch'el fé portato da li egregi         43
Romani incontro a Brenno, incontro a Pirro,
incontro a li altri principi e collegi;

  onde Torquato e Quinzio, che dal cirro          46
negletto fu nomato, i Deci e ' Fabi
ebber la fama che volontier mirro.

  Esso atterrò l'orgoglio de li Aràbi            49
che di retro ad Anibale passaro
l'alpestre rocce, Po, di che tu labi.

  Sott' esso giovanetti trïunfaro                 52
Scipïone e Pompeo; e a quel colle
sotto 'l qual tu nascesti parve amaro.

  Poi, presso al tempo che tutto 'l ciel volle   55
redur lo mondo a suo modo sereno,
Cesare per voler di Roma il tolle.

  E quel che fé da Varo infino a Reno,           58
Isàra vide ed Era e vide Senna
e ogne valle onde Rodano è pieno.

  Quel che fé poi ch'elli uscì di Ravenna        61
e saltò Rubicon, fu di tal volo,
che nol seguiteria lingua né penna.

  Inver' la Spagna rivolse lo stuolo,            64
poi ver' Durazzo, e Farsalia percosse
sì ch'al Nil caldo si sentì del duolo.

  Antandro e Simeonta, onde si mosse,            67
rivide e là dov' Ettore si cuba;
e mal per Tolomeo poscia si scosse.

  Da indi scese folgorando a Iuba;              70
onde si volse nel vostro occidente,
ove sentia la pompeana tuba.

  Di quel che fé col baiulo seguente,           73
Bruto con Cassio ne l'inferno latra,
e Modena e Perugia fu dolente.

Because of it, sad Cleopatra weeps            76
still; as she fled that standard, from the asp
she drew a sudden and atrocious death.

And, with that very bearer, it then reached            79
the Red Sea shore: with him, that emblem brought
the world such peace that Janus' shrine was shut.

But what the standard that has made me speak            82
had done before or then was yet to do
throughout the mortal realm where it holds rule,

comes to seem faint and insignificant            85
if one, with clear sight and pure sentiment,
sees what it did in the third Caesar's hand;

for the true Justice that inspires me            88
granted to it—in that next Caesar's hand—
the glory of avenging His own wrath.

Now marvel here at what I show to you:            91
with Titus—afterward—it hurried toward
avenging vengeance for the ancient sin.

And when the Lombard tooth bit Holy Church,            94
then Charlemagne, under the Eagle's wings,
through victories he gained, brought help to her.

Now you can judge those I condemned above,            97
and judge how such men have offended, have
become the origin of all your evils.

For some oppose the universal emblem            100
with yellow lilies; others claim that emblem
for party: it is hard to see who is worse.

Let Ghibellines pursue their undertakings            103
beneath another sign, for those who sever
this sign and justice are bad followers.

And let not this new Charles strike at it with            106
his Guelphs—but let him fear the claws that stripped
a more courageous lion of its hide.

The sons have often wept for a father's fault;            109
and let this son not think that God will change
the emblem of His force for Charles's lilies.

This little planet is adorned with spirits            112
whose acts were righteous, but who acted for
the honor and the fame that they would gain:

and when desires tend toward earthly ends,            115
then, so deflected, rays of the true love
mount toward the life above with lesser force.

Piangene ancor la trista Cleopatra,                    76
che, fuggendoli innanzi, dal colubro
la morte prese subitana e atra.

Con costui corse infino al lito rubro;                 79
con costui puose il mondo in tanta pace,
che fu serrato a Giano il suo delubro.

Ma ciò che 'l segno che parlar mi face                 82
fatto avea prima e poi era fatturo
per lo regno mortal ch'a lui soggiace,

diventa in apparenza poco e scuro,                     85
se in mano al terzo Cesare si mira
con occhio chiaro e con affetto puro;

ché la viva giustizia che mi spira,                    88
li concedette, in mano a quel ch'i' dico,
gloria di far vendetta a la sua ira.

Or qui t'ammira in ciò ch'io ti replìco:              91
poscia con Tito a far vendetta corse
de la vendetta del peccato antico.

E quando il dente longobardo morse                     94
la Santa Chiesa, sotto le sue ali
Carlo Magno, vincendo, la soccorse.

Omai puoi giudicar di quei cotali                      97
ch'io accusai di sopra e di lor falli,
che son cagion di tutti vostri mali.

L'uno al pubblico segno i gigli gialli                 100
oppone, e l'altro appropria quello a parte,
sì ch'è forte a veder chi più si falli.

Faccian li Ghibellin, faccian lor arte                 103
sott' altro segno, ché mal segue quello
sempre chi la giustizia e lui diparte;

e non l'abbatta esto Carlo novello                     106
coi Guelfi suoi, ma tema de li artigli
ch'a più alto leon trasser lo vello.

Molte fïate già pianser li figli                       109
per la colpa del padre, e non si creda
che Dio trasmuti l'armi per suoi gigli!

Questa picciola stella si correda                      112
d'i buoni spirti che son stati attivi
perché onore e fama li succeda:

e quando li disiri poggian quivi,                      115
sì disvïando, pur convien che i raggi
del vero amore in sù poggin men vivi.

But part of our delight is measuring 118
rewards against our merit, and we see
that our rewards are neither less nor more.

Thus does the Living Justice make so sweet 121
the sentiments in us, that we are free
of any turning toward iniquity.

Differing voices join to sound sweet music; 124
so do the different orders in our life
render sweet harmony among these spheres.

And in this very pearl there also shines 127
the light of Romeo, of one whose acts,
though great and noble, met ungratefulness.

And yet those Provençals who schemed against him 130
had little chance to laugh, for he who finds
harm to himself in others' righteous acts

takes the wrong path. Of Raymond Berenger's 133
four daughters, each became a queen—and this,
poor and a stranger, Romeo accomplished.

Then Berenger was moved by vicious tongues 136
to ask this just man for accounting—one
who, given ten, gave Raymond five and seven.

And Romeo, the poor, the old, departed; 139
and were the world to know the heart he had
while begging, crust by crust, for his life-bread,

it—though it praise him now—would praise him more."

Ma nel commensurar d'i nostri gaggi 118
col merto è parte di nostra letizia,
perché non li vedem minor né maggi.

Quindi addolcisce la viva giustizia 121
in noi l'affetto sì, che non si puote
torcer già mai ad alcuna nequizia.

Diverse voci fanno dolci note; 124
così diversi scanni in nostra vita
rendon dolce armonia tra queste rote.

E dentro a la presente margarita 127
luce la luce di Romeo, di cui
fu l'ovra grande e bella mal gradita.

Ma i Provenzai che fecer contra lui 130
non hanno riso; e però mal cammina
qual si fa danno del ben fare altrui.

Quattro figlie ebbe, e ciascuna reina, 133
Ramondo Beringhiere, e ciò li fece
Romeo, persona umìle e peregrina.

E poi il mosser le parole biece 136
a dimandar ragione a questo giusto,
che li assegnò sette e cinque per diece,

indi partissi povero e vetusto; 139
e se 'l mondo sapesse il cor ch'elli ebbe
mendicando sua vita a frusto a frusto,

assai lo loda, e più lo loderebbe." 142

# CANTO VII

"*Hosanna, sanctus Deus sabaòth,*
*superillustrans claritate tua*
*felices ignes horum malacòth!*"
    Thus, even as he wheeled to his own music,        4
I saw that substance sing, that spirit-flame
above whom double lights were twinned; and he
    and his companions moved within their dance,        7
and as if they were swiftest sparks, they sped
out of my sight because of sudden distance.
    I was perplexed, and to myself, I said:        10
"Tell her! Tell her! Tell her, the lady who
can slake my thirst with her sweet drops"; and yet
    the reverence that possesses all of me,        13
even on hearing only *Be* and *ice,*
had bowed my head—I seemed a man asleep.
    But Beatrice soon ended that; for she        16
began to smile at me so brightly that,
even in fire, a man would still feel glad.
    "According to my never-erring judgment,        19
the question that perplexes you is how
just vengeance can deserve just punishment;
    but I shall quickly free your mind from doubt;        22
and listen carefully; the words I speak
will bring the gift of a great truth in reach.
    Since he could not endure the helpful curb        25
on his willpower, the man who was not born,
damning himself, damned all his progeny.
    For this, mankind lay sick, in the abyss        28
of a great error, for long centuries,
until the Word of God willed to descend
    to where the nature that was sundered from        31
its Maker was united to His person
by the sole act of His eternal Love.

*Still the Second Heaven: the Sphere of Mercury. Disappearance of Justinian and his fellow spirits in the wake of hymning and dancing. Beatrice's explanations of Justinian's references to Christ's death as God's just vengeance and the destruction of Jerusalem as vengeance for just vengeance; human corruptibility; the mysteries of Salvation and Resurrection.*

"Osanna, sanctus Deus sabaòth,
superillustrans claritate tua
felices ignes horum malacòth!"

Così, volgendosi a la nota sua, 4
fu viso a me cantare essa sustanza,
sopra la qual doppio lume s'addua;

ed essa e l'altre mossero a sua danza, 7
e quasi velocissime faville
mi si velar di sùbita distanza.

Io dubitava e dicea "Dille, dille!" 10
fra me, "dille" dicea, "a la mia donna
che mi diseta con le dolci stille."

Ma quella reverenza che s'indonna 13
di tutto me, pur per *Be* e per *ice*,
mi richinava come l'uom ch'assonna.

Poco sofferse me cotal Beatrice 16
e cominciò, raggiandomi d'un riso
tal, che nel foco faria l'uom felice:

"Secondo mio infallibile avviso, 19
come giusta vendetta giustamente
punita fosse, t'ha in pensier miso;

ma io ti solverò tosto la mente; 22
e tu ascolta, ché le mie parole
di gran sentenza ti faran presente.

Per non soffrire a la virtù che vole 25
freno a suo prode, quell' uom che non nacque,
dannando sé, dannò tutta sua prole;

onde l'umana specie inferma giacque 28
giù per secoli molti in grande errore,
fin ch'al Verbo di Dio discender piacque

u' la natura, che dal suo fattore 31
s'era allungata, unì a sé in persona
con l'atto sol del suo etterno amore.

Now set your sight on what derives from that.    34
This nature, thus united to its Maker,
was good and pure, even as when created;
    but in itself, this nature had been banished    37
from paradise, because it turned aside
from its own path, from truth, from its own life.
    Thus, if the penalty the Cross inflicted    40
is measured by the nature He assumed,
no one has ever been so justly stung;
    yet none was ever done so great a wrong,    43
if we regard the Person made to suffer,
He who had gathered in Himself that nature.
    Thus, from one action, issued differing things:    46
God and the Jews were pleased by one same death;
earth trembled for that death and Heaven opened.
    You need no longer find it difficult    49
to understand when it is said that just
vengeance was then avenged by a just court.
    But I now see your understanding tangled    52
by thought on thought into a knot, from which,
with much desire, your mind awaits release.
    You say: 'What I have heard is clear to me;    55
but this is hidden from me—why God willed
precisely this pathway for our redemption.'
    Brother, this ordinance is buried from    58
the eyes of everyone whose intellect
has not matured within the flame of love.
    Nevertheless, since there is much attempting    61
to find this point, but little understanding,
I shall tell why that way was the most fitting.
    The Godly Goodness that has banished every    64
envy from Its own Self, burns in Itself;
and sparkling so, It shows eternal beauties.
    All that derives directly from this Goodness    67
is everlasting, since the seal of Goodness
impresses an imprint that never alters.
    Whatever rains from It immediately    70
is fully free, for it is not constrained
by any influence of other things.
    Even as it conforms to that Goodness,    73
so does it please It more; the Sacred Ardor
that gleams in all things is most bright within

Or drizza il viso a quel ch'or si ragiona: 34
questa natura al suo fattore unita,
qual fu creata, fu sincera e buona;

    ma per sé stessa pur fu ella sbandita 37
di paradiso, però che si torse
da via di verità e da sua vita.

    La pena dunque che la croce porse 40
s'a la natura assunta si misura,
nulla già mai sì giustamente morse;

    e così nulla fu di tanta ingiura, 43
guardando a la persona che sofferse,
in che era contratta tal natura.

    Però d'un atto uscir cose diverse: 46
ch'a Dio e a' Giudei piacque una morte;
per lei tremò la terra e 'l ciel s'aperse.

    Non ti dee oramai parer più forte, 49
quando si dice che giusta vendetta
poscia vengiata fu da giusta corte.

    Ma io veggi' or la tua mente ristretta 52
di pensiero in pensier dentro ad un nodo,
del qual con gran disio solver s'aspetta.

    Tu dici: 'Ben discerno ciò ch'i' odo; 55
ma perché Dio volesse, m'è occulto,
a nostra redenzion pur questo modo.'

    Questo decreto, frate, sta sepulto 58
a li occhi di ciascuno il cui ingegno
ne la fiamma d'amor non è adulto.

    Veramente, però ch'a questo segno 61
molto si mira e poco si discerne,
dirò perché tal modo fu più degno.

    La divina bontà, che da sé sperne 64
ogne livore, ardendo in sé, sfavilla
sì che dispiega le bellezze etterne.

    Ciò che da lei sanza mezzo distilla 67
non ha poi fine, perché non si move
la sua imprenta quand' ella sigilla.

    Ciò che da essa sanza mezzo piove 70
libero è tutto, perché non soggiace
a la virtute de le cose nove.

    Più l'è conforme, e però più le piace; 73
ché l'ardor santo ch'ogne cosa raggia,
ne la più somigliante è più vivace.

those things most like Itself. The human being          76
has all these gifts, but if it loses one,
then its nobility has been undone.

Only man's sin annuls man's liberty,          79
makes him unlike the Highest Good, so that,
in him, the brightness of Its light is dimmed;

and man cannot regain his dignity          82
unless, where sin left emptiness, man fills
that void with just amends for evil pleasure.

For when your nature sinned so totally          85
within its seed, then, from these dignities,
just as from Paradise, that nature parted;

and they could never be regained—if you          88
consider carefully—by any way
that did not pass across one of these fords:

either through nothing other than His mercy,          91
God had to pardon man, or of himself
man had to proffer payment for his folly.

Now fix your eyes on the profundity          94
of the Eternal Counsel; heed as closely
as you are able to, my reasoning.

Man, in his limits, could not recompense;          97
for no obedience, no humility,
he offered later could have been so deep

that it could match the heights he meant to reach          100
through disobedience; man lacked the power
to offer satisfaction by himself.

Thus there was need for God, through His own ways,          103
to bring man back to life intact—I mean
by one way or by both. But since a deed

pleases its doer more, the more it shows          106
the goodness of the heart from which it springs,
the Godly Goodness that imprints the world

was happy to proceed through both its ways          109
to raise you up again. Nor has there been,
nor will there be, between the final night

and the first day, a chain of actions so          112
lofty and so magnificent as He
enacted when He followed His two ways;

for God showed greater generosity          115
in giving His own self that man might be
able to rise, than if He simply pardoned;

Di tutte queste dote s'avvantaggia 76
l'umana creatura, e s'una manca,
di sua nobilità convien che caggia.

Solo il peccato è quel che la disfranca 79
e falla dissimìle al sommo bene,
per che del lume suo poco s'imbianca;

e in sua dignità mai non rivene, 82
se non rïempie, dove colpa vòta,
contra mal dilettar con giuste pene.

Vostra natura, quando peccò *tota* 85
nel seme suo, da queste dignitadi,
come di paradiso, fu remota;

né ricovrar potiensi, se tu badi 88
ben sottilmente, per alcuna via,
sanza passar per un di questi guadi:

o che Dio solo per sua cortesia 91
dimesso avesse, o che l'uom per sé isso
avesse sodisfatto a sua follia.

Ficca mo l'occhio per entro l'abisso 94
de l'etterno consiglio, quanto puoi
al mio parlar distrettamente fisso.

Non potea l'uomo ne' termini suoi 97
mai sodisfar, per non potere ir giuso
con umiltate obedïendo poi,

quanto disobediendo intese ir suso; 100
e questa è la cagion per che l'uom fue
da poter sodisfar per sé dischiuso.

Dunque a Dio convenia con le vie sue 103
riparar l'omo a sua intera vita,
dico con l'una, o ver con amendue.

Ma perché l'ovra tanto è più gradita 106
da l'operante, quanto più appresenta
de la bontà del core ond' ell' è uscita,

la divina bontà che 'l mondo imprenta, 109
di proceder per tutte le sue vie,
a rilevarvi suso, fu contenta.

Né tra l'ultima notte e 'l primo die 112
sì alto o sì magnifico processo,
o per l'una o per l'altra, fu o fie:

ché più largo fu Dio a dar sé stesso 115
per far l'uom sufficiente a rilevarsi,
che s'elli avesse sol da sé dimesso;

for every other means fell short of justice,                    118
except the way whereby the Son of God
humbled Himself when He became incarnate.

Now to give all your wishes full content,                       121
I go back to explain one point, so that
you, too, may see it plainly, as I do.

You say: 'I see that water, see that fire                       124
and air and earth and all that they compose
come to corruption, and endure so briefly;

and yet these, too, were things created; if                    127
what has been said above is true, then these
things never should be subject to corruption.'

Brother, the angels and the pure country                       130
where you are now—these may be said to be
created, as they are, in all their being;

whereas the elements that you have mentioned,                   133
as well as those things that are made from them,
receive their form from a created power.

The matter they contain had been created,                       136
just as within the stars that wheel about them,
the power to give form had been created.

The rays and motion of the holy lights                          139
draw forth the soul of every animal
and plant from matter able to take form;

but your life is breathed forth immediately                     142
by the Chief Good, who so enamors it
of His own Self that it desires Him always.

So reasoning, you also can deduce                               145
your resurrection; you need but remember
the way in which your human flesh was fashioned

when both of the first parents were created."                   148

e tutti li altri modi erano scarsi 118
a la giustizia, se 'l Figliuol di Dio
non fosse umilïato ad incarnarsi.

  Or per empierti bene ogne disio, 121
ritorno a dichiararti in alcun loco,
perché tu veggi lì così com' io.

  Tu dici: 'Io veggio l'acqua, io veggio il foco, 124
l'aere e la terra e tutte lor misture
venire a corruzione, e durar poco;

  e queste cose pur furon creature; 127
per che, se ciò ch'è detto è stato vero,
esser dovrien da corruzion sicure.'

  Li angeli, frate, e 'l paese sincero 130
nel qual tu se', dir si posson creati,
sì come sono, in loro essere intero;

  ma li alimenti che tu hai nomati 133
e quelle cose che di lor si fanno
da creata virtù sono informati.

  Creata fu la materia ch'elli hanno; 136
creata fu la virtù informante
in queste stelle che 'ntorno a lor vanno.

  L'anima d'ogne bruto e de le piante 139
di complession potenzïata tira
lo raggio e 'l moto de le luci sante;

  ma vostra vita sanza mezzo spira 142
la somma beninanza, e la innamora
di sé sì che poi sempre la disira.

  E quinci puoi argomentare ancora 145
vostra resurrezion, se tu ripensi
come l'umana carne fessi allora

    che li primi parenti intrambo fensi." 148

OVERLEAF:
*The Crucifixion*

# CANTO VIII

The world, when still in peril, thought that, wheeling,
in the third epicycle, Cyprian
the fair sent down her rays of frenzied love,

so that, in ancient error, ancient peoples                    4
not only honored her with sacrifices
and votive cries, but honored, too, Diöne

and Cupid, one as mother, one as son                          7
of Cyprian, and told how Cupid sat
in Dido's lap; and gave the name of her

with whom I have begun this canto, to                         10
the planet that is courted by the sun,
at times behind her and at times in front.

I did not notice my ascent to it,                             13
yet I was sure I was in Venus when
I saw my lady grow more beautiful.

And just as, in a flame, a spark is seen,                     16
and as, in plainsong, voice in voice is heard—
one holds the note, the other comes and goes—

I saw in that light other wheeling lamps,                     19
some more and some less swift, yet in accord,
I think, with what their inner vision was.

Winds, seen or unseen, never have descended                  22
so swiftly from cold clouds as not to seem
impeded, slow, to any who had seen

those godly lights approaching us, halting                    25
the circling dance those spirits had begun
within the heaven of high Seraphim;

and a *"Hosanna"* sounded from within                         28
their front ranks—such that I have never been
without desire to hear it sound again.

Then one drew nearer us, and he began                         31
alone: "We all are ready at your pleasure,
so that you may receive delight from us.

Origin of the planet Venus's name. Ascent to the Third Heaven,
the Sphere of Venus. Charles Martel. His discourse on fathers
and sons and the vicissitudes of heredity, and then on the need
to respect men's natural dispositions.

Solea creder lo mondo in suo periclo
che la bella Ciprigna il folle amore
raggiasse, volta nel terzo epiciclo;

per che non pur a lei faceano onore                    4
di sacrificio e di votivo grido
le genti antiche ne l'antico errore;

ma Dïone onoravano e Cupido,                           7
quella per madre sua, questo per figlio,
e dicean ch'el sedette in grembo a Dido;

e da costei ond' io principio piglio                   10
pigliavano il vocabol de la stella
che 'l sol vagheggia or da coppa or da ciglio.

Io non m'accorsi del salire in ella;                   13
ma d'esservi entro mi fé assai fede
la donna mia ch'i' vidi far più bella.

E come in fiamma favilla si vede,                      16
e come in voce voce si discerne,
quand' una è ferma e altra va e riede,

vid' io in essa luce altre lucerne                     19
muoversi in giro più e men correnti,
al modo, credo, di lor viste interne.

Di fredda nube non disceser venti,                     22
o visibili o no, tanto festini,
che non paressero impediti e lenti

a chi avesse quei lumi divini                          25
veduti a noi venir, lasciando il giro
pria cominciato in li alti Serafini;

e dentro a quei che più innanzi appariro               28
sonava "Osanna" sì, che unque poi
di rïudir non fui sanza disiro.

Indi si fece l'un più presso a noi                     31
e solo incominciò: "Tutti sem presti
al tuo piacer, perché di noi ti gioi.

One circle and one circling and one thirst                                    34
are ours as we revolve with the celestial
Princes whom, from the world, you once invoked:
    'You who, through understanding, move the third                           37
heaven.' Our love is so complete—to bring
you joy, brief respite will not be less sweet.''
    After my eyes had turned with reverence                                   40
to see my lady, after her consent
had brought them reassurance and content,
    they turned back to the light that promised me                            43
so much; and, "Tell me, who are you," I asked
in a voice stamped with loving sentiment.
    And how much larger, brighter did I see                                   46
that spirit grow when, as I spoke, it felt
the new joy that was added to its joys!
    Thus changed, it then replied: "The world held me                        49
briefly below; but had my stay been longer,
much evil that will be, would not have been.
    My happiness, surrounding me with rays,                                   52
keeps me concealed from you; it hides me like
a creature that is swathed in its own silk.
    You loved me much and had good cause for that;                           55
for had I stayed below, I should have showed
you more of my love than the leaves alone.
    The left bank that the Rhone bathes after it                              58
has mingled with the waters of the Sorgue,
awaited me in due time as its lord,
    as did Ausonia's horn, which—south of where                              61
the Tronto and the Verde reach the sea—
Catona, Bari, and Gaeta border.
    Upon my brow a crown already shone—                                       64
the crown of that land where the Danube flows
when it has left behind its German shores.
    And fair Trinacria, whom ashes (these                                     67
result from surging sulphur, not Typhoeus)
cover between Pachynus and Pelorus,
    along the gulf that Eurus vexes most,                                     70
would still await its rulers born—through me—
from Charles and Rudolph, if ill sovereignty,
    which always hurts the heart of subject peoples,                         73
had not provoked Palermo to cry out:
'Die! Die!' And if my brother could foresee

Noi ci volgiam coi principi celesti       34
d'un giro e d'un girare e d'una sete,
ai quali tu del mondo già dicesti:
    '*Voi che 'ntendendo il terzo ciel movete*';       37
e sem sì pien d'amor, che, per piacerti,
non fia men dolce un poco di quïete."

    Poscia che li occhi miei si fuoro offerti       40
a la mia donna reverenti, ed essa
fatti li avea di sé contenti e certi,
    rivolsersi a la luce che promessa       43
tanto s'avea, e "Deh, chi siete?" fue
la voce mia di grande affetto impressa.

    E quanta e qual vid' io lei far piùe       46
per allegrezza nova che s'accrebbe,
quando parlai, a l'allegrezze sue!
    Così fatta, mi disse: "Il mondo m'ebbe       49
giù poco tempo; e se più fosse stato,
molto sarà di mal, che non sarebbe.

    La mia letizia mi ti tien celato       52
che mi raggia dintorno e mi nasconde
quasi animal di sua seta fasciato.
    Assai m'amasti, e avesti ben onde;       55
che s'io fossi giù stato, io ti mostrava
di mio amor più oltre che le fronde.

    Quella sinistra riva che si lava       58
di Rodano poi ch'è misto con Sorga,
per suo segnore a tempo m'aspettava,
    e quel corno d'Ausonia che s'imborga       61
di Bari e di Gaeta e di Catona,
da ove Tronto e Verde in mare sgorga.

    Fulgeami già in fronte la corona       64
di quella terra che 'l Danubio riga
poi che le ripe tedesche abbandona.
    E la bella Trinacria, che caliga       67
tra Pachino e Peloro, sopra 'l golfo
che riceve da Euro maggior briga,
    non per Tifeo ma per nascente solfo,       70
attesi avrebbe li suoi regi ancora,
nati per me di Carlo e di Ridolfo,
    se mala segnoria, che sempre accora       73
li popoli suggetti, non avesse
mosso Palermo a gridar: 'Mora, mora!'

what ill-rule brings, he would already flee                    76
from Catalonia's grasping poverty,
aware that it may cause him injury;

for truly there is need for either him                          79
or others to prevent his loaded boat
from having to take on still greater loads.

His niggard nature is descended from                            82
one who was generous; and he needs soldiers
who are not bent on filling up their coffers."

"My lord, since I believe that you perceive                     85
completely—where all good begins and ends—
the joy I see within myself on hearing

your words to me, my joy is felt more freely;                   88
and I joy, too, in knowing you are blessed,
since you perceived this as you gazed at God.

You made me glad; so may you clear the doubt                    91
that rose in me when you—before—described
how from a gentle seed, harsh fruit derives."

These were my words to him, and he replied:                     94
"If I can show one certain truth to you,
you will confront what now is at your back.

The Good that moves and makes content the realm                 97
through which you now ascend, makes providence
act as a force in these great heavens' bodies;

and in the Mind that, in itself, is perfect,                    100
not only are the natures of His creatures
but their well-being, too, provided for;

and thus, whatever this bow shoots must fall                    103
according to a providential end,
just like a shaft directed to its target.

Were this not so, the heavens you traverse                      106
would bring about effects in such a way
that they would not be things of art but shards.

That cannot be unless the Minds that move                       109
these planets are defective and, defective,
the First Mind, which had failed to make them perfect.

Would you have this truth still more clear to you?"             112
I: "No. I see it is impossible
for nature to fall short of what is needed."

He added: "Tell me, would a man on earth                        115
be worse if he were not a citizen?"
"Yes," I replied, "and here I need no proof."

E se mio frate questo antivedesse, 76
l'avara povertà di Catalogna
già fuggeria, perché non li offendesse;

ché veramente proveder bisogna 79
per lui, o per altrui, sì ch'a sua barca
carcata più d'incarco non si pogna.

La sua natura, che di larga parca 82
discese, avria mestier di tal milizia
che non curasse di mettere in arca."

"Però ch'i' credo che l'alta letizia 85
che 'l tuo parlar m'infonde, segnor mio,
là 've ogne ben si termina e s'inizia,

per te si veggia come la vegg' io, 88
grata m'è più; e anco quest' ho caro
perché 'l discerni rimirando in Dio.

Fatto m'hai lieto, e così mi fa chiaro, 91
poi che, parlando, a dubitar m'hai mosso
com' esser può, di dolce seme, amaro."

Questo io a lui; ed elli a me: "S'io posso 94
mostrarti un vero, a quel che tu dimandi
terrai lo viso come tien lo dosso.

Lo ben che tutto il regno che tu scandi 97
volge e contenta, fa esser virtute
sua provedenza in questi corpi grandi.

E non pur le nature provedute 100
sono in la mente ch'è da sé perfetta,
ma esse insieme con la lor salute:

per che quantunque quest' arco saetta 103
disposto cade a proveduto fine,
sì come cosa in suo segno diretta.

Se ciò non fosse, il ciel che tu cammine 106
producerebbe sì li suoi effetti,
che non sarebbero arti, ma ruine;

e ciò esser non può, se li 'ntelletti 109
che muovon queste stelle non son manchi,
e manco il primo, che non li ha perfetti.

Vuo' tu che questo ver più ti s'imbianchi?" 112
E io "Non già; ché impossibil veggio
che la natura, in quel ch'è uopo, stanchi."

Ond' elli ancora: "Or dì: sarebbe il peggio 115
per l'omo in terra, se non fosse cive?"
"Sì," rispuos' io; "e qui ragion non cheggio."

"Can there be citizens if men below                    118
are not diverse, with diverse duties? No,
if what your master writes is accurate."

Until this point that shade went on, deducing;         121
then he concluded: "Thus, the roots from which
your tasks proceed must needs be different:

so, one is born a Solon, one a Xerxes,                 124
and one a Melchizedek, and another,
he who flew through the air and lost his son.

Revolving nature, serving as a seal                    127
for mortal wax, plies well its art, but it
does not distinguish one house from another.

Thus, even from the seed, Esau takes leave             130
of Jacob; and because he had a father
so base, they said Quirinus was Mars' son.

Engendered natures would forever take                  133
the path of those who had engendered them,
did not Divine provision intervene.

Now that which stood behind you, stands in front:      136
but so that you may know the joy you give me,
I now would cloak you with a corollary.

Where Nature comes upon discrepant fortune,            139
like any seed outside its proper region,
Nature will always yield results awry.

But if the world below would set its mind              142
on the foundation Nature lays as base
to follow, it would have its people worthy.

But you twist to religion one whose birth              145
made him more fit to gird a sword, and make
a king of one more fit for sermoning,

so that the track you take is off the road."           148

"E puot' elli esser, se giù non si vive 118
diversamente per diversi offici?
Non, se 'l maestro vostro ben vi scrive."

Sì venne deducendo infino a quici; 121
poscia conchiuse: "Dunque esser diverse
convien di vostri effetti le radici:

per ch'un nasce Solone e altro Serse, 124
altro Melchisedèch e altro quello
che, volando per l'aere, il figlio perse.

La circular natura, ch'è suggello 127
a la cera mortal, fa ben sua arte,
ma non distingue l'un da l'altro ostello.

Quinci addivien ch'Esaù si diparte 130
per seme da Iacòb; e vien Quirino
da sì vil padre, che si rende a Marte.

Natura generata il suo cammino 133
simil farebbe sempre a' generanti,
se non vincesse il proveder divino.

Or quel che t'era dietro t'è davanti: 136
ma perché sappi che di te mi giova,
un corollario voglio che t'ammanti.

Sempre natura, se fortuna trova 139
discorde a sé, com' ogne altra semente
fuor di sua regïon, fa mala prova.

E se 'l mondo là giù ponesse mente 142
al fondamento che natura pone,
seguendo lui, avria buona la gente.

Ma voi torcete a la religïone 145
tal che fia nato a cignersi la spada,
e fate re di tal ch'è da sermone;

onde la traccia vostra è fuor di strada." 148

# CANTO IX

Fair Clemence, after I had been enlightened
by your dear Charles, he told me how his seed
would be defrauded, but he said: "Be silent

    and let the years revolve." All I can say           4
is this: lament for vengeance well-deserved
will follow on the wrongs you are to suffer.

    And now the life-soul of that holy light           7
turned to the Sun that fills it even as
the Goodness that suffices for all things.

    Ah, souls seduced and creatures without reverence,     10
who twist your hearts away from such a Good,
who let your brows be bent on emptiness!

    And here another of those splendors moved         13
toward me; and by its brightening without,
it showed its wish to please me. Beatrice,

    whose eyes were fixed on me, as they had been       16
before, gave me the precious certainty
that she consented to my need to speak.

    "Pray, blessed spirit, may you remedy—           19
quickly—my wish to know," I said. "Give me
proof that you can reflect the thoughts I think."

    At which that light, one still unknown to me,        22
out of the depth from which it sang before,
continued as if it rejoiced in kindness:

    "In that part of indecent Italy              25
that lies between Rialto and the springs
from which the Brenta and the Piave stream,

    rises a hill—of no great height—from which       28
a firebrand descended, and it brought
much injury to all the land about.

    Both he and I were born of one same root:         31
Cunizza was my name, and I shine here
because this planet's radiance conquered me.

*The Third Heaven: the Sphere of Venus. The prophecy of*
*Charles Martel. Cunizza da Romano and her prophecy. Folco*
*of Marseille, who points out Rahab, and then denounces con-*
*temporary ecclesiastics and prophesies the regeneration of the*
*Church.*

Da poi che Carlo tuo, bella Clemenza,
m'ebbe chiarito, mi narrò li 'nganni
che ricever dovea la sua semenza;

   ma disse: "Taci e lascia muover li anni";      4
sì ch'io non posso dir se non che pianto
giusto verrà di retro ai vostri danni.

   E già la vita di quel lume santo      7
rivolta s'era al Sol che la rïempie
come quel ben ch'a ogne cosa è tanto.

   Ahi anime ingannate e fatture empie,      10
che da sì fatto ben torcete i cuori,
drizzando in vanità le vostre tempie!

   Ed ecco un altro di quelli splendori      13
ver' me si fece, e 'l suo voler piacermi
significava nel chiarir di fori.

   Li occhi di Beatrice, ch'eran fermi      16
sovra me, come pria, di caro assenso
al mio disio certificato fermi.

   "Deh, metti al mio voler tosto compenso,      19
beato spirto," dissi, "e fammi prova
ch'i' possa in te refletter quel ch'io penso!"

   Onde la luce che m'era ancor nova,      22
del suo profondo, ond' ella pria cantava,
seguette come a cui di ben far giova:

   "In quella parte de la terra prava      25
italica che siede tra Rïalto
e le fontane di Brenta e di Piava,

   si leva un colle, e non surge molt' alto,      28
là onde scese già una facella
che fece a la contrada un grande assalto.

   D'una radice nacqui e io ed ella:      31
Cunizza fui chiamata, e qui refulgo
perché mi vinse il lume d'esta stella;

But in myself I pardon happily                                        34
the reason for my fate; I do not grieve—
and vulgar minds may find this hard to see.

    Of the resplendent, precious jewel that stands                   37
most close to me within our heaven, much
fame still remains and will not die away

    before this hundredth year returns five times:                  40
see then if man should not seek excellence—
that his first life bequeath another life.

    And this, the rabble that is now enclosed                        43
between the Adige and Tagliamento
does not consider, nor does it repent

    despite its scourgings; and since it would shun                  46
its duty, at the marsh the Paduans
will stain the river-course that bathes Vicenza;

    and where the Sile and Cagnano flow                              49
in company, one lords it, arrogant;
the net to catch him is already set.

    Feltre shall yet lament the treachery                            52
of her indecent shepherd—act so filthy
that for the like none ever entered prison.

    The vat to hold the blood of the Ferrarese                       55
would be too large indeed, and weary he
who weighs it ounce by ounce—the vat that he,

    generous priest, will offer up to show                           58
fidelity to his Guelph party; and
such gifts will suit the customs of that land.

    Above are mirrors—Thrones is what you call them—                 61
and from them God in judgment shines on us;
and thus we think it right to say such things."

    Here she was silent and appeared to me                           64
to turn toward other things, reentering
the wheeling dance where she had been before.

    The other joy, already known to me                               67
as precious, then appeared before my eyes
like a pure ruby struck by the sun's rays.

    On high, joy is made manifest by brightness,                     70
as, here on earth, by smiles; but down below,
the shade grows darker when the mind feels sorrow.

    "God can see all," I said, "and, blessed spirit,                 73
your vision is contained in Him, so that
no wish can ever hide itself from you.

ma lietamente a me medesma indulgo 34
la cagion di mia sorte, e non mi noia;
che parria forse forte al vostro vulgo.

    Di questa luculenta e cara gioia 37
del nostro cielo che più m'è propinqua,
grande fama rimase; e pria che moia,

    questo centesimo anno ancor s'incinqua: 40
vedi se far si dee l'omo eccellente,
sì ch'altra vita la prima relinqua.

    E ciò non pensa la turba presente 43
che Tagliamento e Adice richiude,
né per esser battuta ancor si pente;

    ma tosto fia che Padova al palude 46
cangerà l'acqua che Vincenza bagna,
per essere al dover le genti crude;

    e dove Sile e Cagnan s'accompagna, 49
tal signoreggia e va con la testa alta,
che già per lui carpir si fa la ragna.

    Piangerà Feltro ancora la difalta 52
de l'empio suo pastor, che sarà sconcia
sì, che per simil non s'entrò in malta.

    Troppo sarebbe larga la bigoncia 55
che ricevesse il sangue ferrarese,
e stanco chi 'l pesasse a oncia a oncia,

    che donerà questo prete cortese 58
per mostrarsi di parte; e cotai doni
conformi fieno al viver del paese.

    Sù sono specchi, voi dicete Troni, 61
onde refulge a noi Dio giudicante;
sì che questi parlar ne paion buoni."

    Qui si tacette; e fecemi sembiante 64
che fosse ad altro volta, per la rota
in che si mise com' era davante.

    L'altra letizia, che m'era già nota 67
per cara cosa, mi si fece in vista
qual fin balasso in che lo sol percuota.

    Per letiziar là sù fulgor s'acquista, 70
sì come riso qui; ma giù s'abbuia
l'ombra di fuor, come la mente è trista.

    "Dio vede tutto, e tuo veder s'inluia," 73
diss' io, "beato spirto, sì che nulla
voglia di sé a te puot' esser fuia.

Your voice has always made the heavens glad,            76
as has the singing of the pious fires
that make themselves a cowl of their six wings:
    why then do you not satisfy my longings?            79
I would not have to wait for your request
if I could enter you as you do me."
    "The widest valley into which the waters            82
spread from the sea that girds the world," his words
began, "between discrepant shores, extends
    eastward so far against the sun, that when          85
those waters end at the meridian,
that point—when they began—was the horizon.
    I lived along the shoreline of that valley          88
between the Ebro and the Magra, whose
brief course divides the Genoese and Tuscans.
    Beneath the same sunset, the same sunrise,          91
lie both Bougie and my own city, which
once warmed its harbor with its very blood.
    Those men to whom my name was known, called me  94
Folco; and even as this sphere receives
my imprint, so was I impressed with its;
    for even Belus' daughter, wronging both            97
Sychaeus and Creusa, did not burn
more than I did, as long as I was young;
    nor did the Rhodopean woman whom                   100
Demophoön deceived, nor did Alcides
when he enclosed Iole in his heart.
    Yet one does not repent here; here one smiles—     103
not for the fault, which we do not recall,
but for the Power that fashioned and foresaw.
    For here we contemplate the art adorned            106
by such great love, and we discern the good
through which the world above forms that below.
    But so that all your longings born within          109
this sphere may be completely satisfied
when you bear them away, I must continue.
    You wish to know what spirit is within             112
the light that here beside me sparkles so,
as would a ray of sun in limpid water.
    Know then that Rahab lives serenely in             115
that light, and since her presence joins our order,
she seals that order in the highest rank.

Dunque la voce tua, che 'l ciel trastulla          76
sempre col canto di quei fuochi pii
che di sei ali facen la coculla,
   perché non satisface a' miei disii?          79
Già non attendere' io tua dimanda,
s'io m'intuassi, come tu t'inmii."
   "La maggior valle in che l'acqua si spanda,"          82
incominciaro allor le sue parole,
"fuor di quel mar che la terra inghirlanda,
   tra ' discordanti liti contra 'l sole          85
tanto sen va, che fa meridïano
là dove l'orizzonte pria far suole.
   Di quella valle fu' io litorano          88
tra Ebro e Macra, che per cammin corto
parte lo Genovese dal Toscano.
   Ad un occaso quasi e ad un orto          91
Buggea siede e la terra ond' io fui,
che fé del sangue suo già caldo il porto.
   Folco mi disse quella gente a cui          94
fu noto il nome mio; e questo cielo
di me s'imprenta, com' io fe' di lui;
   ché più non arse la figlia di Belo,          97
noiando e a Sicheo e a Creusa,
di me, infin che si convenne al pelo;
   né quella Rodopëa che delusa          100
fu da Demofoonte, né Alcide
quando Iole nel core ebbe rinchiusa.
   Non però qui si pente, ma si ride,          103
non de la colpa, ch'a mente non torna,
ma del valor ch'ordinò e provide.
   Qui si rimira ne l'arte ch'addorna          106
cotanto affetto, e discernesi 'l bene
per che 'l mondo di sù quel di giù torna.
   Ma perché tutte le tue voglie piene          109
ten porti che son nate in questa spera,
procedere ancor oltre mi convene.
   Tu vuo' saper chi è in questa lumera          112
che qui appresso me così scintilla
come raggio di sole in acqua mera.
   Or sappi che là entro si tranquilla          115
Raab; e a nostr' ordine congiunta,
di lei nel sommo grado si sigilla.

This heaven, where the shadow cast by earth          118
comes to a point, had Rahab as the first
soul to be taken up when Christ triumphed.

    And it was right to leave her in this heaven     121
as trophy of the lofty victory
that Christ won, palm on palm, upon the cross,

    for she had favored the initial glory           124
of Joshua within the Holy Land—
which seldom touches the Pope's memory.

    Your city, which was planted by that one        127
who was the first to turn against his Maker,
the one whose envy cost us many tears—

    produces and distributes the damned flower      130
that turns both sheep and lambs from the true course,
for of the shepherd it has made a wolf.

    For this the Gospel and the great Church Fathers  133
are set aside and only the Decretals
are studied—as their margins clearly show.

    On these the Pope and cardinals are intent.     136
Their thoughts are never bent on Nazareth,
where Gabriel's open wings were reverent.

    And yet the hill of Vatican as well             139
as other noble parts of Rome that were
the cemetery for Peter's soldiery

    will soon be freed from priests' adultery."     142

Da questo cielo, in cui l'ombra s'appunta 118
che 'l vostro mondo face, pria ch'altr' alma
del trïunfo di Cristo fu assunta.

Ben si convenne lei lasciar per palma 121
in alcun cielo de l'alta vittoria
che s'acquistò con l'una e l'altra palma,

perch' ella favorò la prima gloria 124
di Iosüè in su la Terra Santa,
che poco tocca al papa la memoria.

La tua città, che di colui è pianta 127
che pria volse le spalle al suo fattore
e di cui è la 'nvidia tanto pianta,

produce e spande il maladetto fiore 130
c'ha disvïate le pecore e li agni,
però che fatto ha lupo del pastore.

Per questo l'Evangelio e i dottor magni 133
son derelitti, e solo ai Decretali
si studia, sì che pare a' lor vivagni.

A questo intende il papa e ' cardinali; 136
non vanno i lor pensieri a Nazarette,
là dove Gabrïello aperse l'ali.

Ma Vaticano e l'altre parti elette 139
di Roma che son state cimitero
a la milizia che Pietro seguette,

tosto libere fien de l'avoltero." 142

OVERLEAF:
*Thomas Aquinas and the Other 11 Lights*

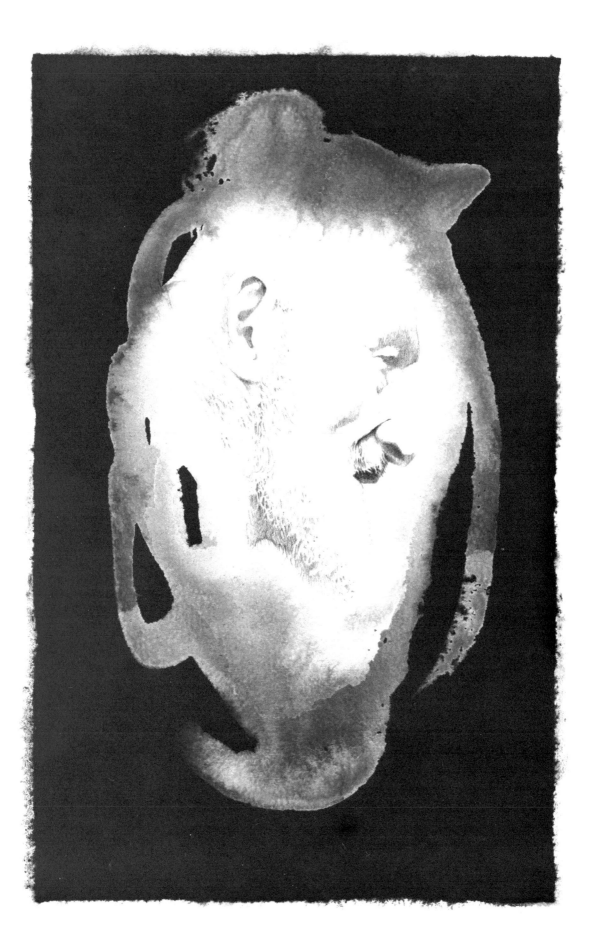

# CANTO X

Gazing upon His Son with that Love which
One and the Other breathe eternally,
the Power—first and inexpressible—

made everything that wheels through mind and space    4
so orderly that one who contemplates
that harmony cannot but taste of Him.

Then, reader, lift your eyes with me to see    7
the high wheels; gaze directly at that part
where the one motion strikes against the other;

and there begin to look with longing at    10
that Master's art, which in Himself he loves
so much that his eye never parts from it.

See there the circle branching from that cross-point    13
obliquely: zodiac to bear the planets
that satisfy the world in need of them.

For if the planets' path were not aslant,    16
much of the heavens' virtue would be wasted
and almost every power on earth be dead;

and if the zodiac swerved more or less    19
far from the straight course, then earth's harmony
would be defective in both hemispheres.

Now, reader, do not leave your bench, but stay    22
to think on that of which you have foretaste;
you will have much delight before you tire.

I have prepared your fare; now feed yourself,    25
because that matter of which I am made
the scribe calls all my care unto itself.

The greatest minister of nature—he    28
who imprints earth with heaven's worth and, with
his light, provides the measurement for time—

since he was in conjunction with the part    31
I noted, now was wheeling through the spirals
where he appears more early every day.

*Divine wisdom and the harmony of Creation. Ascent to the*
*Fourth Heaven, the Sphere of the Sun. Thanksgiving to God.*
*St. Thomas and the other eleven spirits, who form a crown*
*around Beatrice and Dante.*

Guardando nel suo Figlio con l'Amore
che l'uno e l'altro etternalmente spira,
lo primo e ineffabile Valore

quanto per mente e per loco si gira                    4
con tant' ordine fé, ch'esser non puote
sanza gustar di lui chi ciò rimira.

Leva dunque, lettore, a l'alte rote                    7
meco la vista, dritto a quella parte
dove l'un moto e l'altro si percuote;

e lì comincia a vagheggiar ne l'arte                   10
di quel maestro che dentro a sé l'ama,
tanto che mai da lei l'occhio non parte.

Vedi come da indi si dirama                            13
l'oblico cerchio che i pianeti porta,
per sodisfare al mondo che li chiama.

Che se la strada lor non fosse torta,                  16
molta virtù nel ciel sarebbe in vano,
e quasi ogne potenza qua giù morta;

e se dal dritto più o men lontano                      19
fosse 'l partire, assai sarebbe manco
e giù e sù de l'ordine mondano.

Or ti riman, lettor, sovra 'l tuo banco,               22
dietro pensando a ciò che si preliba,
s'esser vuoi lieto assai prima che stanco.

Messo t'ho innanzi; omai per te ti ciba;               25
ché a sé torce tutta la mia cura
quella materia ond' io son fatto scriba.

Lo ministro maggior de la natura,                      28
che del valor del ciel lo mondo imprenta
e col suo lume il tempo ne misura,

con quella parte che sù si rammenta                    31
congiunto, si girava per le spire
in che più tosto ognora s'appresenta;

And I was with him, but no more aware 34
of the ascent than one can be aware
of any sudden thought before it starts.
　The one who guides me so from good to better 37
is Beatrice, and on our path her acts
have so much swiftness that they span no time.
　How bright within themselves must be the lights 40
I saw on entering the Sun, for they
were known to me by splendor, not by color!
　Though I should call on talent, craft, and practice, 43
my telling cannot help them be imagined;
but you can trust—and may you long to see it.
　And if our fantasies fall short before 46
such heights, there is no need to wonder; for
no eye has seen light brighter than the Sun's.
　Such was the sphere of His fourth family, 49
whom the High Father always satisfies,
showing how he engenders and breathes forth.
　And Beatrice began: "Give thanks, give thanks 52
to Him, the angels' Sun, who, through His grace,
has lifted you to this embodied sun."
　No mortal heart was ever so disposed 55
to worship, or so quick to yield itself
to God with all its gratefulness, as I
　was when I heard those words, and all my love 58
was so intent on Him that Beatrice
was then eclipsed within forgetfulness.
　And she was not displeased, but smiled at this, 61
so that the splendor of her smiling eyes
divided my rapt mind between two objects.
　And I saw many lights, alive, most bright; 64
we formed the center, they became a crown,
their voices even sweeter than their splendor:
　just so, at times, we see Latona's daughter 67
circled when saturated air holds fast
the thread that forms the girdle of her halo.
　In Heaven's court, from which I have returned, 70
one finds so many fair and precious gems
that are not to be taken from that kingdom:
　one of those gems, the song those splendors sang. 73
He who does not take wings to reach that realm,
may wait for tidings of it from the mute.

e io era con lui; ma del salire      34
non m'accors' io, se non com' uom s'accorge,
anzi 'l primo pensier, del suo venire.

    E Bëatrice quella che sì scorge      37
di bene in meglio, sì subitamente
che l'atto suo per tempo non si sporge.

    Quant' esser convenia da sé lucente      40
quel ch'era dentro al sol dov' io entra'mi,
non per color, ma per lume parvente!

    Perch' io lo 'ngegno e l'arte e l'uso chiami,      43
sì nol direi che mai s'imaginasse;
ma creder puossi e di veder si brami.

    E se le fantasie nostre son basse      46
a tanta altezza, non è maraviglia;
ché sopra 'l sol non fu occhio ch'andasse.

    Tal era quivi la quarta famiglia      49
de l'alto Padre, che sempre la sazia,
mostrando come spira e come figlia.

    E Bëatrice cominciò: "Ringrazia,      52
ringrazia il Sol de li angeli, ch'a questo
sensibil t'ha levato per sua grazia."

    Cor di mortal non fu mai sì digesto      55
a divozione e a rendersi a Dio
con tutto 'l suo gradir cotanto presto,

    come a quelle parole mi fec' io;      58
e sì tutto 'l mio amore in lui si mise,
che Bëatrice eclissò ne l'oblio.

    Non le dispiacque, ma sì se ne rise,      61
che lo splendor de li occhi suoi ridenti
mia mente unita in più cose divise.

    Io vidi più folgór vivi e vincenti      64
far di noi centro e di sé far corona,
più dolci in voce che in vista lucenti:

    così cinger la figlia di Latona      67
vedem talvolta, quando l'aere è pregno,
sì che ritenga il fil che fa la zona.

    Ne la corte del cielo, ond' io rivegno,      70
si trovan molte gioie care e belle
tanto che non si posson trar del regno;

    e 'l canto di quei lumi era di quelle;      73
chi non s'impenna sì che là sù voli,
dal muto aspetti quindi le novelle.

After those ardent suns, while singing so,       76
had wheeled three times around us, even as
stars that are close to the fixed poles, they seemed

    to me like women who, though not released      79
from dancing, pause in silence, listening
until new notes invite to new dancing.

    And from within one light I heard begin:      82
"Because the ray of grace, from which true love
is kindled first and then, in loving, grows,

    shines with such splendor, multiplied, in you,      85
that it has led you up the stair that none
descends who will not climb that stair again,

    whoever would refuse to quench your thirst      88
with wine from his flask, would be no more free
than water that does not flow toward the sea.

    You want to know what plants bloom in this garland      91
that, circling, contemplates with love the fair
lady who strengthens your ascent to heaven.

    I was a lamb among the holy flock      94
that Dominic leads on the path where one
may fatten well if one does not stray off.

    He who is nearest on my right was both      97
my brother and my teacher: from Cologne,
Albert, and I am Thomas of Aquino.

    If you would know who all the others are,      100
then even as I speak let your eyes follow,
making their way around the holy wreath.

    That next flame issues from the smile of Gratian,      103
who served one and the other court of law
so well that his work pleases Paradise.

    That other, who adorns our choir next—      106
he was that Peter who, like the poor widow,
offered his treasure to the Holy Church.

    The fifth light, and the fairest light among us,      109
breathes forth such love that all the world below
hungers for tidings of it; in that flame

    there is the lofty mind where such profound      112
wisdom was placed that, if the truth be true,
no other ever rose with so much vision.

    Next you can see the radiance of that candle      115
which, in the flesh, below, beheld most deeply
the angels' nature and their ministry.

Poi, sì cantando, quelli ardenti soli                              76
si fuor girati intorno a noi tre volte,
come stelle vicine a' fermi poli,

    donne mi parver, non da ballo sciolte,                         79
ma che s'arrestin tacite, ascoltando
fin che le nove note hanno ricolte.

    E dentro a l'un senti' cominciar: "Quando                      82
lo raggio de la grazia, onde s'accende
verace amore e che poi cresce amando,

    multiplicato in te tanto resplende,                            85
che ti conduce su per quella scala
u' sanza risalir nessun discende;

    qual ti negasse il vin de la sua fiala                         88
per la tua sete, in libertà non fora
se non com' acqua ch'al mar non si cala.

    Tu vuo' saper di quai piante s'infiora                         91
questa ghirlanda che 'ntorno vagheggia
la bella donna ch'al ciel t'avvalora.

    Io fui de li agni de la santa greggia                          94
che Domenico mena per cammino
u' ben s'impingua se non si vaneggia.

    Questi che m'è a destra più vicino,                            97
frate e maestro fummi, ed esso Alberto
è di Cologna, e io Thomas d' Aquino.

    Se sì di tutti li altri esser vuo' certo,                      100
di retro al mio parlar ten vien col viso
girando su per lo beato serto.

    Quell' altro fiammeggiare esce del riso                        103
di Grazïan, che l'uno e l'altro foro
aiutò sì che piace in paradiso.

    L'altro ch'appresso addorna il nostro coro,                    106
quel Pietro fu che con la poverella
offerse a Santa Chiesa suo tesoro.

    La quinta luce, ch'è tra noi più bella,                        109
spira di tale amor, che tutto 'l mondo
là giù ne gola di saper novella:

    entro v'è l'alta mente u' sì profondo                          112
saver fu messo, che, se 'l vero è vero,
a veder tanto non surse il secondo.

    Appresso vedi il lume di quel cero                             115
che giù in carne più a dentro vide
l'angelica natura e 'l ministero.

Within the other little light there smiles 118
that champion of the Christian centuries
whose narrative was used by Augustine.

Now, if your mind's eye, following my praising, 121
was drawn from light to light, you must already
be thirsting for the eighth: within that light,

because he saw the Greatest Good, rejoices 124
the blessed soul who makes the world's deceit
most plain to all who hear him carefully.

The flesh from which his soul was banished lies 127
below, within Cieldauro, and he came
from martyrdom and exile to this peace.

Beyond, you see, flaming, the ardent spirits 130
of Isidore and Bede and Richard—he
whose meditation made him more than man.

This light from whom your gaze returns to me 133
contains a spirit whose oppressive thoughts
made him see death as coming much too slowly:

it is the everlasting light of Siger, 136
who when he lectured in the Street of Straw,
demonstrated truths that earned him envy."

Then, like a clock that calls us at the hour 139
in which the bride of God, on waking, sings
matins to her Bridegroom, encouraging

His love (when each clock-part both drives and draws), 142
chiming the sounds with notes so sweet that those
with spirit well-disposed feel their love grow;

so did I see the wheel that moved in glory 145
go round and render voice to voice with such
sweetness and such accord that they can not

be known except where joy is everlasting. 148

Ne l'altra piccioletta luce ride       118
quello avvocato de' tempi cristiani
del cui latino Augustin si provide.

   Or se tu l'occhio de la mente trani       121
di luce in luce dietro a le mie lode,
già de l'ottava con sete rimani.

   Per vedere ogne ben dentro vi gode       124
l'anima santa che 'l mondo fallace
fa manifesto a chi di lei ben ode.

   Lo corpo ond' ella fu cacciata giace       127
giuso in Cieldauro; ed essa da martiro
e da essilio venne a questa pace.

   Vedi oltre fiammeggiar l'ardente spiro       130
d'Isidoro, di Beda e di Riccardo,
che a considerar fu più che viro.

   Questi onde a me ritorna il tuo riguardo,       133
è 'l lume d'uno spirto che 'n pensieri
gravi a morir li parve venir tardo:

   essa è luce etterna di Sigieri,       136
che, leggendo nel Vico de li Strami,
silogizzò invidïosi veri."

   Indi, come orologio che ne chiami       139
ne l'ora che la sposa di Dio surge
a mattinar lo sposo perché l'ami,

   che l'una parte e l'altra tira e urge,       142
tin tin sonando con sì dolce nota,
che 'l ben disposto spirto d'amor turge;

   così vid' ïo la gloriosa rota       145
muoversi e render voce a voce in tempra
e in dolcezza ch'esser non pò nota

   se non colà dove gioir s'insempra.       148

# CANTO XI

O senseless cares of mortals, how deceiving
are syllogistic reasonings that bring
your wings to flight so low, to earthly things!
    One studied law and one the *Aphorisms*           4
of the physicians; one was set on priesthood
and one, through force or fraud, on rulership;
    one meant to plunder, one to politick;             7
one labored, tangled in delights of flesh,
and one was fully bent on indolence;
    while I, delivered from our servitude            10
to all these things, was in the height of heaven
with Beatrice, so gloriously welcomed.
    After each of those spirits had returned           13
to that place in the ring where it had been,
it halted, like a candle in its stand.
    And from within the splendor that had spoken     16
to me before, I heard him, as he smiled—
become more radiant, more pure—begin:
    "Even as I grow bright within Its rays,          19
so, as I gaze at the Eternal Light,
I can perceive your thoughts and see their cause.
    You are in doubt; you want an explanation      22
in language that is open and expanded,
so clear that it contents your understanding
    of two points: where I said, 'They fatten well,'   25
and where I said, 'No other ever rose'—
and here one has to make a clear distinction.
    The Providence that rules the world with wisdom   28
so fathomless that creatures' intellects
are vanquished and can never probe its depth,
    so that the Bride of Him who, with loud cries,    31
had wed her with His blessed blood, might meet
her Love with more fidelity and more

*The Fourth Heaven: the Sphere of the Sun. The senseless cares*
*of mortals. The long clarification by St. Thomas of his comment*
*on his own order, the Dominicans. His telling of the life of St.*
*Francis, who wed Poverty and founded the Franciscans.*

O insensata cura de' mortali,
quanto son difettivi silogismi
quei che ti fanno in basso batter l'ali!

Chi dietro a *iura* e chi ad amforismi      4
sen giva, e chi seguendo sacerdozio,
e chi regnar per forza o per sofismi,

e chi rubare e chi civil negozio,      7
chi nel diletto de la carne involto
s'affaticava e chi si dava a l'ozio,

quando, da tutte queste cose sciolto,      10
con Bëatrice m'era suso in cielo
cotanto glorïosamente accolto.

Poi che ciascuno fu tornato ne lo      13
punto del cerchio in che avanti s'era,
fermossi, come a candellier candelo.

E io senti' dentro a quella lumera      16
che pria m'avea parlato, sorridendo
incominciar, faccendosi più mera:

"Così com' io del suo raggio resplendo,      19
sì, riguardando ne la luce etterna,
li tuoi pensieri onde cagioni apprendo.

Tu dubbi, e hai voler che si ricerna      22
in sì aperta e 'n sì distesa lingua
lo dicer mio, ch'al tuo sentir si sterna,

ove dinanzi dissi: 'U' ben s'impingua,'      25
e là u' dissi: 'Non nacque il secondo';
e qui è uopo che ben si distingua.

La provedenza, che governa il mondo      28
con quel consiglio nel quale ogne aspetto
creato è vinto pria che vada al fondo,

però che andasse ver' lo suo diletto      31
la sposa di colui ch'ad alte grida
disposò lei col sangue benedetto,

assurance in herself, on her behalf                          34
commanded that there be two princes, one
on this side, one on that side, as her guides.

    One prince was all seraphic in his ardor;          37
the other, for his wisdom, had possessed
the splendor of cherubic light on earth.

    I shall devote my tale to one, because          40
in praising either prince one praises both:
the labors of the two were toward one goal.

    Between Topino's stream and that which flows    43
down from the hill the blessed Ubaldo chose,
from a high peak there hangs a fertile slope;

    from there Perugia feels both heat and cold      46
at Porta Sole, while behind it sorrow
Nocera and Gualdo under their hard yoke.

    From this hillside, where it abates its rise,    49
a sun was born into the world, much like
this sun when it is climbing from the Ganges.

    Therefore let him who names this site not say    52
*Ascesi,* which would be to say too little,
but *Orient,* if he would name it rightly.

    That sun was not yet very distant from           55
his rising, when he caused the earth to take
some comfort from his mighty influence;

    for even as a youth, he ran to war               58
against his father, on behalf of her—
the lady unto whom, just as to death,

    none willingly unlocks the door; before         61
his spiritual court *et coram patre,*
he wed her; day by day he loved her more.

    She was bereft of her first husband; scorned,   64
obscure, for some eleven hundred years,
until that sun came, she had had no suitor.

    Nor did it help her when men heard that he       67
who made earth tremble found her unafraid—
serene, with Amyclas—when he addressed her;

    nor did her constancy and courage help           70
when she, even when Mary stayed below,
suffered with Christ upon the cross. But so

    that I not tell my tale too darkly, you          73
may now take Francis and take Poverty
to be the lovers meant in my recounting.

in sé sicura e anche a lui più fida,       34
due principi ordinò in suo favore,
che quinci e quindi le fosser per guida.

  L'un fu tutto serafico in ardore;       37
l'altro per sapïenza in terra fue
di cherubica luce uno splendore.

  De l'un dirò, però che d'amendue       40
si dice l'un pregiando, qual ch'om prende,
perch' ad un fine fur l'opere sue.

  Intra Tupino e l'acqua che discende       43
del colle eletto dal beato Ubaldo,
fertile costa d'alto monte pende,

  onde Perugia sente freddo e caldo       46
da Porta Sole; e di rietro le piange
per grave giogo Nocera con Gualdo.

  Di questa costa, là dov' ella frange       47
più sua rattezza, nacque al mondo un sole,
come fa questo talvolta di Gange.

  Però chi d'esso loco fa parole,       52
non dica Ascesi, ché direbbe corto,
ma Orïente, se proprio dir vuole.

  Non era ancor molto lontan da l'orto,       55
ch'el cominciò a far sentir la terra
de la sua gran virtute alcun conforto;

  ché per tal donna, giovinetto, in guerra       58
del padre corse, a cui, come a la morte,
la porta del piacer nessun diserra;

  e dinanzi a la sua spirital corte       61
*et coram patre* le si fece unito;
poscia di dì in dì l'amò più forte.

  Questa, privata del primo marito,       64
millecent' anni e più dispetta e scura
fino a costui si stette sanza invito;

  né valse udir che la trovò sicura       67
con Amiclate, al suon de la sua voce,
colui ch'a tutto 'l mondo fé paura;

  né valse esser costante né feroce,       70
sì che, dove Maria rimase giuso,
ella con Cristo pianse in su la croce.

  Ma perch' io non proceda troppo chiuso,       73
Francesco e Povertà per questi amanti
prendi oramai nel mio parlar diffuso.

Their harmony and their glad looks, their love      76
and wonder and their gentle contemplation,
served others as a source of holy thoughts;
   so much so, that the venerable Bernard      79
went barefoot first; he hurried toward such peace;
and though he ran, he thought his pace too slow.
   O wealth unknown! O good that is so fruitful!      82
Egidius goes barefoot, and Sylvester,
behind the groom—the bride delights them so.
   Then Francis—father, master—goes his way      85
with both his lady and his family,
the lowly cord already round their waists.
   Nor did he lower his eyes in shame because      88
he was the son of Pietro Bernardone,
nor for the scorn and wonder he aroused;
   but like a sovereign, he disclosed in full—      91
to Innocent—the sternness of his rule;
from him he had the first seal of his order.
   And after many of the poor had followed      94
Francis, whose wondrous life were better sung
by glory's choir in the Empyrean,
   the sacred purpose of this chief of shepherds      97
was then encircled with a second crown
by the Eternal Spirit through Honorius.
   And after, in his thirst for martyrdom,      100
within the presence of the haughty Sultan,
he preached of Christ and those who followed Him.
   But, finding hearers who were too unripe      103
to be converted, he—not wasting time—
returned to harvest the Italian fields;
   there, on the naked crag between the Arno      106
and Tiber, he received the final seal
from Christ; and this, his limbs bore for two years.
   When He who destined Francis to such goodness      109
was pleased to draw him up to the reward
that he had won through his humility,
   then to his brothers, as to rightful heirs,      112
Francis commended his most precious lady,
and he bade them to love her faithfully;
   and when, returning to its kingdom, his      115
bright soul wanted to set forth from her bosom,
it, for its body, asked no other bier.

La lor concordia e i lor lieti sembianti,                    76
amore e maraviglia e dolce sguardo
facieno esser cagion di pensier santi;
   tanto che 'l venerabile Bernardo                    79
si scalzò prima, e dietro a tanta pace
corse e, correndo, li parve esser tardo.
   Oh ignota ricchezza! oh ben ferace!                    82
Scalzasi Egidio, scalzasi Silvestro
dietro a lo sposo, sì la sposa piace.
   Indi sen va quel padre e quel maestro                    85
con la sua donna e con quella famiglia
che già legava l'umile capestro.
   Né li gravò viltà di cuor le ciglia                    88
per esser fi' di Pietro Bernardone,
né per parer dispetto a maraviglia;
   ma regalmente sua dura intenzione                    91
ad Innocenzio aperse, e da lui ebbe
primo sigillo a sua religïone.
   Poi che la gente poverella crebbe                    94
dietro a costui, la cui mirabil vita
meglio in gloria del ciel si canterebbe,
   di seconda corona redimita                    97
fu per Onorio da l'Etterno Spiro
la santa voglia d'esto archimandrita.
   E poi che, per la sete del martiro,                    100
ne la presenza del Soldan superba
predicò Cristo e li altri che 'l seguiro,
   e per trovare a conversione acerba                    103
troppo la gente e per non stare indarno,
redissi al frutto de l'italica erba,
   nel crudo sasso intra Tevero e Arno                    106
da Cristo prese l'ultimo sigillo,
che le sue membra due anni portarno.
   Quando a colui ch'a tanto ben sortillo                    109
piacque di trarlo suso a la mercede
ch'el meritò nel suo farsi pusillo,
   a' frati suoi, sì com' a giuste rede,                    112
raccomandò la donna sua più cara,
e comandò che l'amassero a fede;
   e del suo grembo l'anima preclara                    115
mover si volle, tornando al suo regno,
e al suo corpo non volle altra bara.

Consider now that man who was a colleague                              118
worthy of Francis; with him, in high seas,
he kept the bark of Peter on true course.

Such was our patriarch; thus you can see                               121
that those who follow him as he commands,
as cargo carry worthy merchandise.

But now his flock is grown so greedy for                               124
new nourishment that it must wander far,
in search of strange and distant grazing lands;

and as his sheep, remote and vagabond,                                 127
stray farther from his side, at their return
into the fold, their lack of milk is greater.

Though there are some indeed who, fearing harm,                        130
stay near the shepherd, they are few in number—
to cowl them would require little cloth.

Now if my words are not too dim and distant,                           133
if you have listened carefully to them,
if you can call to mind what has been said,

then part of what you wish to know is answered,                        136
for you will see the splinters on the plant
and see what my correction meant: 'Where one

may fatten well, *if one does not stray off.*'"                        139

Pensa oramai qual fu colui che degno     118
collega fu a mantener la barca
di Pietro in alto mar per dritto segno;

e questo fu il nostro patrïarca;     121
per che qual segue lui, com' el comanda,
discerner puoi che buone merce carca.

Ma 'l suo pecuglio di nova vivanda     124
è fatto ghiotto, sì ch'esser non puote
che per diversi salti non si spanda;

e quanto le sue pecore remote     127
e vagabunde più da esso vanno,
più tornano a l'ovil di latte vòte.

Ben son di quelle che temono 'l danno     130
e stringonsi al pastor; ma son sì poche,
che le cappe fornisce poco panno.

Or, se le mie parole non son fioche,     133
se la tua audïenza è stata attenta,
se ciò ch'è detto a la mente revoche,

in parte fia la tua voglia contenta,     136
perché vedrai la pianta onde si scheggia,
e vedra' il corrègger che argomenta

'U' ben s'impingua, se non si vaneggia.' "     139

OVERLEAF:
*Sts. Francis and Dominic*

# CANTO XII

No sooner had the blessed flame begun
to speak its final word than the millstone
of holy lights began to turn, but it
    was not yet done with one full revolution        4
before another ring surrounded it,
and motion matched with motion, song with song—
    a song that, sung by those sweet instruments,        7
surpasses so our Muses and our Sirens
as firstlight does the light that is reflected.
    Just as, concentric, like in color, two        10
rainbows will curve their way through a thin cloud
when Juno has commanded her handmaid,
    the outer rainbow echoing the inner,        13
much like the voice of one—the wandering nymph—
whom love consumed as sun consumes the mist
    (and those two bows let people here foretell,        16
by reason of the pact God made with Noah,
that flood will never strike the world again):
    so the two garlands of those everlasting        19
roses circled around us, and so did
the outer circle mime the inner ring.
    When dance and jubilation, festival        22
of song and flame that answered flame, of light
with light, of gladness and benevolence,
    in one same instant, with one will, fell still        25
(just as the eyes, when moved by their desire,
can only close and open in accord),
    then from the heart of one of the new lights        28
there came a voice, and as I turned toward it,
I seemed a needle turning to the polestar;
    and it began: "The love that makes me fair        31
draws me to speak about the other leader
because of whom my own was so praised here.

*Still the Fourth Heaven: the Sphere of the Sun. The secondary crown of twelve spirits. St. Bonaventure, a Franciscan. His praise of St. Dominic. The life of St. Dominic. Denunciation of degenerate Franciscans. St. Bonaventure's presentation of the other eleven spirits in his ring.*

Sì tosto come l'ultima parola
la benedetta fiamma per dir tolse,
a rotar cominciò la santa mola;

e nel suo giro tutta non si volse                    4
prima ch'un'altra di cerchio la chiuse,
e moto a moto e canto a canto colse;

canto che tanto vince nostre muse,                   7
nostre serene in quelle dolci tube,
quanto primo splendor quel ch'e' refuse.

Come se volgon per tenera nube                      10
due archi paralelli e concolori,
quando Iunone a sua ancella iube,

nascendo di quel d'entro quel di fori,              13
a guisa del parlar di quella vaga
ch'amor consunse come sol vapori,

e fanno qui la gente esser presaga,                 16
per lo patto che Dio con Noè puose,
del mondo che già mai più non s'allaga:

così di quelle sempiterne rose                      19
volgiensi circa noi le due ghirlande,
e sì l'estrema a l'intima rispuose.

Poi che 'l tripudio e l'altra festa grande,         22
sì del cantare e sì del fiammeggiarsi
luce con luce gaudïose e blande,

insieme a punto e a voler quetarsi,                 25
pur come li occhi ch'al piacer che i move
conviene insieme chiudere e levarsi;

del cor de l'una de le luci nove                     28
si mosse voce, che l'ago a la stella
parer mi fece in volgermi al suo dove;

e cominciò: "L'amor che mi fa bella                  31
mi tragge a ragionar de l'altro duca
per cui del mio sì ben ci si favella.

Where one is, it is right to introduce                    34
the other: side by side, they fought, so may
they share in glory and together gleam.

Christ's army, whose rearming cost so dearly,             37
was slow, uncertain of itself, and scanty
behind its ensign, when the Emperor

who rules forever helped his ranks in danger—            40
only out of His grace and not their merits.
And, as was said, He then sustained His bride,

providing her with two who could revive                  43
a straggling people: champions who would
by doing and by preaching bring new life.

In that part of the West where gentle zephyr             46
rises to open those new leaves in which
Europe appears reclothed, not far from where,

behind the waves that beat upon the coast,               49
the sun, grown weary from its lengthy course,
at times conceals itself from all men's eyes—

there, Calaroga, blessed by fortune, sits                52
under the aegis of the mighty shield
on which the lion loses and prevails.

Within its walls was born the loving vassal              55
of Christian faith, the holy athlete, one
kind to his own and harsh to enemies;

no sooner was his mind created than                      58
it was so full of living force that it,
still in his mother's womb, made her prophetic.

Then, at the sacred font, where Faith and he             61
brought mutual salvation as their dowry,
the rites of their espousal were complete.

The lady who had given the assent                        64
for him saw, in a dream, astonishing
fruit that would spring from him and from his heirs.

And that his name might echo what he was,                67
a spirit moved from here to have him called
by the possessive of the One by whom

he was possessed completely. Dominic                     70
became his name; I speak of him as one
whom Christ chose as the worker in His garden.

He seemed the fitting messenger and servant              73
of Christ: the very first love that he showed
was for the first injunction Christ had given.

Degno è che, dov' è l'un, l'altro s'induca:    34
sì che, com' elli ad una militaro,
così la gloria loro insieme luca.

  L'essercito di Cristo, che sì caro    37
costò a rïarmar, dietro a la 'nsegna
si movea tardo, sospeccioso e raro,

  quando lo 'mperador che sempre regna    40
provide a la milizia, ch'era in forse,
per sola grazia, non per esser degna;

  e, come è detto, a sua sposa soccorse    43
con due campioni, al cui fare, al cui dire
lo popol disvïato si raccorse.

  In quella parte ove surge ad aprire    46
Zeffiro dolce le novelle fronde
di che si vede Europa rivestire,

  non molto lungi al percuoter de l'onde    49
dietro a le quali, per la lunga foga,
lo sol talvolta ad ogne uom si nasconde,

  siede la fortunata Calaroga    52
sotto la protezion del grande scudo
in che soggiace il leone e soggioga:

  dentro vi nacque l'amoroso drudo    55
de la fede cristiana, il santo atleta
benigno a' suoi e a' nemici crudo;

  e come fu creata, fu repleta    58
sì la sua mente di viva vertute
che, ne la madre, lei fece profeta.

  Poi che le sponsalizie fuor compiute    61
al sacro fonte intra lui e la Fede,
u' si dotar di mutüa salute,

  la donna che per lui l'assenso diede,    64
vide nel sonno il mirabile frutto
ch'uscir dovea di lui e de le rede;

  e perché fosse qual era in costrutto,    67
quinci si mosse spirito a nomarlo
del possessivo di cui era tutto.

  Domenico fu detto; e io ne parlo    70
sì come de l'agricola che Cristo
elesse a l'orto suo per aiutarlo.

  Ben parve messo e famigliar di Cristo:    73
ché 'l primo amor che 'n lui fu manifesto,
fu al primo consiglio che diè Cristo.

His nurse would often find him on the ground,     76
alert and silent, in a way that said:
'It is for this that I have come.' Truly,
   his father was Felice and his mother     79
Giovanna if her name, interpreted,
is in accord with what has been asserted.
   Not for the world, for which men now travail     82
along Taddeo's way or Ostian's,
but through his love of the true manna, he
   became, in a brief time, so great a teacher     85
that he began to oversee the vineyard
that withers when neglected by its keeper.
   And from the seat that once was kinder to     88
the righteous poor (and now has gone astray,
not in itself, but in its occupant),
   he did not ask to offer two or three     91
for six, nor for a vacant benefice,
nor *decimus, quae sunt pauperum Dei*—
   but pleaded for the right to fight against     94
the erring world, to serve the seed from which
there grew the four-and-twenty plants that ring you.
   Then he, with both his learning and his zeal,     97
and with his apostolic office, like
a torrent hurtled from a mountain source,
   coursed, and his impetus, with greatest force,     100
struck where the thickets of the heretics
offered the most resistance. And from him
   there sprang the streams with which the catholic     103
garden has found abundant watering,
so that its saplings have more life, more green.
   If such was one wheel of the chariot     106
in which the Holy Church, in her defense,
taking the field, defeated enemies
   within, then you must see the excellence     109
of him—the other wheel—whom Thomas praised
so graciously before I made my entry.
   And yet the track traced by the outer rim     112
of that wheel is abandoned now—as in
a cask of wine when crust gives way to mold.
   His family, which once advanced with steps     115
that followed his footprints, has now turned back:
its forward foot now seeks the foot that lags.

Spesse fïate fu tacito e desto
trovato in terra da la sua nutrice,
come dicesse: 'Io son venuto a questo.'

    Oh padre suo veramente Felice!            79
oh madre sua veramente Giovanna,
se, interpretata, val come si dice!

    Non per lo mondo, per cui mo s'affanna      82
di retro ad Ostïense e a Taddeo,
ma per amor de la verace manna

    in picciol tempo gran dottor si feo;        85
tal che si mise a circüir la vigna
che tosto imbianca, se 'l vignaio è reo.

    E a la sedia che fu già benigna          88
più a' poveri giusti, non per lei,
ma per colui che siede, che traligna,

    non dispensare o due o tre per sei,        91
non la fortuna di prima vacante,
non *decimas, quae sunt pauperum Dei*,

    addimandò, ma contro al mondo errante     94
licenza di combatter per lo seme
del qual ti fascian ventiquattro piante.

    Poi, con dottrina e con volere insieme,     97
con l'officio appostolico si mosse
quasi torrente ch'alta vena preme;

    e ne li sterpi eretici percosse         100
l'impeto suo, più vivamente quivi
dove le resistenze eran più grosse.

    Di lui si fecer poi diversi rivi         103
onde l'orto catolico si riga,
sì che i suoi arbuscelli stan più vivi.

    Se tal fu l'una rota de la biga         106
in che la Santa Chiesa si difese
e vinse in campo la sua civil briga,

    ben ti dovrebbe assai esser palese       109
l'eccellenza de l'altra, di cui Tomma
dinanzi al mio venir fu sì cortese.

    Ma l'orbita che fé la parte somma       112
di sua circunferenza, è derelitta,
sì ch'è la muffa dov' era la gromma.

    La sua famiglia, che si mosse dritta      115
coi piedi a le sue orme, è tanto volta,
che quel dinanzi a quel di retro gitta;

And soon we are to see, at harvest time, 118
the poor grain gathered, when the tares will be
denied a place within the bin—and weep.

I do admit that, if one were to search 121
our volume leaf by leaf, he might still read
one page with, 'I am as I always was';

but those of Acquasparta or Casale 124
who read our Rule are either given to
escaping it or making it too strict.

I am the living light of Bonaventure 127
of Bagnorea; in high offices
I always put the left-hand interests last.

Illuminato and Augustine are here; 130
they were among the first unshod poor brothers
to wear the cord, becoming friends of God.

Hugh of St. Victor, too, is here with them; 133
Peter of Spain, who, with his twelve books, glows
on earth below; and Peter Book-Devourer,

Nathan the prophet, Anselm, and Chrysostom 136
the Metropolitan, and that Donatus
who deigned to deal with that art which comes first.

Rabanus, too, is here; and at my side 139
shines the Calabrian Abbot Joachim,
who had the gift of the prophetic spirit.

To emulate so great a paladin, 142
the glowing courtesy and the discerning
language of Thomas urged me on and stirred,

with me, the souls that form this company." 145

e tosto si vedrà de la ricolta        118
de la mala coltura, quando il loglio
si lagnerà che l'arca li sia tolta.

  Ben dico, chi cercasse a foglio a foglio        121
nostro volume, ancor troveria carta
u' leggerebbe 'I' mi son quel ch'i' soglio';

  ma non fia da Casal né d'Acquasparta,        124
là onde vegnon tali a la scrittura,
ch'uno la fugge e altro la coarta.

  Io son la vita di Bonaventura        127
da Bagnoregio, che ne' grandi offici
sempre pospuosi la sinistra cura.

  Illuminato e Augustin son quici,        130
che fuor de' primi scalzi poverelli
che nel capestro a Dio si fero amici.

  Ugo da San Vittore è qui con elli,        133
e Pietro Mangiadore e Pietro Spano,
lo qual giù luce in dodici libelli;

  Natàn profeta e 'l metropolitano        136
Crisostomo e Anselmo e quel Donato
ch'a la prim' arte degnò porre mano.

  Rabano è qui, e lucemi dallato        139
il calavrese abate Giovacchino
di spirito profetico dotato.

  Ad inveggiar cotanto paladino        142
mi mosse l'infiammata cortesia
di fra Tommaso e 'l discreto latino;

  e mosse meco questa compagnia."        145

# CANTO XIII

Let him imagine, who would rightly seize
what I saw now—and let him while I speak
retain that image like a steadfast rock—
in heaven's different parts, those fifteen stars          4
that quicken heaven with such radiance
as to undo the air's opacities;
let him imagine, too, that Wain which stays              7
within our heaven's bosom night and day,
so that its turning never leaves our sight;
let him imagine those two stars that form                10
the mouth of that Horn which begins atop
the axle round which the first wheel revolves;
then see these join to form two signs in heaven—        13
just like the constellation that was shaped
by Minos' daughter when she felt death's chill—
two signs with corresponding radii,                     16
revolving so that one sign moves in one
direction, and the other in a second;
and he will have a shadow—as it were—                   19
of the true constellation, the double dance
that circled round the point where I was standing:
a shadow—since its truth exceeds our senses,            22
just as the swiftest of all heavens is
more swift than the Chiana's sluggishness.
They sang no Bacchus there, they sang no Paean,         25
but sang three Persons in the divine nature,
and in one Person the divine and human.
The singing and the dance fulfilled their measure;     28
and then those holy lights gave heed to us,
rejoicing as they turned from task to task.
The silence of the blessed fellowship                   31
was broken by the very light from which
I heard the wondrous life of God's poor man;

*Still the Fourth Heaven: the Sphere of the Sun. Invitation to the reader to exercise his astronomical fantasy. Dance and song of the two rings of spirits. St. Thomas on the wisdom of King Solomon. St. Thomas's warning against hasty judgments.*

Imagini, chi bene intender cupe
quel ch'i' or vidi—e ritegna l'image,
mentre ch'io dico, come ferma rupe—,
    quindici stelle che 'n diverse plage                   4
lo cielo avvivan di tanto sereno
che soperchia de l'aere ogne compage;
    imagini quel carro a cu' il seno                        7
basta del nostro cielo e notte e giorno,
sì ch'al volger del temo non vien meno;
    imagini la bocca di quel corno                          10
che si comincia in punta de lo stelo
a cui la prima rota va dintorno,
    aver fatto di sé due segni in cielo,                    13
qual fece la figliuola di Minoi
allora che sentì di morte il gelo;
    e l'un ne l'altro aver li raggi suoi,                   16
e amendue girarsi per maniera
che l'uno andasse al primo e l'altro al poi;
    e avrà quasi l'ombra de la vera                         19
costellazione e de la doppia danza
che circulava il punto dov' io era:
    poi ch'è tanto di là da nostra usanza,                  22
quanto di là dal mover de la Chiana
si move il ciel che tutti li altri avanza.
    Lì si cantò non Bacco, non Peana,                       25
ma tre persone in divina natura,
e in una persona essa e l'umana.
    Compié 'l cantare e 'l volger sua misura;              28
e attesersi a noi quei santi lumi,
felicitando sé di cura in cura.
    Ruppe il silenzio ne' concordi numi                     31
poscia la luce in che mirabil vita
del poverel di Dio narrata fumi,

that light said: "Since one stalk is threshed, and since          34
its grain is in the granary already,
sweet love leads me to thresh the other stalk.
    You think that any light which human nature          37
can rightfully possess was all infused
by that Force which had shaped both of these two:
    the one out of whose chest was drawn the rib          40
from which was formed the lovely cheek whose palate
was then to prove so costly to the world;
    and One whose chest was transfixed by the lance,          43
who satisfied all past and future sins,
outweighing them upon the scales of justice.
    Therefore you wondered at my words when I—          46
before—said that no other ever vied
with that great soul enclosed in the fifth light.
    Now let your eyes hold fast to my reply,          49
and you will see: truth centers both my speech
and your belief, just like a circle's center.
    Both that which never dies and that which dies          52
are only the reflected light of that
Idea which our Sire, with Love, begets;
    because the living Light that pours out so          55
from Its bright Source that It does not disjoin
from It or from the Love intrined with them,
    through Its own goodness gathers up Its rays          58
within nine essences, as in a mirror,
Itself eternally remaining One.
    From there, from act to act, light then descends          61
down to the last potentialities,
where it is such that it engenders nothing
    but brief contingent things, by which I mean          64
the generated things the moving heavens
bring into being, with or without seed.
    The wax of such things and what shapes that wax          67
are not immutable; and thus, beneath
Idea's stamp, light shines through more or less.
    Thus it can be that, in the selfsame species,          70
some trees bear better fruit and some bear worse,
and men are born with different temperaments.
    For were the wax appropriately readied,          73
and were the heaven's power at its height,
the brightness of the seal would show completely;

e disse: "Quando l'una paglia è trita,  34
quando la sua semenza è già riposta,
a batter l'altra dolce amor m'invita.

    Tu credi che nel petto onde la costa  37
si trasse per formar la bella guancia
il cui palato a tutto 'l mondo costa,

    e in quel che, forato da la lancia,  40
e prima e poscia tanto sodisfece,
che d'ogne colpa vince la bilancia,

    quantunque a la natura umana lece  43
aver di lume, tutto fosse infuso
da quel valor che l'uno e l'altro fece;

    e però miri a ciò ch'io dissi suso,  46
quando narrai che non ebbe 'l secondo
lo ben che ne la quinta luce è chiuso.

    Or apri li occhi a quel ch'io ti rispondo,  49
e vedräi il tuo credere e 'l mio dire
nel vero farsi come centro in tondo.

    Ciò che non more e ciò che può morire  52
non è se non splendor di quella idea
che partorisce, amando, il nostro Sire;

    ché quella viva luce che sì mea  55
dal suo lucente, che non si disuna
da lui né da l'amor ch'a lor s'intrea,

    per sua bontate il suo raggiare aduna,  58
quasi specchiato, in nove sussistenze,
etternalmente rimanendosi una.

    Quindi discende a l'ultime potenze  61
giù d'atto in atto, tanto divenendo,
che più non fa che brevi contingenze;

    e queste contingenze essere intendo  64
le cose generate, che produce
con seme e sanza seme il ciel movendo.

    La cera di costoro e chi la duce  67
non sta d'un modo; e però sotto 'l segno
idëale poi più e men traluce.

    Ond' elli avvien ch'un medesimo legno,  70
secondo specie, meglio e peggio frutta;
e voi nascete con diverso ingegno.

    Se fosse a punto la cera dedutta  73
e fosse il cielo in sua virtù supprema,
la luce del suggel parrebbe tutta;

but Nature always works defectively— 76
she passes on that light much like an artist
who knows his craft but has a hand that trembles.

Yet where the ardent Love prepares and stamps 79
the lucid Vision of the primal Power,
a being then acquires complete perfection.

In that way, earth was once made worthy of 82
the full perfection of a living being;
thus was the Virgin made to be with child.

So that I do approve of the opinion 85
you hold: that human nature never was
nor shall be what it was in those two persons.

Now if I said no more beyond this point, 88
your words might well begin, 'How is it, then,
with your assertion of his matchless vision?'

But so that the obscure can be made plain, 91
consider who he was, what was the cause
of his request when he was told, 'Do ask.'

My words did not prevent your seeing clearly 94
that it was as a king that he had asked
for wisdom that would serve his royal task—

and not to know the number of the angels 97
on high or, if combined with a contingent,
*necesse* ever can produce *necesse*,

or *si est dare primum motum esse*, 100
or if, within a semicircle, one
can draw a triangle with no right angle.

Thus, if you note both what I said and say, 103
by 'matchless vision' it is kingly prudence
my arrow of intention means to strike;

and if you turn clear eyes to that word 'rose,' 106
you'll see that it referred to kings alone—
kings, who are many, and the good are rare.

Take what I said with this distinction then; 109
in that way it accords with what you thought
of the first father and of our Beloved.

And let this weigh as lead to slow your steps, 112
to make you move as would a weary man
to *yes* or *no* when you do not see clearly:

whether he would affirm or would deny, 115
he who decides without distinguishing
must be among the most obtuse of men;

ma la natura la dà sempre scema,     76
similemente operando a l'artista
ch'a l'abito de l'arte ha man che trema.

   Però se 'l caldo amor la chiara vista     79
de la prima virtù dispone e segna,
tutta la perfezion quivi s'acquista.

   Così fu fatta già la terra degna     82
di tutta l'animal perfezïone;
così fu fatta la Vergine pregna;

   sì ch'io commendo tua oppinïone,     85
che l'umana natura mai non fue
né fia qual fu in quelle due persone.

   Or s'i' non procedesse avanti pìue,     88
'Dunque, come costui fu sanza pare?'
comincerebber le parole tue.

   Ma perché paia ben ciò che non pare,     91
pensa chi era, e la cagion che 'l mosse,
quando fu detto 'Chiedi,' a dimandare.

   Non ho parlato sì, che tu non posse     94
ben veder ch'el fu re, che chiese senno
acciò che re sufficïente fosse;

   non per sapere il numero in che enno     97
li motor di qua sù, o se *necesse*
con contingente mai *necesse* fenno;

   non *si est dare primum motum esse*,     100
o se del mezzo cerchio far si puote
trïangol sì ch'un retto non avesse.

   Onde, se ciò ch'io dissi e questo note,     103
regal prudenza è quel vedere impari
in che lo stral di mia intenzion percuote;

   e se al "surse" drizzi li occhi chiari,     106
vedrai aver solamente respetto
ai regi, che son molti, e ' buon son rari.

   Con questa distinzion prendi 'l mio detto;     109
e così puote star con quel che credi
del primo padre e del nostro Diletto.

   E questo ti sia sempre piombo a' piedi,     112
per farti mover lento com' uom lasso
e al sì e al no che tu non vedi:

   ché quelli è tra li stolti bene a basso,     115
che sanza distinzione afferma e nega
ne l'un così come ne l'altro passo;

opinion—hasty—often can incline                118
to the wrong side, and then affection for
one's own opinion binds, confines the mind.
    Far worse than uselessly he leaves the shore    121
(more full of error than he was before)
who fishes for the truth but lacks the art.
    Of this, Parmenides, Melissus, Bryson,        124
are clear proofs to the world, and many others
who went their way but knew not where it went;
    so did Sabellius and Arius                    127
and other fools—like concave blades that mirror—
who rendered crooked the straight face of Scriptures.
    So, too, let men not be too confident         130
in judging—witness those who, in the field,
would count the ears before the corn is ripe;
    for I have seen, all winter through, the brier    133
display itself as stiff and obstinate,
and later, on its summit, bear the rose;
    and once I saw a ship sail straight and swift    136
through all its voyaging across the sea,
then perish at the end, at harbor entry.
    Let not Dame Bertha or Master Martin think    139
that they have shared God's Counsel when they see
one rob and see another who donates:
    the last may fall, the other may be saved."    142

perch' elli 'ncontra che più volte piega     118
l'oppinïon corrente in falsa parte,
e poi l'affetto l'intelletto lega.

  Vie più che 'ndarno da riva si parte,     121
perché non torna tal qual e' si move,
chi pesca per lo vero e non ha l'arte.

  E di ciò sono al mondo aperte prove     124
Parmenide, Melisso e Brisso e molti,
li quali andaro e non sapëan dove;

  sì fé Sabellio e Arrio e quelli stolti     127
che furon come spade a le Scritture
in render torti li diritti volti.

  Non sien le genti, ancor, troppo sicure     130
a giudicar, sì come quei che stima
le biade in campo pria che sien mature;

  ch'i' ho veduto tutto 'l verno prima     133
lo prun mostrarsi rigido e feroce,
poscia portar la rosa in su la cima;

  e legno vidi già dritto e veloce     136
correr lo mar per tutto suo cammino,
perire al fine a l'intrar de la foce.

  Non creda donna Berta e ser Martino,     139
per vedere un furare, altro offerere,
vederli dentro al consiglio divino;

  ché quel può surgere, e quel può cadere."     142

OVERLEAF:
*The Resurrection*

# CANTO XIV

From rim to center, center out to rim,
so does the water move in a round vessel,
as it is struck without, or struck within.
    What I am saying fell most suddenly          4
into my mind, as soon as Thomas's
glorious living flame fell silent, since
    between his speech and that of Beatrice,      7
a similarity was born. And she,
when he was done, was pleased to start with this:
    "He does not tell you of it—not with speech   10
nor in his thoughts as yet—but this man needs
to reach the root of still another truth.
    Do tell him if that light with which your soul  13
blossoms will stay with you eternally
even as it is now; and if it stays,
    do tell him how, when you are once again       16
made visible, it will be possible
for you to see such light and not be harmed."
    As dancers in a ring, when drawn and driven    19
by greater gladness, lift at times their voices
and dance their dance with more exuberance,
    so, when they heard that prompt, devout request,  22
the blessed circles showed new joyousness
in wheeling dance and in amazing song.
    Whoever weeps because on earth we die          25
that we may live on high, has never seen
eternal showers that bring refreshment there.
    That One and Two and Three who ever lives      28
and ever reigns in Three and Two and One,
not circumscribed and circumscribing all,
    was sung three times by each and all those souls  31
with such a melody that it would be
appropriate reward for every merit.

*Still the Fourth Heaven: the Sphere of the Sun. Beatrice's*
*request to the spirits to resolve Dante's query concerning the*
*radiance of the spirits after the Resurrection. Solomon's reply.*
*Appearance of new spirits. Ascent to the Fifth Heaven, the*
*Sphere of Mars. The vision of a cross and Christ. The rapture*
*of Dante.*

Dal centro al cerchio, e sì dal cerchio al centro
movesi l'acqua in un ritondo vaso,
secondo ch'è percosso fuori o dentro:

ne la mia mente fé sùbito caso                                    4
questo ch'io dico, sì come si tacque
la glorïosa vita di Tommaso,

per la similitudine che nacque                                   7
del suo parlare e di quel di Beatrice,
a cui sì cominciar, dopo lui, piacque:

"A costui fa mestieri, e nol vi dice                             10
né con la voce né pensando ancora,
d'un altro vero andare a la radice.

Diteli se la luce onde s'infiora                                 13
vostra sustanza, rimarrà con voi
etternalmente sì com' ell' è ora;

e se rimane, dite come, poi                                      16
che sarete visibili rifatti,
esser porà ch'al veder non vi nòi."

Come, da più letizia pinti e tratti,                             19
a la fiata quei che vanno a rota
levan la voce e rallegrano li atti,

così, a l'orazion pronta e divota,                               22
li santi cerchi mostrar nova gioia
nel torneare e ne la mira nota.

Qual si lamenta perché qui si moia                               25
per viver colà sù, non vide quive
lo refrigerio de l'etterna ploia.

Quell' uno e due e tre che sempre vive                           28
e regna sempre in tre e 'n due e 'n uno,
non circunscritto, e tutto circunscrive,

tre volte era cantato da ciascuno                                31
di quelli spiriti con tal melodia,
ch'ad ogne merto saria giusto muno.

And I could hear within the smaller circle's     34
divinest light a modest voice (perhaps
much like the angel's voice in speech to Mary)
reply: "As long as the festivity     37
of Paradise shall be, so long shall our
love radiate around us such a garment.
Its brightness takes its measure from our ardor,     40
our ardor from our vision, which is measured
by what grace each receives beyond his merit.
When, glorified and sanctified, the flesh     43
is once again our dress, our persons shall,
in being all complete, please all the more;
therefore, whatever light gratuitous     46
the Highest Good gives us will be enhanced—
the light that will allow us to see Him;
that light will cause our vision to increase,     49
the ardor vision kindles to increase,
the brightness born of ardor to increase.
Yet even as a coal engenders flame,     52
but with intenser glow outshines it, so
that in that flame the coal persists, it shows;
so will the brightness that envelops us     55
be then surpassed in visibility
by reborn flesh, which earth now covers up.
Nor will we tire when faced with such bright light,     58
for then the body's organs will have force
enough for all in which we can delight."
One and the other choir seemed to me     61
so quick and keen to say "Amen" that they
showed clearly how they longed for their dead bodies—
not only for themselves, perhaps, but for     64
their mothers, fathers, and for others dear
to them before they were eternal flames.
And—look!—beyond the light already there,     67
an added luster rose around those rings,
even as a horizon brightening.
And even as, at the approach of evening,     70
new lights begin to show along the sky,
so that the sight seems and does not seem real,
it seemed to me that I began to see     73
new spirits there, forming a ring beyond
the choirs with their two circumferences.

E io udi' ne la luce più dia                                           34
del minor cerchio una voce modesta,
forse qual fu da l'angelo a Maria,
    risponder: "Quanto fia lunga la festa           37
di paradiso, tanto il nostro amore
si raggerà dintorno cotal vesta.
    La sua chiarezza séguita l'ardore;              40
l'ardor la visïone, e quella è tanta,
quant' ha di grazia sovra suo valore.
    Come la carne glorïosa e santa                 43
fia rivestita, la nostra persona
più grata fia per esser tutta quanta;
    per che s'accrescerà ciò che ne dona            46
di gratüito lume il sommo bene,
lume ch'a lui veder ne condiziona;
    onde la visïon crescer convene,                49
crescer l'ardor che di quella s'accende,
crescer lo raggio che da esso vene.
    Ma sì come carbon che fiamma rende,            52
e per vivo candor quella soverchia,
sì che la sua parvenza si difende;
    così questo folgór che già ne cerchia          55
fia vinto in apparenza da la carne
che tutto dì la terra ricoperchia;
    né potrà tanta luce affaticarne:               58
ché li organi del corpo saran forti
a tutto ciò che potrà dilettarne."
    Tanto mi parver sùbiti e accorti               61
e l'uno e l'altro coro a dicer "Amme!"
che ben mostrar disio d'i corpi morti:
    forse non pur per lor, ma per le mamme,         64
per li padri e per li altri che fuor cari
anzi che fosser sempiterne fiamme.
    Ed ecco intorno, di chiarezza pari,            67
nascere un lustro sopra quel che v'era,
per guisa d'orizzonte che rischiari.
    E sì come al salir di prima sera                70
comincian per lo ciel nove parvenze,
sì che la vista pare e non par vera,
    parvemi lì novelle sussistenze                 73
cominciare a vedere, e fare un giro
di fuor da l'altre due circunferenze.

O the true sparkling of the Holy Ghost— 76
how rapid and how radiant before
my eyes that, overcome, could not sustain it!

But, smiling, Beatrice then showed to me 79
such loveliness—it must be left among
the visions that take flight from memory.

From this my eyes regained the strength to look 82
above again; I saw myself translated
to higher blessedness, alone with my

lady; and I was sure that I had risen 85
because the smiling star was red as fire—
beyond the customary red of Mars.

With all my heart and in that language which 88
is one for all, for this new grace I gave
to God my holocaust, appropriate.

Though in my breast that burning sacrifice 91
was not completed yet, I was aware
that it had been accepted and auspicious;

for splendors, in two rays, appeared to me, 94
so radiant and fiery that I said:
"O Helios, you who adorn them thus!"

As, graced with lesser and with larger lights 97
between the poles of the world, the Galaxy
gleams so that even sages are perplexed;

so, constellated in the depth of Mars, 100
those rays described the venerable sign
a circle's quadrants form where they are joined.

And here my memory defeats my wit: 103
Christ's flaming from that cross was such that I
can find no fit similitude for it.

But he who takes his cross and follows Christ 106
will pardon me again for my omission—
my seeing Christ flash forth undid my force.

Lights moved along that cross from horn to horn 109
and from the summit to the base, and as
they met and passed, they sparkled, radiant:

so, straight and slant and quick and slow, one sees 112
on earth the particles of bodies, long
and short, in shifting shapes, that move along

the ray of light that sometimes streaks across 115
the shade that men devise with skill and art
to serve as their defense against the sun.

Oh vero sfavillar del Santo Spiro!    76
come si fece sùbito e candente
a li occhi miei che, vinti, nol soffriro!

  Ma Bëatrice sì bella e ridente    79
mi si mostrò, che tra quelle vedute
si vuol lasciar che non seguir la mente.

  Quindi ripreser li occhi miei virtute    82
a rilevarsi; e vidimi translato
sol con mia donna in più alta salute.

  Ben m'accors' io ch'io era più levato,    85
per l'affocato riso de la stella,
che mi parea più roggio che l'usato.

  Con tutto 'l core e con quella favella    88
ch'è una in tutti, a Dio feci olocausto,
qual conveniesi a la grazia novella.

  E non er' anco del mio petto essausto    89
l'ardor del sacrificio, ch'io conobbi
esso litare stato accetto e fausto;

  ché con tanto lucore e tanto robbi    94
m'apparvero splendor dentro a due raggi,
ch'io dissi: "O Eliòs che sì li addobbi!"

  Come distinta da minori e maggi    97
lumi biancheggia tra ' poli del mondo
Galassia sì, che fa dubbiar ben saggi;

  sì costellati facean nel profondo    100
Marte quei raggi il venerabil segno
che fan giunture di quadranti in tondo.

  Qui vince la memoria mia lo 'ngegno;    103
ché quella croce lampeggiava Cristo,
sì ch'io non so trovare essempro degno;

  ma chi prende sua croce e segue Cristo,    106
ancor mi scuserà di quel ch'io lasso,
vedendo in quell' albor balenar Cristo.

  Di corno in corno e tra la cima e 'l basso    109
si movien lumi, scintillando forte
nel congiugnersi insieme e nel trapasso:

  così si veggion qui diritte e torte,    112
veloci e tarde, rinovando vista,
le minuzie d'i corpi, lunghe e corte,

  moversi per lo raggio onde si lista    115
talvolta l'ombra che, per sua difesa,
la gente con ingegno e arte acquista.

And just as harp and viol, whose many chords    118
are tempered, taut, produce sweet harmony
although each single note is not distinct,

so, from the lights that then appeared to me,    121
out from that cross there spread a melody
that held me rapt, although I could not tell

what hymn it was. I knew it sang high praise,    124
since I heard "Rise" and "Conquer," but I was
as one who hears but cannot seize the sense.

Yet I was so enchanted by the sound    127
that until then no thing had ever bound
me with such gentle bonds. My words may seem

presumptuous, as though I dared to deem    130
a lesser thing the lovely eyes that bring
to my desire, as it gazes, peace.

But he who notes that, in ascent, her eyes—    133
all beauty's living seals—gain force, and notes
that I had not yet turned to them in Mars,

can then excuse me—just as I accuse    136
myself, thus to excuse myself—and see
that I speak truly: here her holy beauty

is not denied—ascent makes it more perfect.    139

E come giga e arpa, in tempra tesa      118
di molte corde, fa dolce tintinno
a tal da cui la nota non è intesa,
     così da' lumi che lì m'apparinno      121
s'accogliea per la croce una melode
che mi rapiva, sanza intender l'inno.
     Ben m'accors' io ch'elli era d'alte lode,      124
però ch'a me venìa "Resurgi" e "Vinci"
come a colui che non intende e ode.
     Io m'innamorava tanto quinci,      127
che 'nfino a lì non alcuna cosa
che mi legasse con sì dolci vinci.
     Forse la mia parola par troppo osa,      130
posponendo il piacer de li occhi belli,
ne' quai mirando mio disio ha posa;
     ma chi s'avvede che i vivi suggelli      133
d'ogne bellezza più fanno più suso,
e ch'io non m'era lì rivolto a quelli,
     escusar puommi di quel ch'io m'accuso      136
per escusarmi, e vedermi dir vero:
ché 'l piacer santo non è qui dischiuso,
     perché si fa, montando, più sincero.

# CANTO XV

Generous will—in which is manifest
always the love that breathes toward righteousness,
as in contorted will is greediness—

imposing silence on that gentle lyre,                              4
brought quiet to the consecrated chords
that Heaven's right hand slackens and draws taut.

Can souls who prompted me to pray to them,                        7
by falling silent all in unison,
be deaf to men's just prayers? Then he may grieve

indeed and endlessly—the man who leaves                           10
behind such love and turns instead to seek
things that do not endure eternally.

As, through the pure and tranquil skies of night,                 13
at times a sudden fire shoots, and moves
eyes that were motionless—a fire that seems

a star that shifts its place, except that in                      16
that portion of the heavens where it flared,
nothing is lost, and its own course is short—

so, from the horn that stretches on the right,                    19
down to the foot of that cross, a star ran
out of the constellation glowing there;

nor did that gem desert the cross's track,                        22
but coursed along the radii, and seemed
just like a flame that alabaster screens.

With such affection did Anchises' shade                           25
reach out (if we may trust our greatest muse)
when in Elysium he saw his son.

"O blood of mine—o the celestial grace                            28
bestowed beyond all measure—unto whom
as unto you was Heaven's gate twice opened?"

That light said this; and thus, I heeded him.                     31
Then, looking back to see my lady, I,
on this side and on that, was stupefied;

*The Fifth Heaven: the Sphere of Mars. The silence of the
blessed spirits. Cacciaguida, who reveals himself as Dante's
ancestor. Cacciaguida on the Florence of his times and his life
there, and on his death in the Holy Land in the Second Crusade,
where he served the emperor Conrad.*

Benigna volontade in che si liqua
sempre l'amor che drittamente spira,
come cupidità fa ne la iniqua,

silenzio puose a quella dolce lira,                                    4
e fece quïetar le sante corde
che la destra del cielo allenta e tira.

Come saranno a' giusti preghi sorde                                    7
quelle sustanze che, per darmi voglia
ch'io le pregassi, a tacer fur concorde?

Bene è che sanza termine si doglia                                     10
chi, per amor di cosa che non duri
etternalmente, quello amor si spoglia.

Quale per li seren tranquilli e puri                                   13
discorre ad ora ad or sùbito foco,
movendo li occhi che stavan sicuri,

e pare stella che tramuti loco,                                        16
se non che da la parte ond' e' s'accende
nulla sen perde, ed esso dura poco:

tale dal corno che 'n destro si stende                                 19
a piè di quella croce corse un astro
de la costellazion che lì resplende;

né si partì la gemma dal suo nastro,                                   22
ma per la lista radïal trascorse,
che parve foco dietro ad alabastro.

Sì pïa l'ombra d'Anchise si porse,                                     25
se fede merta nostra maggior musa,
quando in Eliso del figlio s'accorse.

"*O sanguis meus, o superinfusa*                                       28
*gratia Deï, sicut tibi cui*
*bis unquam celi ianüa reclusa?*"

Così quel lume: ond' io m'attesi a lui;                                31
poscia rivolsi a la mia donna il viso,
e quinci e quindi stupefatto fui;

for in the smile that glowed within her eyes,                34
I thought that I—with mine—had touched the height
of both my blessedness and paradise.

Then—and he was a joy to hear and see—                       37
that spirit added to his first words things
that were too deep to meet my understanding.

Not that he chose to hide his sense from me;                 40
necessity compelled him; he conceived
beyond the mark a mortal mind can reach.

And when his bow of burning sympathy                         43
was slack enough to let his speech descend
to meet the limit of our intellect,

these were the first words where I caught the sense:         46
"Blessed be you, both Three and One, who show
such favor to my seed." And he continued:

"The long and happy hungering I drew                         49
from reading that great volume where both black
and white are never changed, you—son—have now

appeased within this light in which I speak                  52
to you; for this, I owe my gratitude
to her who gave you wings for your high flight.

You think your thoughts flow into me from Him                55
who is the First—as from the number one,
the five and six derive, if one is known—

and so you do not ask me who I am                            58
and why I seem more joyous to you than
all other spirits in this festive throng.

Your thought is true, for both the small and great           61
of this life gaze into that mirror where,
before you think, your thoughts have been displayed.

But that the sacred love in which I keep                     64
my vigil with unending watchfulness,
the love that makes me thirst with sweet desire,

be better satisfied, let your voice—bold,                    67
assured, and glad—proclaim your will and longing,
to which my answer is decreed already."

I turned to Beatrice, but she heard me                       70
before I spoke; her smile to me was signal
that made the wings of my desire grow.

Then I began: "As soon as you beheld                         73
the First Equality, both intellect
and love weighed equally for each of you,

ché dentro a li occhi suoi ardeva un riso        34
tal, ch'io pensai co' miei toccar lo fondo
de la mia gloria e del mio paradiso.

    Indi, a udire e a veder giocondo,        37
giunse lo spirto al suo principio cose,
ch'io non lo 'ntesi, sì parlò profondo;

    né per elezïon mi si nascose,        40
ma per necessità, ché 'l suo concetto
al segno d'i mortal si soprapuose.

    E quando l'arco de l'ardente affetto        43
fu sì sfogato, che 'l parlar discese
inver' lo segno del nostro intelletto,

    la prima cosa che per me s'intese,        46
"Benedetto sia tu," fu, "trino e uno,
che nel mio seme se' tanto cortese!"

    E seguì: "Grato e lontano digiuno,        49
tratto leggendo del magno volume
du' non si muta mai bianco né bruno,

    solvuto hai, figlio, dentro a questo lume        52
in ch'io ti parlo, mercé di colei
ch'a l'alto volo ti vestì le piume.

    Tu credi che a me tuo pensier mei        55
da quel ch'è primo, così come raia
da l'un, se si conosce, il cinque e 'l sei;

    e però ch'io mi sia e perch' io paia        58
più gaudïoso a te, non mi domandi,
che alcun altro in questa turba gaia.

    Tu credi 'l vero; ché i minori e ' grandi        61
di questa vita miran ne lo speglio
in che, prima che pensi, il pensier pandi;

    ma perché 'l sacro amore in che io veglio        64
con perpetüa vista e che m'asseta
di dolce disïar, s'adempia meglio,

    la voce tua sicura, balda e lieta        67
suoni la volontà, suoni 'l disio,
a che la mia risposta è già decreta!"

    Io mi volsi a Beatrice, e quella udio        70
pria ch'io parlassi, e arrisemi un cenno
che fece crescer l'ali al voler mio.

    Poi cominciai così: "L'affetto e 'l senno,        73
come la prima equalità v'apparse,
d'un peso per ciascun di voi si fenno,

because the Sun that brought you light and heat     76
possesses heat and light so equally
that no thing matches His equality;
    whereas in mortals, word and sentiment—     79
to you, the cause of this is evident—
are wings whose featherings are disparate.
    I—mortal—feel this inequality;     82
thus, it is only with my heart that I
can offer thanks for your paternal greeting.
    Indeed I do beseech you, living topaz,     85
set in this precious jewel as a gem:
fulfill my longing—let me know your name."
    "O you, my branch in whom I took delight     88
even awaiting you, I am your root,"
so he, in his reply to me, began,
    then said: "The man who gave your family     91
its name, who for a century and more
has circled the first ledge of Purgatory,
    was son to me and was your great-grandfather;     94
it is indeed appropriate for you
to shorten his long toil with your good works.
    Florence, within her ancient ring of walls—     97
that ring from which she still draws tierce and nones—
sober and chaste, lived in tranquillity.
    No necklace and no coronal were there,     100
and no embroidered gowns; there was no girdle
that caught the eye more than the one who wore it.
    No daughter's birth brought fear unto her father,     103
for age and dowry then did not imbalance—
to this side and to that—the proper measure.
    There were no families that bore no children;     106
and Sardanapalus was still a stranger—
not come as yet to teach in the bedchamber.
    Not yet had your Uccellatoio's rise     109
outdone the rise of Monte Mario,
which, too, will be outdone in its decline.
    I saw Bellincione Berti girt     112
with leather and with bone, and saw his wife
come from her mirror with her face unpainted.
    I saw dei Nerli and del Vecchio     115
content to wear their suits of unlined skins,
and saw their wives at spindle and at spool.

però che 'l sol che v'allumò e arse,        76
col caldo e con la luce è sì iguali,
che tutte simiglianze sono scarse.

   Ma voglia e argomento ne' mortali,        79
per la cagion ch'a voi è manifesta,
diversamente son pennuti in ali;

   ond' io, che son mortal, mi sento in questa        82
disagguaglianza, e però non ringrazio
se non col core a la paterna festa.

   Ben supplico io a te, vivo topazio        85
che questa gioia prezïosa ingemmi,
perché mi facci del tuo nome sazio."

   "O fronda mia in che io compiacemmi        88
pur aspettando, io fui la tua radice":
cotal principio, rispondendo, femmi.

   Poscia mi disse: "Quel da cui si dice        91
tua cognazione e che cent' anni e piùe
girato ha 'l monte in la prima cornice,

   mio figlio fu e tuo bisavol fue:        94
ben si convien che la lunga fatica
tu li raccorci con l'opere tue.

   Fiorenza dentro da la cerchia antica,        97
ond' ella toglie ancora e terza e nona,
si stava in pace, sobria e pudica.

   Non avea catenella, non corona,        100
non gonne contigiate, non cintura
che fosse a veder più che la persona.

   Non faceva, nascendo, ancor paura        103
la figlia al padre, ché 'l tempo e la dote
non fuggien quinci e quindi la misura.

   Non avea case di famiglia vòte;        106
non v'era giunto ancor Sardanapalo
a mostrar ciò che 'n camera si puote.

   Non era vinto ancora Montemalo        109
dal vostro Uccellatoio, che, com' è vinto
nel montar sù, così sarà nel calo.

   Bellincion Berti vid' io andar cinto        112
di cuoio e d'osso, e venir da lo specchio
la donna sua sanza 'l viso dipinto;

   e vidi quel d'i Nerli e quel del Vecchio        115
esser contenti a la pelle scoperta,
e le sue donne al fuso e al pennecchio.

O happy wives! Each one was sure of her          118
own burial place, and none—for France's sake—
as yet was left deserted in her bed.

 One woman watched with loving care the cradle          121
and, as she soothed her infant, used the way
of speech with which fathers and mothers play;

 another, as she drew threads from the distaff,          124
would tell, among her household, tales of Trojans,
and tales of Fiesole, and tales of Rome.

 A Lapo Salterello, a Cianghella,          127
would then have stirred as much dismay as now
a Cincinnatus and Cornelia would.

 To such a life—so tranquil and so lovely—          130
of citizens in true community,
into so sweet a dwelling place did Mary,

 invoked in pains of birth, deliver me;          133
and I, within your ancient Baptistery,
at once became Christian and Cacciaguida.

 Moronto was my brother, and Eliseo;          136
my wife came from the valley of the Po—
the surname that you bear was brought by her.

 In later years I served the Emperor          139
Conrad—and my good works so gained his favor
that he gave me the girdle of his knighthood.

 I followed him to war against the evil          142
of that law whose adherents have usurped—
this, through your Pastors' fault—your just possessions.

 There, by that execrable race, I was          145
set free from fetters of the erring world,
the love of which defiles so many souls.

 From martyrdom I came unto this peace."          148

Oh fortunate! ciascuna era certa 118
de la sua sepultura, e ancor nulla
era per Francia nel letto diserta.

L'una vegghiava a studio de la culla, 121
e, consolando, usava l'idïoma
che prima i padri e le madri trastulla;

l'altra, traendo a la rocca la chioma, 124
favoleggiava con la sua famiglia
d'i Troiani, di Fiesole e di Roma.

Saria tenuta allor tal maraviglia 127
una Cianghella, un Lapo Salterello,
qual or saria Cincinnato e Corniglia.

A così riposato, a così bello 130
viver di cittadini, a così fida
cittadinanza, a così dolce ostello,

Maria mi diè, chiamata in alte grida; 133
e ne l'antico vostro Batisteo
insieme fui cristiano e Cacciaguida.

Moronto fu mio frate ed Eliseo; 136
mia donna venne a me di val di Pado,
e quindi il sopranome tuo si feo.

Poi seguitai lo 'mperador Currado; 139
ed el mi cinse de la sua milizia,
tanto per bene ovrar li venni in grado.

Dietro li andai incontro a la nequizia 142
di quella legge il cui popolo usurpa,
per colpa d'i pastor, vostra giustizia.

Quivi fu' io da quella gente turpa 145
disviluppato dal mondo fallace,
lo cui amor molt' anime deturpa;

e venni dal martiro a questa pace." 148

OVERLEAF:
*The Evocation of Florence*

# CANTO XVI

If here below, where sentiment is far
too weak to withstand error, I should see
men glorying in you, nobility

of blood—a meager thing!—I should not wonder,         4
for even where desire is not awry,
I mean in Heaven, I too felt such pride.

You are indeed a cloak that soon wears out,           7
so that if, day by day, we add no patch,
then circling time will trim you with its shears.

My speech began again with *you,* the word            10
that Rome was the first city to allow,
although her people seldom speak it now;

at this word, Beatrice, somewhat apart,               13
smiling, seemed like the woman who had coughed—
so goes the tale—at Guinevere's first fault.

So did my speech begin: "You are my father;           16
you hearten me to speak with confidence;
you raise me so that I am more than I.

So many streams have filled my mind with gladness—    19
so many, and such gladness, that mind must
rejoice that it can bear this and not burst.

Then tell me, founder of my family,                   22
who were your ancestors and, in your boyhood,
what were the years the records registered;

and tell me of the sheepfold of St. John—            25
how numerous it was, who in that flock
were worthy of the highest offices."

As at the breathing of the winds, a coal             28
will quicken into flame, so I saw that
light glow at words that were affectionate;

and as, before my eyes, it grew more fair,           31
so, with a voice more gentle and more sweet—
not in our modern speech—it said to me:

*Still the Fifth Heaven: the Sphere of Mars. Pride in birth.*
*Dante's queries to Cacciaguida. Cacciaguida's replies: the date*
*of his birth, his ancestors, the population and notable families*
*of Florence in Cacciaguida's time.*

O poca nostra nobiltà di sangue,
se glorïar di te la gente fai
qua giù dove l'affetto nostro langue,

    mirabil cosa non mi sarà mai:                    4
ché là dove appetito non si torce,
dico nel cielo, io me ne gloriai.

    Ben se' tu manto che tosto raccorce:            7
sì che, se non s'appon di dì in die,
lo tempo va dintorno con le force.

    Dal "voi" che prima a Roma s'offerie,          10
in che la sua famiglia men persevra,
ricominciaron le parole mie;

    onde Beatrice, ch'era un poco scevra,          13
ridendo, parve quella che tossio
al primo fallo scritto di Ginevra.

    Io cominciai: "Voi siete il padre mio;         16
voi mi date a parlar tutta baldezza;
voi mi levate sì, ch'i' son più ch'io.

    Per tanti rivi s'empie d'allegrezza            19
la mente mia, che di sé fa letizia
perché può sostener che non si spezza.

    Ditemi dunque, cara mia primizia,             22
quai fuor li vostri antichi e quai fuor li anni
che si segnaro in vostra püerizia;

    ditemi de l'ovil di San Giovanni              25
quanto era allora, e chi eran le genti
tra esso degne di più alti scanni."

    Come s'avviva a lo spirar d'i venti            28
carbone in fiamma, così vid' io quella
luce risplendere a' miei blandimenti;

    e come a li occhi miei si fé più bella,        31
così con voce più dolce e soave,
ma non con questa moderna favella,

"Down from that day when *Ave* was pronounced,                34
until my mother (blessed now), by giving
birth, eased the burden borne in bearing me,

this fire of Mars had come five-hundred-fifty                37
and thirty more times to its Lion—there
to be rekindled underneath its paw.

My ancestors and I were born just where                40
the runner in your yearly games first comes
upon the boundary of the final ward.

That is enough concerning my forebears:                43
what were their names, from where they came—of that,
silence, not speech, is more appropriate.

All those who, at that time, between the Baptist                46
and Mars, were capable of bearing arms,
numbered one fifth of those who live there now.

But then the citizens, now mixed with Campi,                49
with the Certaldo, and with the Figline,
were pure down to the humblest artisan.

Oh, it would be far better if you had                52
those whom I mention as your neighbors (and
your boundaries at Galuzzo and Trespiano),

than to have them within, to bear the stench                55
of Aguglione's wretch and Signa's wretch,
whose sharp eyes now on barratry are set.

If those who, in the world, go most astray                58
had not seen Caesar with stepmothers' eyes,
but, like a mother to her son, been kind,

then one who has become a Florentine                61
trader and money changer would have stayed
in Semifonte, where his fathers peddled,

the Counts would still be lords of Montemurlo,                64
the Cerchi would be in Acone's parish,
perhaps the Buondelmonti in Valdigreve.

The mingling of the populations led                67
to evil in the city, even as
food piled on food destroys the body's health;

the blind bull falls more quickly, more headlong,                70
than does the blind lamb; and the one blade can
often cut more and better than five swords.

Consider Luni, Urbisaglia, how                73
they went to ruin (Sinigaglia follows,
and Chiusi, too, will soon have vanished); then,

dissemi: "Da quel dì che fu detto 'Ave'    34
al parto in che mia madre, ch'è or santa,
s'alleviò di me ond' era grave,

    al suo Leon cinquecento cinquanta    37
e trenta fiate venne questo foco
a rinfiammarsi sotto la sua pianta.

    Li antichi miei e io nacqui nel loco    40
dove si truova pria l'ultimo sesto
da quei che corre il vostro annüal gioco.

    Basti d'i miei maggiori udirne questo:    43
chi ei si fosser e onde venner quivi,
più è tacer che ragionare onesto.

    Tutti color ch'a quel tempo eran ivi    46
da poter arme tra Marte e 'l Batista,
erano il quinto di quei ch'or son vivi.

    Ma la cittadinanza, ch'è or mista    49
di Campi, di Certaldo e di Fegghine,
pura vediesi ne l'ultimo artista.

    Oh quanto fora meglio esser vicine    52
quelle genti ch'io dico, e al Galluzzo
e a Trespiano aver vostro confine,

    che averle dentro e sostener lo puzzo    55
del villan d'Aguglion, di quel da Signa,
che già per barattare ha l'occhio aguzzo!

    Se la gente ch'al mondo più traligna    58
non fosse stata a Cesare noverca,
ma come madre a suo figlio benigna,

    tal fatto è fiorentino e cambia e merca,    61
che si sarebbe vòlto a Simifonti,
là dove andava l'avolo a la cerca;

    sariesi Montemurlo ancor de' Conti;    64
sarieno i Cerchi nel piovier d'Acone,
e forse in Valdigrieve i Buondelmonti.

    Sempre la confusion de le persone    67
principio fu del mal de la cittade,
come del vostro il cibo che s'appone;

    e cieco toro più avaccio cade    70
che cieco agnello; e molte volte taglia
più e meglio una che le cinque spade.

    Se tu riguardi Luni e Orbisaglia    73
come sono ite, e come se ne vanno
di retro ad esse Chiusi e Sinigaglia,

if you should hear of families undone, 76
you will find nothing strange or difficult
in that—since even cities meet their end.

All things that you possess, possess their death, 79
just as you do; but in some things that last
long, death can hide from you whose lives are short.

And even as the heaven of the moon, 82
revolving, respiteless, conceals and then
reveals the shores, so Fortune does with Florence;

therefore, there is no cause for wonder in 85
what I shall tell of noble Florentines,
of those whose reputations time has hidden.

I saw the Ughi, saw the Catellini, 88
Filippi, Greci, Ormanni, Alberichi,
famed citizens already in decline,

and saw, as great as they were venerable, 91
dell'Arca with della Sannella, and
Ardinghi, Soldanieri, and Bostichi.

Nearby the gate that now is burdened with 94
new treachery that weighs so heavily
that it will bring the vessel to shipwreck,

there were the Ravignani, from whose line 97
Count Guido comes and all who—since—derive
their name from the illustrious Bellincione.

And della Pressa knew already how 100
to rule; and Galigaio, in his house,
already had the gilded hilt and pommel.

The stripe of Vair had mightiness already, 103
as did the Giuochi, Galli, and Barucci,
Fifanti, and Sacchetti, and those who

blush for the bushel; and the stock from which 106
spring the Calfucci was already mighty,
and Sizzi and Arrigucci were already

raised to high office. Oh, how great were those 109
I saw—whom pride laid low! And the gold balls,
in all of her great actions, flowered Florence.

Such were the ancestors of those who now, 112
whenever bishops' sees are vacant, grow
fat as they sit in church consistories.

The breed—so arrogant and dragonlike 115
in chasing him who flees, but lamblike, meek
to him who shows his teeth or else his purse—

udir come le schiatte si disfanno
non ti parrà nova cosa né forte,
poscia che le cittadi termine hanno.

  Le vostre cose tutte hanno lor morte,      79
sì come voi; ma celasi in alcuna
che dura molto, e le vite son corte.

  E come 'l volger del ciel de la luna      82
cuopre e discuopre i liti sanza posa,
così fa di Fiorenza la Fortuna:

  per che non dee parer mirabil cosa      85
ciò ch'io dirò de li alti Fiorentini
onde è la fama nel tempo nascosa.

  Io vidi li Ughi e vidi i Catellini,      88
Filippi, Greci, Ormanni e Alberichi,
già nel calare, illustri cittadini;

  e vidi così grandi come antichi,      91
con quel de la Sannella, quel de l'Arca,
e Soldanieri e Ardinghi e Bostichi.

  Sovra la porta ch'al presente è carca      94
di nova fellonia di tanto peso
che tosto fia iattura de la barca,

  erano i Ravignani, ond' è disceso      97
il conte Guido e qualunque del nome
de l'alto Bellincione ha poscia preso.

  Quel de la Pressa sapeva già come      100
regger si vuole, e avea Galigaio
dorata in casa sua già l'elsa e 'l pome.

  Grand' era già la colonna del Vaio,      103
Sacchetti, Giuochi, Fifanti e Barucci
e Galli e quei ch'arrossan per lo staio.

  Lo ceppo di che nacquero i Calfucci      106
era già grande, e già eran tratti
a le curule Sizii e Arrigucci.

  Oh quali io vidi quei che son disfatti      109
per lor superbia! e le palle de l'oro
fiorian Fiorenza in tutt' i suoi gran fatti.

  Così facieno i padri di coloro      112
che, sempre che la vostra chiesa vaca,
si fanno grassi stando a consistoro.

  L'oltracotata schiatta che s'indraca      115
dietro a chi fugge, e a chi mostra 'l dente
o ver la borsa, com' agnel si placa,

was on the rise already, but of stock                                118
so mean that Ubertin Donato, when
his father-in-law made him kin to them,
    was scarcely pleased. Already Caponsacco        121
had come from Fiesole down to the market;
already citizens of note were Guida
    and Infangato. I shall tell a thing               124
incredible and true: the gateway through
the inner walls was named for the della Pera.
    All those whose arms bear part of the fair ensign  127
of the great baron—he whose memory
and worth are honored on the feast of Thomas—
    received knighthood and privilege from him,       130
though he whose coat of arms has fringed that ensign
has taken sides now with the populace.
    The Gualterotti and the Importuni                 133
were there already; were the Borgo spared
new neighbors, it would still be tranquil there.
    The house of Amidei, with which your sorrows      136
began—by reason of its just resentment,
which ruined you and ended years of gladness—
    was honored then, as were its close companions.   139
O Buondelmonte, through another's counsel,
you fled your wedding pledge, and brought such evil!
    Many would now rejoice, who still lament,         142
if when you first approached the city, God
had given you unto the river Ema!
    But Florence, in her final peace, was fated       145
to offer up—unto that mutilated
stone guardian upon her bridge—a victim.
    These were the families, and others with them:    148
the Florence that I saw—in such repose
that there was nothing to have caused her sorrow.
    These were the families: with them I saw          151
her people so acclaimed and just, that on
her staff the lily never was reversed,
    nor was it made bloodred by factious hatred."     154

già venìa sù, ma di picciola gente;                118
sì che non piacque ad Ubertin Donato
che poï il suocero il fé lor parente.

Già era 'l Caponsacco nel mercato                  121
disceso giù da Fiesole, e già era
buon cittadino Giuda e Infangato.

Io dirò cosa incredibile e vera:                    124
nel picciol cerchio s'entrava per porta
che si nomava da quei de la Pera.

Ciascun che de la bella insegna porta              127
del gran barone il cui nome e 'l cui pregio
la festa di Tommaso riconforta,

da esso ebbe milizia e privilegio;                 130
avvegna che con popol si rauni
oggi colui che la fascia col fregio.

Già eran Gualterotti e Importuni;                  133
e ancor saria Borgo più quïeto,
se di novi vicin fosser digiuni.

La casa di che nacque il vostro fleto,             136
per lo giusto disdegno che v'ha morti
e puose fine al vostro viver lieto,

era onorata, essa e suoi consorti:                 139
o Buondelmonte, quanto mal fuggisti
le nozze süe per li altrui conforti!

Molti sarebber lieti, che son tristi,              142
se Dio t'avesse conceduto ad Ema
la prima volta ch'a città venisti.

Ma conveniesi, a quella pietra scema               145
che guarda 'l ponte, che Fiorenza fesse
vittima ne la sua pace postrema.

Con queste genti, e con altre con esse,            148
vid' io Fiorenza in sì fatto riposo,
che non avea cagione onde piangesse.

Con queste genti vid' io glorïoso                  151
e giusto il popol suo, tanto che 'l giglio
non era ad asta mai posto a ritroso,

né per divisïon fatto vermiglio."                  154

# CANTO XVII

Like Phaethon (one who still makes fathers wary
of sons) when he had heard insinuations,
and he, to be assured, came to Clymene,

such was I and such was I seen to be                                    4
by Beatrice and by the holy lamp
that—earlier—had shifted place for me.

Therefore my lady said to me: "Display                                 7
the flame of your desire, that it may
be seen well-stamped with your internal seal,

not that we need to know what you'd reveal,                            10
but that you learn the way that would disclose
your thirst, and you be quenched by what we pour."

"O my dear root, who, since you rise so high,                          13
can see the Point in which all times are present—
for just as earthly minds are able to

see that two obtuse angles cannot be                                   16
contained in a triangle, you can see
contingent things before they come to be—

while I was in the company of Virgil,                                  19
both on the mountain that heals souls and when
descending to the dead world, what I heard

about my future life were grievous words—                             22
although, against the blows of chance I feel
myself as firmly planted as a cube.

Thus my desire would be appeased if I                                  25
might know what fortune is approaching me:
the arrow one foresees arrives more gently."

So did I speak to the same living light                                28
that spoke to me before; as Beatrice
had wished, what was my wish was now confessed.

Not with the maze of words that used to snare                          31
the fools upon this earth before the Lamb
of God who takes away our sins was slain,

*Still the Fifth Heaven: the Sphere of Mars. Dante's asking*
*Cacciaguida for word on what future awaits Dante. Caccia-*
*guida's prophecy concerning Dante's exile and tribulations.*
*Words of comfort from Cacciaguida, and his urging of Dante*
*to fearless fulfillment of his poetic mission.*

Qual venne a Climenè, per accertarsi
di ciò ch'avëa incontro a sé udito,
quei ch'ancor fa li padri ai figli scarsi;

   tal era io, e tal era sentito              4
e da Beatrice e da la santa lampa
che pria per me avea mutato sito.

   Per che mia donna "Manda fuor la vampa     7
del tuo disio," mi disse, "sì ch'ella esca
segnata bene de la interna stampa:

   non perché nostra conoscenza cresca        10
per tuo parlare, ma perché t'ausi
a dir la sete, sì che l'uom ti mesca."

   "O cara piota mia che sì t'insusi,           13
che, come veggion le terrene menti
non capere in trïangol due ottusi,

   così vedi le cose contingenti            16
anzi che sieno in sé, mirando il punto
a cui tutti li tempi son presenti;

   mentre ch'io era a Virgilio congiunto     19
su per lo monte che l'anime cura
e discendendo nel mondo defunto,

   dette mi fuor di mia vita futura         22
parole gravi, avvegna ch'io mi senta
ben tetragono ai colpi di ventura;

   per che la voglia mia saria contenta     25
d'intender qual fortuna mi s'appressa:
ché saetta previsa vien più lenta."

   Così diss' io a quella luce stessa        28
che pria m'avea parlato; e come volle
Beatrice, fu la mia voglia confessa.

   Né per ambage, in che la gente folle     31
già s'inviscava pria che fosse anciso
l'Agnel di Dio che le peccata tolle,

but with words plain and unambiguous,                              34
that loving father, hidden, yet revealed
by his own smile, replied: "Contingency,

while not extending past the book in which               37
your world of matter has been writ, is yet
in the Eternal Vision all depicted

(but this does not imply necessity,                              40
just as a ship that sails downstream is not
determined by the eye that watches it).

And from that Vision—just as from an organ          43
the ear receives a gentle harmony—
what time prepares for you appears to me.

Hippolytus was forced to leave his Athens          46
because of his stepmother, faithless, fierce;
and so must you depart from Florence: this

is willed already, sought for, soon to be               49
accomplished by the one who plans and plots
where—every day—Christ is both sold and bought.

The blame, as usual, will be cried out               52
against the injured party; but just vengeance
will serve as witness to the truth that wields it.

You shall leave everything you love most dearly:     55
this is the arrow that the bow of exile
shoots first. You are to know the bitter taste

of others' bread, how salt it is, and know          58
how hard a path it is for one who goes
descending and ascending others' stairs.

And what will be most hard for you to bear          61
will be the scheming, senseless company
that is to share your fall into this valley;

against you they will be insane, completely          64
ungrateful and profane; and yet, soon after,
not you but they will have their brows bloodred.

Of their insensate acts, the proof will be          67
in the effects; and thus, your honor will
be best kept if your party is your self.

Your first refuge and your first inn shall be       70
the courtesy of the great Lombard, he
who on the ladder bears the sacred bird;

and so benign will be his care for you               73
that, with you two, in giving and in asking,
that shall be first which is, with others, last.

ma per chiare parole e con preciso 34
latin rispuose quello amor paterno,
chiuso e parvente del suo proprio riso:

    "La contingenza, che fuor del quaderno 37
de la vostra matera non si stende,
tutta è dipinta nel cospetto etterno;

    necessità però quindi non prende 40
se non come dal viso in che si specchia
nave che per torrente giù discende.

    Da indi, sì come viene ad orecchia 43
dolce armonia da organo, mi viene
a vista il tempo che ti s'apparecchia.

    Qual si partio Ipolito d'Atene 46
per la spietata e perfida noverca,
tal di Fiorenza partir ti convene.

    Questo si vuole e questo già si cerca, 49
e tosto verrà fatto a chi ciò pensa
là dove Cristo tutto dì si merca.

    La colpa seguirà la parte offensa 52
in grido, come suol; ma la vendetta
fia testimonio al ver che la dispensa.

    Tu lascerai ogne cosa diletta 55
più caramente; e questo è quello strale
che l'arco de lo essilio pria saetta.

    Tu proverai sì come sa di sale 58
lo pane altrui, e come è duro calle
lo scendere e 'l salir per l'altrui scale.

    E quel che più ti graverà le spalle, 61
sarà la compagnia malvagia e scempia
con la qual tu cadrai in questa valle;

    che tutta ingrata, tutta matta ed empia 64
si farà contr' a te; ma, poco appresso,
ella, non tu, n'avrà rossa la tempia.

    Di sua bestialitate il suo processo 67
farà la prova; sì ch'a te fia bello
averti fatta parte per te stesso.

    Lo primo tuo refugio e 'l primo ostello 70
sarà la cortesia del gran Lombardo
che 'n su la scala porta il santo uccello;

    ch'in te avrà sì benigno riguardo, 73
che del fare e del chieder, tra voi due,
fia primo quel che tra li altri è più tardo.

You shall—beside him—see one who, at birth,                    76
had so received the seal of this strong star
that what he does will be remarkable.

People have yet to notice him because                          79
he is a boy—for nine years and no more
have these spheres wheeled around him—but before

the Gascon gulls the noble Henry, some                         82
sparks will have marked the virtue of the Lombard:
hard labor and his disregard for silver.

His generosity is yet to be                                    85
so notable that even enemies
will never hope to treat it silently.

Put trust in him and in his benefits:                          88
his gifts will bring much metamorphosis—
rich men and beggars will exchange their states.

What I tell you about him you will bear                        91
inscribed within your mind—but hide it there";
and he told things beyond belief even

for those who will yet see them. Then he added:               94
"Son, these are glosses of what you had heard;
these are the snares that hide beneath brief years.

Yet I'd not have you envying your neighbors;                  97
your life will long outlast the punishment
that is to fall upon their treacheries."

After that holy soul had, with his silence,                  100
showed he was freed from putting in the woof
across the web whose warp I set for him,

I like a man who, doubting, craves for counsel               103
from one who sees and rightly wills and loves,
replied to him: "I clearly see, my father,

how time is hurrying toward me in order                      106
to deal me such a blow as would be most
grievous for him who is not set for it;

thus, it is right to arm myself with foresight,             109
that if I lose the place most dear, I may
not lose the rest through what my poems say.

Down in the world of endless bitterness,                     112
and on the mountain from whose lovely peak
I was drawn upward by my lady's eyes,

and afterward, from light to light in Heaven,               115
I learned that which, if I retell it, must
for many have a taste too sharp, too harsh;

Con lui vedrai colui che 'mpresso fue,                          76
nascendo, sì da questa stella forte,
che notabili fier l'opere sue.

   Non se ne son le genti ancora accorte                    79
per la novella età, ché pur nove anni
son queste rote intorno di lui torte;

   ma pria che 'l Guasco l'alto Arrigo inganni,           82
parran faville de la sua virtute
in non curar d'argento né d'affanni.

   Le sue magnificenze conosciute                          85
saranno ancora, sì che ' suoi nemici
non ne potran tener le lingue mute.

   A lui t'aspetta e a' suoi benefici;                     88
per lui fia trasmutata molta gente,
cambiando condizion ricchi e mendici;

   e portera'ne scritto ne la mente                        91
di lui, e nol dirai"; e disse cose
incredibili a quei che fier presente.

   Poi giunse: "Figlio, queste son le chiose              94
di quel che ti fu detto; ecco le 'nsidie
che dietro a pochi giri son nascose.

   Non vo' però ch'a' tuoi vicini invidie,                 97
poscia che s'infutura la tua vita
via più là che 'l punir di lor perfidie."

   Poi che, tacendo, si mostrò spedita                    100
l'anima santa di metter la trama
in quella tela ch'io le porsi ordita,

   io cominciai, come colui che brama,                    103
dubitando, consiglio da persona
che vede e vuol dirittamente e ama:

   "Ben veggio, padre mio, sì come sprona                 106
lo tempo verso me, per colpo darmi
tal, ch'è più grave a chi più s'abbandona;

   per che di provedenza è buon ch'io m'armi,            109
sì che, se loco m'è tolto più caro,
io non perdessi li altri per miei carmi.

   Giù per lo mondo sanza fine amaro,                     112
e per lo monte del cui bel cacume
li occhi de la mia donna mi levaro,

   e poscia per lo ciel, di lume in lume,                 115
ho io appreso quel che s'io ridico,
a molti fia sapor di forte agrume;

yet if I am a timid friend of truth,                                          118
I fear that I may lose my life among
those who will call this present, ancient times."

    The light in which there smiled the treasure I                121
had found within it, first began to dazzle,
as would a golden mirror in the sun,

    then it replied: "A conscience that is dark—            124
either through its or through another's shame—
indeed will find that what you speak is harsh.

    Nevertheless, all falsehood set aside,                      127
let all that you have seen be manifest,
and let them scratch wherever it may itch.

    For if, at the first taste, your words molest,             130
they will, when they have been digested, end
as living nourishment. As does the wind,

    so shall your outcry do—the wind that sends           133
its roughest blows against the highest peaks;
that is no little cause for claiming honor.

    Therefore, within these spheres, upon the mountain,   136
and in the dismal valley, you were shown
only those souls that unto fame are known—

    because the mind of one who hears will not               139
put doubt to rest, put trust in you, if given
examples with their roots unknown and hidden,

    or arguments too dim, too unapparent."                     142

e s'io al vero son timido amico,       118
temo di perder viver tra coloro
che questo tempo chiameranno antico."

    La luce in che rideva il mio tesoro       121
ch'io trovai lì, si fé prima corusca,
quale a raggio di sole specchio d'oro;

    indi rispuose: "Coscïenza fusca       124
o de la propria o de l'altrui vergogna
pur sentirà la tua parola brusca.

    Ma nondimen, rimossa ogne menzogna,       127
tutta tua visïon fa manifesta;
e lascia pur grattar dov' è la rogna.

    Ché se la voce tua sarà molesta       130
nel primo gusto, vital nodrimento
lascerà poi, quando sarà digesta.

    Questo tuo grido farà come vento,       133
che le più alte cime più percuote;
e ciò non fa d'onor poco argomento.

    Però ti son mostrate in queste rote,       136
nel monte e ne la valle dolorosa
pur l'anime che son di fama note,

    che l'animo di quel ch'ode, non posa       139
né ferma fede per essempro ch'aia
la sua radice incognita e ascosa,

    né per altro argomento che non paia."       142

OVERLEAF:
*Diligite . . .*

DILIGITE·IVSTITIAM·QVI·

INVOCANS · TERRAM

# CANTO XVIII

By now that blessed mirror was delighting
in its own inner words; I, tasting mine,
was tempering the bitter with the sweet.

But she, the lady leading me to God,      4
said: "Shift your thoughts: remember—I am close
to Him who lightens every unjust hurt."

Hearing the loving sound my solace spoke,      7
I turned. But here I have to leave untold
what love I saw within her holy eyes,

   not just because I do not trust my speech,      10
but, too, because recall cannot retrieve
that much, unless Another is its guide.

This only—of that moment—can I tell:      13
that even as I gazed at her, my soul
was free from any other need as long

   as the Eternal Loveliness that shone      16
on Beatrice directly, from her eyes,
contented me with the reflected light.

But, conquering my will with her smile's splendor,      19
she told me: "Turn to him and listen—for
not only in my eyes is Paradise."

As, here on earth, at times our sentiment,      22
if it be passionate enough to take
the soul entirely, shows in the face,

   so, in the flaming of the holy fire      25
to which I turned, I saw that he desired
some further words with me. And he began:

"In this fifth resting place, upon the tree      28
that grows down from its crown and endlessly
bears fruit and never loses any leaves,

   are blessed souls that, down below, before      31
they came to heaven, were so notable
that any poem would be enriched by them.

*Still the Fifth Heaven: the Sphere of Mars. The dazzling gaze*
*of Beatrice. Cacciaguida's presentation of other spirits of the*
*cross. Ascent to the Sixth Heaven, the Sphere of Jupiter. Letters*
*and words formed by the spirits in Jupiter. The shaping of the*
*Eagle. Dante's prayer and his denunciation of evil popes,*
*especially John XXII.*

Già si godeva solo del suo verbo
quello specchio beato, e io gustava
lo mio, temprando col dolce l'acerbo;
    e quella donna ch'a Dio mi menava           4
disse: "Muta pensier; pensa ch'i' sono
presso a colui ch'ogne torto disgrava."
    Io mi rivolsi a l'amoroso suono               7
del mio conforto; e qual io allor vidi
ne li occhi santi amor, qui l'abbandono:
    non perch' io pur del mio parlar diffidi,    10
ma per la mente che non può redire
sovra sé tanto, s'altri non la guidi.
    Tanto poss' io di quel punto ridire,      13
che, rimirando lei, lo mio affetto
libero fu da ogne altro disire,
    fin che 'l piacere etterno, che diretto    16
raggiava in Bëatrice, dal bel viso
mi contentava col secondo aspetto.
    Vincendo me col lume d'un sorriso,      19
ella mi disse: "Volgiti e ascolta;
ché non pur ne' miei occhi è paradiso."
    Come si vede qui alcuna volta          22
l'affetto ne la vista, s'elli è tanto,
che da lui sia tutta l'anima tolta,
    così nel fiammeggiar del folgór santo,    25
a ch'io mi volsi, conobbi la voglia
in lui di ragionarmi ancora alquanto.
    El cominciò: "In questa quinta soglia    28
de l'albero che vive de la cima
e frutta sempre e mai non perde foglia,
    spiriti son beati, che giù, prima        31
che venissero al ciel, fuor di gran voce,
sì ch'ogne musa ne sarebbe opima.

Therefore look at the cross, along its horns:    34
those whom I name will race as swiftly as,
within a cloud, its rapid lightnings flash."

Then, just as soon as Joshua was named,    37
I saw a splendor thrust along the cross,
nor did I note the name before the act.

And at the name of noble Maccabeus,    40
I saw another flame wheel round itself,
and gladness was the whip that spurred that top.

So, too, for Charlemagne and Roland—my    43
attentive eye held fast to that pair like
a falconer who tracks his falcon's flight.

The next to draw my eyes along that cross    46
were William and Renouard and, too, Duke Godfrey
and Robert Guiscard. Then, when he had left me

and mingled with the other lights, the soul    49
who had addressed me showed his artistry,
singing among the singers in that sphere.

I turned to my right side to see if I    52
might see if Beatrice had signified
by word or gesture what I was to do

and saw such purity within her eyes,    55
such joy, that her appearance now surpassed
its guise at other times, even the last.

And as, by feeling greater joyousness    58
in doing good, a man becomes aware
that day by day his virtue is advancing,

so I became aware that my revolving    61
with heaven had increased its arc—by seeing
that miracle becoming still more brilliant.

And like the rapid change that one can see    64
in a pale woman's face when it has freed
itself from bearing bashful modesty,

such change I, turning, saw: the red of Mars    67
was gone—and now the temperate sixth star's
white heaven welcomed me into itself.

I saw within that torch of Jupiter    70
the sparkling of the love that it contained
design before my eyes the signs we speak.

And just as birds that rise from riverbanks,    73
as if rejoicing after feeding there,
will form a round flock or another shape,

Però mira ne' corni de la croce:      34
quello ch'io nomerò, lì farà l'atto
che fa in nube il suo foco veloce."

Io vidi per la croce un lume tratto      37
dal nomar Iosuè, com' el si feo;
né mi fu noto il dir prima che 'l fatto.

E al nome de l'alto Macabeo      40
vidi moversi un altro roteando,
e letizia era ferza del paleo.

Così per Carlo Magno e per Orlando      43
due ne seguì lo mio attento sguardo,
com' occhio segue suo falcon volando.

Poscia trasse Guiglielmo e Rinoardo      46
e 'l duca Gottifredi la mia vista
per quella croce, e Ruberto Guiscardo.

Indi, tra l'altre luci mota e mista,      49
mostrommi l'alma che m'avea parlato
qual era tra i cantor del cielo artista.

Io mi rivolsi dal mio destro lato      52
per vedere in Beatrice il mio dovere,
o per parlare o per atto, segnato;

e vidi le sue luci tanto mere,      55
tanto gioconde, che la sua sembianza
vinceva li altri e l'ultimo solere.

E come, per sentir più dilettanza      58
bene operando, l'uom di giorno in giorno
s'accorge che la sua virtute avanza,

sì m'accors' io che 'l mio girare intorno      61
col cielo insieme avea cresciuto l'arco,
veggendo quel miracol più addorno.

E qual è 'l trasmutare in picciol varco      64
di tempo in bianca donna, quando 'l volto
suo si discarchi di vergogna il carco,

tal fu ne li occhi miei, quando fui vòlto,      67
per lo candor de la temprata stella
sesta, che dentro a sé m'avea ricolto.

Io vidi in quella giovïal facella      70
lo sfavillar de l'amor che lì era
segnare a li occhi miei nostra favella.

E come augelli surti di rivera,      73
quasi congratulando a lor pasture,
fanno di sé or tonda or altra schiera,

so, in their lights, the saintly beings sang 76
and, in their flight, the figures that they spelled
were now a *D*, now *I*, and now an *L*.

First, they moved to the rhythm of their song; 79
then, after they had finished forming one
letter, they halted for a while, in silence.

O godly Pegasea, you who give 82
to genius glory and long life, as it,
through you, gives these to kingdoms and to cities,

give me your light that I may emphasize 85
these signs as I inscribed them in my mind:
your power—may it appear in these brief lines!

Those blessed spirits took the shape of five 88
times seven vowels and consonants, and I
noted the parts as they were spelled for me.

DILIGITE JUSTITIAM were the verb 91
and noun that first appeared in that depiction;
QUI IUDICATIS TERRAM followed after.

Then, having formed the *M* of the fifth word, 94
those spirits kept their order; Jupiter's
silver, at that point, seemed embossed with gold.

And I saw other lights descending on 97
the apex of the *M* and, settling, singing—
I think—the Good that draws them to Itself.

Then, as innumerable sparks rise up 100
when one strikes burning logs (and in those sparks
fools have a way of reading auguries),

from that *M* seemed to surge more than a thousand 103
lights; and they climbed, some high, some low, just as
the Sun that kindles them assigned positions.

With each light settled quietly in place, 106
I saw that the array of fire had shaped
the image of an eagle's head and neck.

He who paints there has no one as His guide: 109
He guides Himself; in Him we recognize
the shaping force that flows from nest to nest.

The other lights, who were, it seemed, content 112
at first to form a lily on the *M*,
moving a little, formed the eagle's frame.

O gentle star, what—and how many—gems 115
made plain to me that justice here on earth
depends upon the heaven you engem!

sì dentro ai lumi sante creature
volitando cantavano, e faciensi
or *D*, or *I*, or *L* in sue figure.

Prima, cantando, a sua nota moviensi;          79
poi, diventando l'un di questi segni,
un poco s'arrestavano e taciensi.

O diva Pegasëa che li 'ngegni          82
fai glorïosi e rendili longevi,
ed essi teco le cittadi e ' regni,

illustrami di te, sì ch'io rilevi          85
le lor figure com' io l'ho concette:
paia tua possa in questi versi brevi!

Mostrarsi dunque in cinque volte sette          88
vocali e consonanti; e io notai
le parti sì, come mi parver dette.

"DILIGITE IUSTITIAM," primai          91
fur verbo e nome di tutto 'l dipinto;
"QUI IUDICATIS TERRAM," fur sezzai.

Poscia ne l'emme del vocabol quinto          94
rimasero ordinate; sì che Giove
pareva argento lì d'oro distinto.

E vidi scendere altre luci dove          97
era il colmo de l'emme, e lì quetarsi
cantando, credo, il ben ch'a sé le move.

Poi, come nel percuoter d'i ciocchi arsi          100
surgono innumerabili faville,
onde li stolti sogliono agurarsi,

resurger parver quindi più di mille          103
luci e salir, qual assai e qual poco,
sì come 'l sol che l'accende sortille;

e quïetata ciascuna in suo loco,          106
la testa e 'l collo d'un'aguglia vidi
rappresentare a quel distinto foco.

Quei che dipinge lì, non ha chi 'l guidi;          109
ma esso guida, e da lui si rammenta
quella virtù ch'è forma per li nidi.

L'altra bëatitudo, che contenta          112
pareva prima d'ingigliarsi a l'emme,
con poco moto seguitò la 'mprenta.

O dolce stella, quali e quante gemme          115
mi dimostraro che nostra giustizia
effetto sia del ciel che tu ingemme!

Therefore I pray the Mind in which begin                    118
your motion and your force, to watch that place
which has produced the smoke that dims your rays,

    that once again His anger fall upon                      121
those who would buy and sell within that temple
whose walls were built by miracles and martyrs.

    O hosts of heaven whom I contemplate,                    124
for all who, led by bad example, stray
within the life they live on earth, do pray!

    Men once were used to waging war with swords;            127
now war means seizing here and there the bread
the tender Father would deny to none.

    But you who only write to then erase,                    130
remember this: Peter and Paul, who died
to save the vines you spoil, are still alive.

    Well may you say: "My longing is so bent                 133
on him who chose the solitary life
and for a dance was dragged to martyrdom—

    I do not know the Fisherman or Paul."                    136

Per ch'io prego la mente in che s'inizia                    118
tuo moto e tua virtute, che rimiri
ond' esce il fummo che 'l tuo raggio vizia;
    sì ch'un'altra fïata omai s'adiri                        121
del comperare e vender dentro al templo
che si murò di segni e di martìri.
    O milizia del ciel cu' io contemplo,                     124
adora per color che sono in terra
tutti svïati dietro al malo essemplo!
    Già si solea con le spade far guerra;                    127
ma or si fa togliendo or qui or quivi
lo pan che 'l pïo Padre a nessun serra.
    Ma tu che sol per cancellare scrivi,                     130
pensa che Pietro e Paulo, che moriro
per la vigna che guasti, ancor son vivi.
    Ben puoi tu dire: "I' ho fermo 'l disiro                 133
sì a colui che volle viver solo
e che per salti fu tratto al martiro,
    ch'io non conosco il pescator né Polo."                  136

# CANTO XIX

The handsome image those united souls,
happy within their blessedness, were shaping,
appeared before me now with open wings.
  Each soul seemed like a ruby—one in which          4
a ray of sun burned so, that in my eyes,
it was the total sun that seemed reflected.
  And what I now must tell has never been            7
reported by a voice, inscribed by ink,
never conceived by the imagination;
  for I did see the beak, did hear it speak          10
and utter with its voice both *I* and *mine*
when *we* and *ours* were what, in thought, was meant.
  And it began: "Because I was both just            13
and merciful, I am exalted here
to glory no desire can surpass;
  the memory I left on earth is such                 16
that even the malicious praise it there,
although they do not follow its example."
  Thus one sole warmth is felt from many embers,     19
even as from a multitude of loves
one voice alone rose from the Eagle's image.
  To which I said: "O everlasting flowers            22
of the eternal gladness, who make all
your fragrances appear to me as one,
  do let your breath deliver me from that            25
great fast which kept me hungering so long,
not finding any food for it on earth.
  I know indeed that, though God's Justice has       28
another realm in Heaven as Its mirror,
you here do not perceive it through a veil.
  You know how keenly I prepare myself               31
to listen, and you know what is that doubt
which caused so old a hungering in me."

The Sixth Heaven: the Sphere of Jupiter. The Eagle begins to
speak. Dante's implicit question concerning divine Justice. The
Eagle's voicing of the question and, then, its discourse on the
inscrutability of God's Justice and on salvation. The Eagle's
denunciation of evil Christian rulers.

Parea dinanzi a me con l'ali aperte
la bella image che nel dolce *frui*
liete facevan l'anime conserte;

  parea ciascuna rubinetto in cui               4
raggio di sole ardesse sì acceso,
che ne' miei occhi rifrangesse lui.

  E quel che mi convien ritrar testeso,         7
non portò voce mai, né scrisse incostro,
né fu per fantasia già mai compreso;

  ch'io vidi e anche udi' parlar lo rostro,      10
e sonar ne la voce e "io" e "mio,"
quand' era nel concetto e "noi" e "nostro."

  E cominciò: "Per esser giusto e pio       13
son io qui essaltato a quella gloria
che non si lascia vincere a disio;

  e in terra lasciai la mia memoria         16
sì fatta, che le genti lì malvage
commendan lei, ma non seguon la storia."

  Così un sol calor di molte brage          19
si fa sentir, come di molti amori
usciva solo un suon di quella image.

  Ond' io appresso: "O perpetüi fiori      22
de l'etterna letizia, che pur uno
parer mi fate tutti vostri odori,

  solvetemi, spirando, il gran digiuno      25
che lungamente m'ha tenuto in fame,
non trovandoli in terra cibo alcuno.

  Ben so io che, se 'n cielo altro reame     28
la divina giustizia fa suo specchio,
che 'l vostro non l'apprende con velame.

  Sapete come attento io m'apparecchio     31
ad ascoltar; sapete qual è quello
dubbio che m'è digiun cotanto vecchio."

Just like a falcon set free from its hood,  34
which moves its head and flaps its wings, displaying
its eagerness and proud appearance, so

I saw that ensign do, that Eagle woven  37
of praises of God's grace, accompanied
by songs whose sense those up above enjoy.

Then it began: "The One who turned His compass  40
to mark the world's confines, and in them set
so many things concealed and things revealed,

could not imprint His Power into all  43
the universe without His Word remaining
in infinite excess of such a vessel.

In proof of this, the first proud being, he  46
who was the highest of all creatures, fell—
unripe because he did not wait for light.

Thus it is clear that every lesser nature  49
is—all the more—too meager a container
for endless Good, which is Its own sole measure.

In consequence of this, your vision—which  52
must be a ray of that Intelligence
with which all beings are infused—cannot

of its own nature find sufficient force  55
to see into its origin beyond
what God himself makes manifest to man;

therefore, the vision that your world receives  58
can penetrate into Eternal Justice
no more than eye can penetrate the sea;

for though, near shore, sight reaches the sea floor,  61
you cannot reach it in the open sea;
yet it is there, but hidden by the deep.

Only the light that shines from the clear heaven  64
can never be obscured—all else is darkness
or shadow of the flesh or fleshly poison.

Now is the hiding place of living Justice  67
laid open to you—where it had been hidden
while you addressed it with insistent questions.

For you would say: 'A man is born along  70
the shoreline of the Indus River; none
is there to speak or teach or write of Christ.

And he, as far as human reason sees,  73
in all he seeks and all he does is good:
there is no sin within his life or speech.

Quasi falcone ch'esce del cappello,     34
move la testa e con l'ali si plaude,
voglia mostrando e faccendosi bello,

    vid' io farsi quel segno, che di laude     37
de la divina grazia era contesto,
con canti quai si sa chi là sù gaude.

    Poi cominciò: "Colui che volse il sesto     40
a lo stremo del mondo, e dentro ad esso
distinse tanto occulto e manifesto,

    non poté suo valor sì fare impresso     43
in tutto l'universo, che 'l suo verbo
non rimanesse in infinito eccesso.

    E ciò fa certo che 'l primo superbo,     46
che fu la somma d'ogne creatura,
per non aspettar lume, cadde acerbo;

    e quinci appar ch'ogne minor natura     49
è corto recettacolo a quel bene
che non ha fine e sé con sé misura.

    Dunque vostra veduta, che convene     52
essere alcun de' raggi de la mente
di che tutte le cose son ripiene,

    non pò da sua natura esser possente     55
tanto, che suo principio non discerna
molto di là da quel che l'è parvente.

    Però ne la giustizia sempiterna     58
la vista che riceve il vostro mondo,
com' occhio per lo mare, entro s'interna;

    che, ben che da la proda veggia il fondo,     61
in pelago nol vede; e nondimeno
èli, ma cela lui l'esser profondo.

    Lume non è, se non vien dal sereno     64
che non si turba mai; anzi è tenèbra
od ombra de la carne o suo veleno.

    Assai t'è mo aperta la latebra     67
che t'ascondeva la giustizia viva,
di che facei question cotanto crebra;

    ché tu dicevi: 'Un uom nasce a la riva     70
de l'Indo, e quivi non è chi ragioni
di Cristo né chi legga né chi scriva;

    e tutti suoi voleri e atti buoni     73
sono, quanto ragione umana vede,
sanza peccato in vita o in sermoni.

And that man dies unbaptized, without faith.     76
Where is this justice then that would condemn him?
Where is his sin if he does not believe?'

Now who are you to sit upon the bench,     79
to judge events a thousand miles away,
when your own vision spans so brief a space?

Of course, for him who would be subtle with me,     82
were there no Scriptures to instruct you, then
there would be place for an array of questions.

O earthly animals, o minds obtuse!     85
The Primal Will, which of Itself is good,
from the Supreme Good—Its Self—never moved.

So much is just as does accord with It;     88
and so, created good can draw It to
itself—but It, rayed forth, causes such goods."

Just as, above the nest, the stork will circle     91
when she has fed her fledglings, and as he
whom she has fed looks up at her, so did

the blessed image do, and so did I,     94
the fledgling, while the Eagle moved its wings,
spurred on by many wills in unison.

Wheeling, the Eagle sang, then said: "Even     97
as are my songs to you—past understanding—
such is Eternal Judgment to you mortals."

After the Holy Ghost's bright flames fell silent     100
while still within the sign that made the Romans
revered throughout the world, again the Eagle

began: "No one without belief in Christ     103
has ever risen to this kingdom—either
before or after He was crucified.

But there are many who now cry 'Christ! Christ!'     106
who at the Final Judgment shall be far
less close to Him than one who knows not Christ;

the Ethiopian will shame such Christians     109
when the two companies are separated,
the one forever rich, the other poor.

What shall the Persians, when they come to see     112
that open volume in which they shall read
the misdeeds of your rulers, say to them?

There one shall see, among the deeds of Albert,     115
that which is soon to set the pen in motion,
his making of a desert of Prague's kingdom.

Muore non battezzato e sanza fede:     76
ov' è questa giustizia che 'l condanna?
ov' è colpa sua, se ei non crede?'
   Or tu chi se', che vuo' sedere a scranna,     79
per giudicar di lungi mille miglia
con la veduta corta d'una spanna?
   Certo a colui che meco s'assottiglia,     82
se la Scrittura sovra voi non fosse,
da dubitar sarebbe a maraviglia.
   Oh terreni animali! oh menti grosse!     85
La prima volontà, ch'è da sé buona,
da sé, ch'è sommo ben, mai non si mosse.
   Cotanto è giusto quanto a lei consuona:     88
nullo creato bene a sé la tira,
ma essa, radïando, lui cagiona."
   Quale sovresso il nido si rigira     91
poi c'ha pasciuti la cicogna i figli,
e come quel ch'è pasto la rimira;
   cotal si fece, e sì levài i cigli,     94
la benedetta imagine, che l'ali
movea sospinte da tanti consigli.
   Roteando cantava, e dicea: "Quali     97
son le mie note a te, che non le 'ntendi,
tal è il giudicio etterno a voi mortali."
   Poi si quetaro quei lucenti incendi     100
de lo Spirito Santo ancor nel segno
che fé i Romani al mondo reverendi,
   esso ricominciò: "A questo regno     103
non salì mai chi non credette 'n Cristo,
né pria né poi ch'el si chiavasse al legno.
   Ma vedi: molti gridan 'Cristo, Cristo!'     106
che saranno in giudicio assai men *prope*
a lui, che tal che non conosce Cristo;
   e tai Cristian dannerà l'Etïòpe,     109
quando si partiranno i due collegi,
l'uno in etterno ricco e l'altro inòpe.
   Che poran dir li Perse a' vostri regi,     112
come vedranno quel volume aperto
nel qual si scrivon tutti suoi dispregi?
   Lì si vedrà, tra l'opere d'Alberto,     115
quella che tosto moverà la penna,
per che 'l regno di Praga fia diserto.

There one shall see the grief inflicted on                    118
the Seine by him who falsifies his coins,
one who shall die beneath a wild boar's blow.

That book will show the thirst of arrogance                   121
that drives the Scot and Englishman insane—
unable to remain within their borders.

That book will show the life of lechery                       124
and ease the Spaniard led—and the Bohemian,
who never knew and never wished for valor.

That book will show the Cripple of Jerusalem—                 127
his good deeds labeled with an *I* alone,
whereas his evils will be under M.

That book will show the greed and cowardice                   130
of him who oversees the Isle of Fire,
on which Anchises ended his long life;

and to make plain his paltriness, the letters                 133
that register his deeds will be contracted,
to note much pettiness in little space.

And all shall see the filthiness of both                      136
his uncle and his brother, who dishonored
a family so famous—and two crowns.

And he of Portugal and he of Norway                           139
shall be known in that book, and he of Rascia,
who saw—unluckily—the coin of Venice.

O happy Hungary, if she would let                             142
herself be wronged no more! Happy Navarre,
if mountains that surround her served as armor!

And if Navarre needs token of her future,                     145
now Nicosia and Famagosta offer—
as men must see—lament and anger over

their own beast, with his place beside the others."           148

Lì si vedrà il duol che sovra Senna 118
induce, falseggiando la moneta,
quel che morrà di colpo di cotenna.

Lì si vedrà la superbia ch'asseta, 121
che fa lo Scotto e l'Inghilese folle,
sì che non può soffrir dentro a sua meta.

Vedrassi la lussuria e 'l viver molle 124
di quel di Spagna e di quel di Boemme,
che mai valor non conobbe né volle.

Vedrassi al Ciotto di Ierusalemme 127
segnata con un i la sua bontate,
quando 'l contrario segnerà un emme.

Vedrassi l'avarizia e la viltate 130
di quei che guarda l'isola del foco,
ove Anchise finì la lunga etate;

e a dare ad intender quanto è poco, 133
la sua scrittura fian lettere mozze,
che noteranno molto in parvo loco.

E parranno a ciascun l'opere sozze 136
del barba e del fratel, che tanto egregia
nazione e due corone han fatte bozze.

E quel di Portogallo e di Norvegia 139
lì si conosceranno, e quel di Rascia
che male ha visto il conio di Vinegia.

O beata Ungheria, se non si lascia 142
più malmenare! e beata Navarra,
se s'armasse del monte che la fascia!

E creder de' ciascun che già, per arra 145
di questo, Niccosïa e Famagosta
per la lor bestia si lamenti e garra,

che dal fianco de l'altre non si scosta." 148

OVERLEAF:
*The Eye of the Eagle*

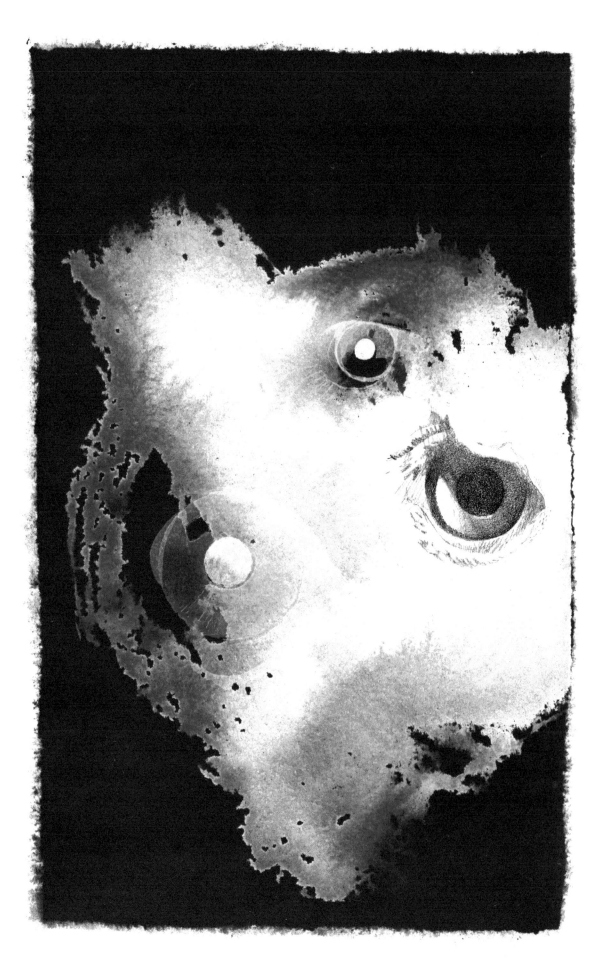

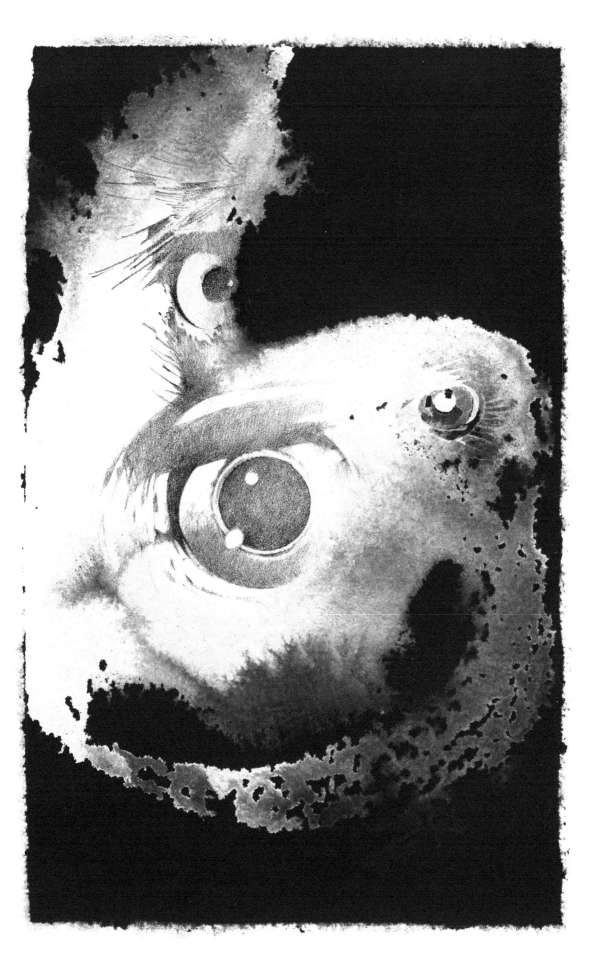

# CANTO XX

When he who graces all the world with light
has sunk so far below our hemisphere
that on all sides the day is spent, the sky,
    which had been lit before by him alone,          4
immediately shows itself again
with many lights reflecting one same source,
    and I remembered this celestial course          7
when, in the blessed beak, the emblem of
the world and of its guardians fell silent;
    for then all of those living lights grew more    10
resplendent, but the songs that they began
were labile—they escape my memory.
    O gentle love that wears a smile as mantle,    13
how ardent was your image in those torches
filled only with the breath of holy thoughts!
    After the precious, gleaming jewels with which    16
the sixth of Heaven's heavens was engemmed
had ended their angelic song in silence,
    I seemed to hear the murmur of a torrent    19
that, limpid, falls from rock to rock, whose flow
shows the abundance of its mountain source.
    Even as sound takes shape at the lute's neck,    22
and even as the wind that penetrates
the blow-hole of the bagpipe, so—with no
    delay—that murmur of the Eagle rose    25
straight up, directly through its neck as if
its neck were hollow; and that murmuring
    became a voice that issued from its beak,    28
taking the shape of words desired by
my heart—and that is where they were transcribed.
    "Now you must watch—and steadily—that part    31
of me that can, in mortal eagles, see
and suffer the sun's force," it then began

*Still the Sixth Heaven: the Sphere of Jupiter. The song of the*
*spirits. The Eagle on the spirits that form its shape. The Eagle*
*on Dante's amazement at seeing the emperor Trajan and the*
*Trojan Ripheus redeemed. Predestination.*

Quando colui che tutto 'l mondo alluma
de l'emisperio nostro sì discende,
che 'l giorno d'ogne parte si consuma,

lo ciel, che sol di lui prima s'accende,　　　　4
subitamente si rifà parvente
per molte luci, in che una risplende;

e questo atto del ciel mi venne a mente,　　　　7
come 'l segno del mondo e de' suoi duci
nel benedetto rostro fu tacente;

però che tutte quelle vive luci,　　　　10
vie più lucendo, cominciaron canti
da mia memoria labili e caduci.

O dolce amor che di riso t'ammanti,　　　　13
quanto parevi ardente in que' flailli,
ch'avieno spirto sol di pensier santi!

Poscia che i cari e lucidi lapilli　　　　16
ond' io vidi ingemmato il sesto lume
puoser silenzio a li angelici squilli,

udir mi parve un mormorar di fiume　　　　19
che scende chiaro giù di pietra in pietra,
mostrando l'ubertà del suo cacume.

E come suono al collo de la cetra　　　　22
prende sua forma, e sì com' al pertugio
de la sampogna vento che penètra,

così, rimosso d'aspettare indugio,　　　　25
quel mormorar de l'aguglia salissi
su per lo collo, come fosse bugio.

Fecesi voce quivi, e quindi uscissi　　　　28
per lo suo becco in forma di parole,
quali aspettava il core ov' io le scrissi.

"La parte in me che vede e pate il sole　　　　31
ne l'aguglie mortali," incominciommi,
"or fisamente riguardar si vole,

to say to me, "because, of all the flames 34
from which I shape my form, those six with which
the eye in my head glows hold highest rank.

He who gleams in the center, my eye's pupil— 37
he was the singer of the Holy Spirit,
who bore the ark from one town to another;

now he has learned the merit will can earn— 40
his song had not been spurred by grace alone,
but his own will, in part, had urged him on.

Of those five flames that, arching, form my brow, 43
he who is nearest to my beak is one
who comforted the widow for her son;

now he has learned the price one pays for not 46
following Christ, through his experience
of this sweet life and of its opposite.

And he whose place is next on the circumference 49
of which I speak, along the upward arc,
delayed his death through truthful penitence;

now he has learned that the eternal judgment 52
remains unchanged, though worthy prayer below
makes what falls due today take place tomorrow.

The next who follows—one whose good intention 55
bore evil fruit—to give place to the Shepherd,
with both the laws and me, made himself Greek;

now he has learned that, even though the world 58
be ruined by the evil that derives
from his good act, that evil does not harm him.

He whom you see—along the downward arc— 61
was William, and the land that mourns his death,
for living Charles and Frederick, now laments;

now he has learned how Heaven loves the just 64
ruler, and he would show this outwardly
as well, so radiantly visible.

Who in the erring world below would hold 67
that he who was the fifth among the lights
that formed this circle was the Trojan Ripheus?

Now he has learned much that the world cannot 70
discern of God's own grace, although his sight
cannot divine, not reach its deepest site."

As if it were a lark at large in air, 73
a lark that sings at first and then falls still,
content with final sweetness that fulfills,

perché d'i fuochi ond' io figura fommi,                        34
quelli onde l'occhio in testa mi scintilla,
e' di tutti lor gradi son li sommi.

   Colui che luce in mezzo per pupilla,                    37
fu il cantor de lo Spirito Santo,
che l'arca traslatò di villa in villa:

   ora conosce il merto del suo canto,                     40
in quanto effetto fu del suo consiglio,
per lo remunerar ch'è altrettanto.

   Dei cinque che mi fan cerchio per ciglio,              43
colui che più al becco mi s'accosta,
la vedovella consolò del figlio:

   ora conosce quanto caro costa                           46
non seguir Cristo, per l'esperïenza
di questa dolce vita e de l'opposta.

   E quel che segue in la circunferenza                    49
di che ragiono, per l'arco superno,
morte indugiò per vera penitenza:

   ora conosce che 'l giudicio etterno                     52
non si trasmuta, quando degno preco
fa crastino là giù de l'odïerno.

   L'altro che segue, con le leggi e meco,                  55
sotto buona intenzion che fé mal frutto,
per cedere al pastor si fece greco:

   ora conosce come il mal dedutto                         58
dal suo bene operar non li è nocivo,
avvegna che sia 'l mondo indi distrutto.

   E quel che vedi ne l'arco declivo,                      61
Guiglielmo fu, cui quella terra plora
che piagne Carlo e Federigo vivo:

   ora conosce come s'innamora                             64
lo ciel del giusto rege, e al sembiante
del suo fulgore il fa vedere ancora.

   Chi crederebbe giù nel mondo errante                    67
che Rifëo Troiano in questo tondo
fosse la quinta de le luci sante?

   Ora conosce assai di quel che 'l mondo                  70
veder non può de la divina grazia,
ben che sua vista non discerna il fondo."

   Quale allodetta che 'n aere si spazia                   73
prima cantando, e poi tace contenta
de l'ultima dolcezza che la sazia,

such seemed to me the image of the seal                76
of that Eternal Pleasure through whose will
each thing becomes the being that it is.

     And though the doubt I felt there was as plain     79
as any colored surface cloaked by glass,
it could not wait to voice itself, but with

     the thrust and weight of urgency it forced         82
"Can such things be?" out from my lips, at which
I saw lights flash—a vast festivity.

     And then the blessed sign—its eye grown still      85
more bright—replied, that I might not be kept
suspended in amazement: "I can see

     that, since you speak of them, you do believe      88
these things but cannot see *how* they may be;
and thus, though you believe them, they are hidden.

     You act as one who apprehends a thing              91
by name but cannot see its quiddity
unless another set it forth to him.

     *Regnum celorum* suffers violence                  94
from ardent love and living hope, for these
can be the conquerors of Heaven's Will;

     yet not as man defeats another man:                97
the Will of God is won because It would
be won and, won, wins through benevolence.

     You were amazed to see the angels' realm           100
adorned with those who were the first and fifth
among the living souls that form my eyebrow.

     When these souls left their bodies, they were not  103
Gentiles—as you believe—but Christians, one
with firm faith in the Feet that suffered, one

     in Feet that were to suffer. One, from Hell,       106
where there is no returning to right will,
returned to his own bones, as the reward

     bestowed upon a living hope, the hope              109
that gave force to the prayers offered God
to resurrect him and convert his will.

     Returning briefly to the flesh, that soul          112
in glory—he of whom I speak—believed
in Him whose power could help him and, believing,

     was kindled to such fire of true love              115
that, when he died a second death, he was
worthy to join in this festivity.

tal mi sembiò l'imago de la 'mprenta 76
de l'etterno piacere, al cui disio
ciascuna cosa qual ell' è diventa.

E avvegna ch'io fossi al dubbiar mio 79
lì quasi vetro a lo color ch'el veste,
tempo aspettar tacendo non patio,

ma de la bocca, "Che cose son queste?" 82
mi pinse con la forza del suo peso:
per ch'io di coruscar vidi gran feste.

Poi appresso, con l'occhio più acceso, 85
lo benedetto segno mi rispuose
per non tenermi in ammirar sospeso:

"Io veggio che tu credi queste cose 88
perch' io le dico, ma non vedi come;
sì che, se son credute, sono ascose.

Fai come quei che la cosa per nome 91
apprende ben, ma la sua quiditate
veder non può se altri non la prome.

Regnum celorum vïolenza pate 94
da caldo amore e da viva speranza,
che vince la divina volontate:

non a guisa che l'omo a l'om sobranza, 97
ma vince lei perché vuole esser vinta,
e, vinta, vince con sua beninanza.

La prima vita del ciglio e la quinta 100
ti fa maravigliar, perché ne vedi
la regïon de li angeli dipinta.

D'i corpi suoi non uscir, come credi, 103
Gentili, ma Cristiani, in ferma fede
quel d'i passuri e quel d'i passi piedi.

Ché l'una de lo 'nferno, u' non si riede 106
già mai a buon voler, tornò a l'ossa;
e ciò di viva spene fu mercede:

di viva spene, che mise la possa 109
ne' prieghi fatti a Dio per suscitarla,
sì che potesse sua voglia esser mossa.

L'anima glorïosa onde si parla, 112
tornata ne la carne, in che fu poco,
credette in lui che potëa aiutarla;

e credendo s'accese in tanto foco 115
di vero amor, ch'a la morte seconda
fu degna di venire a questo gioco.

The other, through the grace that surges from                    118
a well so deep that no created one
has ever thrust his eye to its first source,

    below, set all his love on righteousness,                    121
so that, through grace on grace, God granted him
the sight of our redemption in the future;

    thus he, believing that, no longer suffered                    124
the stench of paganism and rebuked
those who persisted in that perverse way.

    More than a thousand years before baptizing,                    127
to baptize him there were the same three women
you saw along the chariot's right-hand side.

    How distant, o predestination, is                    130
your root from those whose vision does not see
the Primal Cause in Its entirety!

    And, mortals, do take care—judge prudently:                    133
for we, though we see God, do not yet know
all those whom He has chosen; but within

    the incompleteness of our knowledge is                    136
a sweetness, for our good is then refined
in this good, since what God wills, we too will."

    So, from the image God Himself had drawn,                    139
what I received was gentle medicine;
and I saw my shortsightedness plainly.

    And as a lutanist accompanies—                    142
expert—with trembling strings, the expert singer,
by which the song acquires sweeter savor,

    so, while the Eagle spoke—I can remember—                    145
I saw the pair of blessed lights together,
like eyes that wink in concord, move their flames

    in ways that were at one with what he said.                    148

L'altra, per grazia che da sì profonda 118
fontana stilla, che mai creatura
non pinse l'occhio infino a la prima onda,

tutto suo amor là giù pose a drittura: 121
per che, di grazia in grazia, Dio li aperse
l'occhio a la nostra redenzion futura;

ond' ei credette in quella, e non sofferse 124
da indi il puzzo più del paganesmo;
e riprendiene le genti perverse.

Quelle tre donne li fur per battesmo 127
che tu vedesti da la destra rota,
dinanzi al battezzar più d'un millesmo.

O predestinazion, quanto remota 130
è la radice tua da quelli aspetti
che la prima cagion non veggion *tota*!

E voi, mortali, tenetevi stretti 133
a giudicar: ché noi, che Dio vedemo,
non conosciamo ancor tutti li eletti;

ed ènne dolce così fatto scemo, 136
perché il ben nostro in questo ben s'affina,
che quel che vole Iddio, e noi volemo."

Così da quella imagine divina, 139
per farmi chiara la mia corta vista,
data mi fu soave medicina.

E come a buon cantor buon citarista 142
fa seguitar lo guizzo de la corda,
in che più di piacer lo canto acquista,

sì, mentre ch'e' parlò, sì mi ricorda 145
ch'io vidi le due luci benedette,
pur come batter d'occhi si concorda,

con le parole mover le fiammette.

# CANTO XXI

By now my eyes were set again upon
my lady's face, and with my eyes, my mind:
from every other thought, it was withdrawn.
    She did not smile. Instead her speech to me                    4
began: "Were I to smile, then you would be
like Semele when she was turned to ashes,
    because, as you have seen, my loveliness—                      7
which, even as we climb the steps of this
eternal palace, blazes with more brightness—
    were it not tempered here, would be so brilliant              10
that, as it flashed, your mortal faculty
would seem a branch a lightning bolt has cracked.
    We now are in the seventh splendor; this,                     13
beneath the burning Lion's breast, transmits
to earth its rays, with which his force is mixed.
    Let your mind follow where your eyes have led,                16
and let your eyes be mirrors for the figure
that will appear to you within this mirror."
    That man who knows just how my vision pastured                19
upon her blessed face, might recognize
the joy I found when my celestial guide
    had asked of me to turn my mind aside,                        22
were he to weigh my joy when I obeyed
against my joy in contemplating her.
    Within the crystal that—as it revolves                        25
around the earth—bears as its name the name
of that dear king whose rule undid all evil,
    I saw a ladder rising up so high                              28
that it could not be followed by my sight:
its color, gold when gold is struck by sunlight.
    I also saw so many flames descend                             31
those steps that I thought every light displayed
in heaven had been poured out from that place.

*Ascent to the Seventh Heaven, the Sphere of Saturn. The golden*
*ladder. Dante's questions to one of the spirits. The spirit's*
*replies. Another query and a reply concerning predestination.*
*The spirit's identifying of himself as St. Peter Damian, and his*
*denunciation of degenerate prelates. The outcry of the spirits.*

Già eran li occhi miei rifissi al volto
de la mia donna, e l'animo con essi,
e da ogne altro intento s'era tolto.

E quella non ridea; ma "S'io ridessi,"     4
mi cominciò, "tu ti faresti quale
fu Semelè quando di cener fessi:

ché la bellezza mia, che per le scale     7
de l'etterno palazzo più s'accende,
com' hai veduto, quanto più si sale,

se non si temperasse, tanto splende,     10
che 'l tuo mortal podere, al suo fulgore,
sarebbe fronda che trono scoscende.

Noi sem levati al settimo splendore,     13
che sotto 'l petto del Leone ardente
raggia mo misto giù del suo valore.

Ficca di retro a li occhi tuoi la mente,     16
e fa di quelli specchi a la figura
che 'n questo specchio ti sarà parvente."

Qual savesse qual era la pastura     19
del viso mio ne l'aspetto beato
quand' io mi trasmutai ad altra cura,

conoscerebbe quanto m'era a grato     22
ubidire a la mia celeste scorta,
contrapesando l'un con l'altro lato.

Dentro al cristallo che 'l vocabol porta,     25
cerchiando il mondo, del suo caro duce
sotto cui giacque ogne malizia morta,

di color d'oro in che raggio traluce     28
vid' io uno scaleo eretto in suso
tanto, che nol seguiva la mia luce.

Vidi anche per li gradi scender giuso     31
tanti splendor, ch'io pensai ch'ogne lume
che par nel ciel, quindi fosse diffuso.

And just as jackdaws, at the break of day,                    34
together rise—such is their nature's way—
to warm their feathers chilled by night; then some
    fly off and never do return, and some               37
wheel back to that point where they started from,
while others, though they wheel, remain at home;
    such were the ways I saw those splendors take        40
as soon as they had struck a certain step,
where they had thronged as one in radiance.
    The flame that halted nearest us became              43
so bright that in my mind I said: "I see
you clearly signaling to me your love.
    But she from whom I wait for word on how             46
and when to speak and to be silent, pauses;
thus, though I would, I do well not to ask."
    And she who, seeing Him who sees all things,         49
had seen the reason for my silence, said
to me: "Do satisfy your burning longing."
    And I began: "My merit does not make                 52
me worthy of reply, but for the sake
of her who gives me leave to question you—
    a blessed living soul—who hide within                55
your joy, do let me know the reason why
you drew so near to me. And tell me, too,
    why the sweet symphony of Paradise                   58
is silent in this heaven, while, below,
it sounds devoutly through the other spheres."
    "Your hearing is as mortal as your sight;            61
thus, here there is no singing," he replied,
"and Beatrice, in like wise, did not smile.
    When, down the sacred staircase, I descended,        64
I only came to welcome you with gladness—
with words and with the light that mantles me.
    The love that prompted me is not supreme;            67
above, is love that equals or exceeds
my own, as spirit-flames will let you see.
    But the deep charity, which makes us keen            70
to serve the Providence that rules the world,
allots our actions here, as you perceive."
    "O holy lamp," I said, "I do indeed                   73
see how, within this court, it is your free
love that fulfills eternal Providence;

E come, per lo natural costume,      34
le pole insieme, al cominciar del giorno,
si movono a scaldar le fredde piume;

  poi altre vanno via sanza ritorno,      37
altre rivolgon sé onde son mosse,
e altre roteando fan soggiorno;

  tal modo parve me che quivi fosse      40
in quello sfavillar che 'nsieme venne,
sì come in certo grado si percosse.

  E quel che presso più ci si ritenne,      43
si fé sì chiaro, ch'io dicea pensando:
"Io veggio ben l'amor che tu m'accenne.

  Ma quella ond' io aspetto il come e 'l quando      46
del dire e del tacer, si sta; ond' io,
contra 'l disio, fo ben ch'io non dimando."

  Per ch'ella, che vedëa il tacer mio      49
nel veder di colui che tutto vede,
mi disse: "Solvi il tuo caldo disio."

  E io incominciai: "La mia mercede      52
non mi fa degno de la tua risposta;
ma per colei che 'l chieder mi concede,

  vita beata che ti stai nascosta      55
dentro a la tua letizia, fammi nota
la cagion che sì presso mi t'ha posta;

  e dì perché si tace in questa rota      58
la dolce sinfonia di paradiso,
che giù per l'altre suona sì divota."

  "Tu hai l'udir mortal sì come il viso,"      61
rispuose a me; "onde qui non si canta
per quel che Bëatrice non ha riso.

  Giù per li gradi de la scala santa      64
discesi tanto sol per farti festa
col dire e con la luce che mi ammanta;

  né più amor mi fece esser più presta,      67
ché più e tanto amor quinci sù ferve,
sì come il fiammeggiar ti manifesta.

  Ma l'alta carità, che ci fa serve      70
pronte al consiglio che 'l mondo governa,
sorteggia qui sì come tu osserve."

  "Io veggio ben," diss' io, "sacra lucerna,      73
come libero amore in questa corte
basta a seguir la provedenza etterna;

but this seems difficult for me to grasp: 76
why you alone, of those who form these ranks,
were he who was predestined to this task."

And I had yet to reach the final word 79
when that light made a pivot of its midpoint
and spun around as would a swift millstone.

Then, from within its light, that love replied: 82
"Light from the Deity descends on me;
it penetrates the light that enwombs me;

its power, as it joins my power of sight, 85
lifts me so far beyond myself that I
see the High Source from which that light derives.

From this there comes the joy with which I am 88
aflame; I match the clearness of my light
with equal measure of my clear insight.

But even Heaven's most enlightened soul, 91
that Seraph with his eye most set on God,
could not provide the *why,* not satisfy

what you have asked; for deep in the abyss 94
of the Eternal Ordinance, it is
cut off from all created beings' vision.

And to the mortal world, when you return, 97
tell this, lest men continue to trespass
and set their steps toward such a reachless goal.

The mind, bright here, on earth is dulled and smoky. 100
Think: how, below, can mind see that which hides
even when mind is raised to Heaven's height?"

His words so curbed my query that I left 103
behind my questioning; and I drew back
and humbly asked that spirit who he was.

"Not far from your homeland, between two shores 106
of Italy, the stony ridges rise
so high that, far below them, thunder roars.

These ridges form a hump called Catria; 109
a consecrated hermitage beneath
that peak was once devoted just to worship."

So his third speech to me began; then he 112
continued: "There, within that monastery,
in serving God, I gained tenacity:

with food that only olive juice had seasoned, 115
I could sustain with ease both heat and frost,
content within my contemplative thoughts.

ma questo è quel ch'a cerner mi par forte,                    76
perché predestinata fosti sola
a questo officio tra le tue consorte."

Né venni prima a l'ultima parola,                             79
che del suo mezzo fece il lume centro,
girando sé come veloce mola;

poi rispuose l'amor che v'era dentro:                         82
"Luce divina sopra me s'appunta,
penetrando per questa in ch'io m'inventro,

la cui virtù, col mio veder congiunta,                        85
mi leva sopra me tanto, ch'i' veggio
la somma essenza de la quale è munta.

Quinci vien l'allegrezza ond' io fiammeggio;                  88
per ch'a la vista mia, quant' ella è chiara,
la chiarità de la fiamma pareggio.

Ma quell' alma nel ciel che più si schiara,                   91
quel serafin che 'n Dio più l'occhio ha fisso,
a la dimanda tua non satisfara,

però che sì s'innoltra ne lo abisso                           94
de l'etterno statuto quel che chiedi,
che da ogne creata vista è scisso.

E al mondo mortal, quando tu riedi,                           97
questo rapporta, sì che non presumma
a tanto segno più mover li piedi.

La mente, che qui luce, in terra fumma;                       100
onde riguarda come può là giùe
quel che non pote perché 'l ciel l'assumma."

Sì mi prescrisser le parole sue,                              103
ch'io lasciai la quistione e mi ritrassi
a dimandarla umilmente chi fue.

"Tra ' due liti d'Italia surgon sassi,                        106
e non molto distanti a la tua patria,
tanto che ' troni assai suonan più bassi,

e fanno un gibbo che si chiama Catria,                        109
di sotto al quale è consecrato un ermo,
che suole esser disposto a sola latria."

Così ricominciommi il terzo sermo;                            112
e poi, continüando, disse: "Quivi
al servigio di Dio mi fe' sì fermo,

che pur con cibi di liquor d'ulivi                            115
lievemente passava caldi e geli,
contento ne' pensier contemplativi.

That cloister used to offer souls to Heaven,                              118
a fertile harvest, but it now is barren—
as Heaven's punishment will soon make plain.

There I was known as Peter Damian                                        121
and, on the Adriatic shore, was Peter
the Sinner when I served Our Lady's House.

Not much of mortal life was left to me                                   124
when I was sought for, dragged to take that hat
which always passes down from bad to worse.

Once there were Cephas and the Holy Ghost's                              127
great vessel: they were barefoot, they were lean,
they took their food at any inn they found.

But now the modern pastors are so plump                                  130
that they have need of one to prop them up
on this side, one on that, and one in front,

and one to hoist them saddleward. Their cloaks                           133
cover their steeds, two beasts beneath one skin:
o patience, you who must endure so much!"

These words, I saw, had summoned many flames,                            136
descending step by step; I saw them wheel
and, at each turn, become more beautiful.

They joined around him, and they stopped, and raised   139
a cry so deep that nothing here can be
its likeness; but the words they cried I could

not understand—their thunder overcame me.                                142

Render solea quel chiostro a questi cieli 118
fertilemente; e ora è fatto vano,
sì che tosto convien che si riveli.

    In quel loco fu' io Pietro Damiano, 121
e Pietro Peccator fu' ne la casa
di Nostra Donna in sul lito adriano.

    Poca vita mortal m'era rimasa, 124
quando fui chiesto e tratto a quel cappello,
che pur di male in peggio si travasa.

    Venne Cefàs e venne il gran vasello 127
de lo Spirito Santo, magri e scalzi,
prendendo il cibo da qualunque ostello.

    Or voglion quinci e quindi chi rincalzi 130
li moderni pastori e chi li meni,
tanto son gravi, e chi di rietro li alzi.

    Cuopron d'i manti loro i palafreni, 133
sì che due bestie van sott' una pelle:
oh pazïenza che tanto sostieni!"

    A questa voce vid' io più fiammelle 136
di grado in grado scendere e girarsi,
e ogne giro le facea più belle.

    Dintorno a questa vennero e fermarsi, 139
e fero un grido di sì alto suono,
che non potrebbe qui assomigliarsi;

    né io lo 'ntesi, sì mi vinse il tuono. 142

OVERLEAF:
*The Ridges of Catria*

# CANTO XXII

Amazement overwhelming me, I—like
a child who always hurries back to find
that place he trusts the most—turned to my guide;
and like a mother quick to reassure                    4
her pale and panting son with the same voice
that she has often used to comfort him,
she said: "Do you not know you are in Heaven,          7
not know how holy all of Heaven is,
how righteous zeal moves every action here?
Now, since this cry has agitated you                   10
so much, you can conceive how—had you seen
me smile and heard song here—you would have been
confounded; and if you had understood                  13
the prayer within that cry, by now you would
know the revenge you'll see before your death.
The sword that strikes from Heaven's height is neither 16
hasty nor slow, except as it appears
to him who waits for it—who longs or fears.
But turn now toward the other spirits here;            19
for if you set your sight as I suggest,
you will see many who are notable."
As pleased my guide, I turned my eyes and saw          22
a hundred little suns; as these together
cast light, each made the other lovelier.
I stood as one who curbs within himself                25
the goad of longing and, in fear of being
too forward, does not dare to ask a question.
At this, the largest and most radiant                  28
among those pearls moved forward that he might
appease my need to hear who he might be.
Then, in that light, I heard: "Were you to see,        31
even as I do see, the charity
that burns in us, your thoughts would have been uttered.

*Still the Seventh Heaven: the Sphere of Saturn. Beatrice on the
spirits' outcry. St. Benedict and other contemplatives. Dante's
desire to see the face of St. Benedict. St. Benedict on the de-
generacy of the Benedictines. Ascent to the Eighth Heaven, the
Sphere of the Fixed Stars. Invocation to the constellation Gemini.
Dante's earthward gaze.*

Oppresso di stupore, a la mia guida
mi volsi, come parvol che ricorre
sempre colà dove più si confida;

  e quella, come madre che soccorre              4
sùbito al figlio palido e anelo
con la sua voce, che 'l suol ben disporre,

  mi disse: "Non sai tu che tu se' in cielo?       7
e non sai tu che 'l cielo è tutto santo,
e ciò che ci si fa vien da buon zelo?

  Come t'avrebbe trasmutato il canto,           10
e io ridendo, mo pensar lo puoi,
poscia che 'l grido t'ha mosso cotanto;

  nel qual, se 'nteso avessi i prieghi suoi,       13
già ti sarebbe nota la vendetta
che tu vedrai innanzi che tu muoi.

  La spada di qua sù non taglia in fretta      16
né tardo, ma' ch'al parer di colui
che disïando o temendo l'aspetta.

  Ma rivolgiti omai inverso altrui;          19
ch'assai illustri spiriti vedrai,
se com' io dico l'aspetto redui."

  Come a lei piacque, li occhi ritornai,        22
e vidi cento sperule che 'nsieme
più s'abbellivan con mutüi rai.

  Io stava come quei che 'n sé repreme       25
la punta del disio, e non s'attenta
di domandar, sì del troppo si teme;

  e la maggiore e la più luculenta          28
di quelle margherite innanzi fessi,
per far di sé la mia voglia contenta.

  Poi dentro a lei udi': "Se tu vedessi        31
com' io la carità che tra noi arde,
li tuoi concetti sarebbero espressi.

But lest, by waiting, you be slow to reach 34
the high goal of your seeking, I shall answer
what you were thinking when you curbed your speech.

That mountain on whose flank Cassino lies 37
was once frequented on its summit by
those who were still deluded, still awry;

and I am he who was the first to carry 40
up to that peak the name of Him who brought
to earth the truth that lifts us to the heights.

And such abundant grace had brought me light 43
that, from corrupted worship that seduced
the world, I won away the nearby sites.

These other flames were all contemplatives, 46
men who were kindled by the heat that brings
to birth the holy flowers, the holy fruits.

Here is Macarius, here is Romualdus, 49
here are my brothers, those who stayed their steps
in cloistered walls, who kept their hearts steadfast."

I answered: "The affection that you show 52
in speech to me, and kindness that I see
and note within the flaming of your lights,

have given me so much more confidence, 55
just like the sun that makes the rose expand
and reach the fullest flowering it can.

Therefore I pray you, father—and may you 58
assure me that I can receive such grace—
to let me see, unveiled, your human face."

And he: "Brother, your high desire will be 61
fulfilled within the final sphere, as all
the other souls' and my own longing will.

There, each desire is perfect, ripe, intact; 64
and only there, within that final sphere,
is every part where it has always been.

That sphere is not in space and has no poles; 67
our ladder reaches up to it, and that
is why it now is hidden from your sight.

Up to that sphere, Jacob the patriarch 70
could see that ladder's topmost portion reach,
when it appeared to him so thronged with angels.

But no one now would lift his feet from earth 73
to climb that ladder, and my Rule is left
to waste the paper it was written on.

Ma perché tu, aspettando, non tarde                                   34
a l'alto fine, io ti farò risposta
pur al pensier, da che sì ti riguarde.

    Quel monte a cui Cassino è ne la costa            37
fu frequentato già in su la cima
da la gente ingannata e mal disposta;

    e quel son io che sù vi portai prima            40
lo nome di colui che 'n terra addusse
la verità che tanto ci soblima;

    e tanta grazia sopra me relusse,               43
ch'io ritrassi le ville circunstanti
da l'empio cólto che 'l mondo sedusse.

    Questi altri fuochi tutti contemplanti          46
uomini fuoro, accesi di quel caldo
che fa nascere i fiori e ' frutti santi.

    Qui è Maccario, qui è Romoaldo,                 49
qui son li frati miei che dentro ai chiostri
fermar li piedi e tennero il cor saldo."

    E io a lui: "L'affetto che dimostri             52
meco parlando, e la buona sembianza
ch'io veggio e noto in tutti li ardor vostri,

    così m'ha dilatata mia fidanza,                 55
come 'l sol fa la rosa quando aperta
tanto divien quant' ell' ha di possanza.

    Però ti priego, e tu, padre, m'accerta          58
s'io posso prender tanta grazia, ch'io
ti veggia con imagine scoverta."

    Ond' elli: "Frate, il tuo alto disio            61
s'adempierà in su l'ultima spera,
ove s'adempion tutti li altri e 'l mio.

    Ivi è perfetta, matura e intera                 64
ciascuna disïanza; in quella sola
è ogne parte là ove sempr' era,

    perché non è in loco e non s'impola;            67
e nostra scala infino ad essa varca,
onde così dal viso ti s'invola.

    Infin là sù la vide il patriarca                70
Iacobbe porger la superna parte,
quando li apparve d'angeli sì carca.

    Ma, per salirla, mo nessun diparte              73
da terra i piedi, e la regola mia
rimasa è per danno de le carte.

What once were abbey walls are robbers' dens;    76
what once were cowls are sacks of rotten meal.
But even heavy usury does not
    offend the will of God as grievously·    79
as the appropriation of that fruit
which makes the hearts of monks go mad with greed;
    for all within the keeping of the Church    82
belongs to those who ask it in God's name,
and not to relatives or concubines.
    The flesh of mortals yields so easily—    85
on earth a good beginning does not run
from when the oak is born until the acorn.
    Peter began with neither gold nor silver,    88
and I with prayer and fasting, and when Francis
began his fellowship, he did it humbly;
    if you observe the starting point of each,    91
and look again to see where it has strayed,
then you will see how white has gone to gray.
    And yet, the Jordan in retreat, the sea    94
in flight when God had willed it so, were sights
more wonderful than His help here will be."
    So did he speak to me, and he drew back    97
to join his company, which closed, compact;
then, like a whirlwind, upward, all were swept.
    The gentle lady—simply with a sign—    100
impelled me after them and up that ladder,
so did her power overcome my nature;
    and never here below, where our ascent    103
and descent follow nature's law, was there
motion as swift as mine when I took wing.
    So, reader, may I once again return    106
to those triumphant ranks—an end for which
I often beat my breast, weep for my sins—
    more quickly than your finger can withdraw    109
from flame and be thrust into it, I saw,
and was within, the sign that follows Taurus.
    O stars of glory, constellation steeped    112
in mighty force, all of my genius—
whatever be its worth—has you as source:
    with you was born and under you was hidden    115
he who is father of all mortal lives,
when I first felt the air of Tuscany;

Le mura che solieno esser badia
fatte sono spelonche, e le cocolle
sacca son piene di farina ria.

Ma grave usura tanto non si tolle          79
contra 'l piacer di Dio, quanto quel frutto
che fa il cor de' monaci sì folle;

ché quantunque la Chiesa guarda, tutto     82
è de la gente che per Dio dimanda;
non di parenti né d'altro più brutto.

La carne d'i mortali è tanto blanda,       85
che già non basta buon cominciamento
dal nascer de la quercia al far la ghianda.

Pier cominciò sanz' oro e sanz' argento,   88
e io con orazione e con digiuno,
e Francesco umilmente il suo convento;

e se guardi 'l principio di ciascuno,      91
poscia riguardi là dov' è trascorso,
tu vederai del bianco fatto bruno.

Veramente Iordan vòlto retrorso            94
più fu, e 'l mar fuggir, quando Dio volse,
mirabile a veder che qui 'l soccorso."

Così mi disse, e indi si raccolse          97
al suo collegio, e 'l collegio si strinse;
poi, come turbo, in sù tutto s'avvolse.

La dolce donna dietro a lor mi pinse       100
con un sol cenno su per quella scala,
sì sua virtù la mia natura vinse;

né mai qua giù dove si monta e cala        103
naturalmente, fu sì ratto moto
ch'agguagliar si potesse a la mia ala.

S'io torni mai, lettore, a quel divoto     106
trïunfo per lo quale io piango spesso
le mie peccata e 'l petto mi percuoto,

tu non avresti in tanto tratto e messo     109
nel foco il dito, in quant' io vidi 'l segno
che segue il Tauro e fui dentro da esso.

O glorïose stelle, o lume pregno           112
di gran virtù, dal quale io riconosco
tutto, qual che si sia, il mio ingegno,

con voi nasceva e s'ascondeva vosco        115
quelli ch'è padre d'ogne mortal vita,
quand' io senti' di prima l'aere tosco;

and then, when grace was granted me to enter 118
the high wheel that impels your revolutions,
your region was my fated point of entry.

To you my soul now sighs devotedly, 121
that it may gain the force for this attempt,
hard trial that now demands its every strength.

"You are so near the final blessedness," 124
so Beatrice began, "that you have need
of vision clear and keen; and thus, before

you enter farther, do look downward, see 127
what I have set beneath your feet already:
much of the world is there. If you see that,

your heart may then present itself with all 130
the joy it can to the triumphant throng
that goes in gladness through this rounded ether."

My eyes returned through all the seven spheres 133
and saw this globe in such a way that I
smiled at its meager image: I approve

that judgment as the best, which holds this earth 136
to be the least; and he whose thoughts are set
elsewhere, can truly be called virtuous.

I saw Latona's daughter radiant, 139
without the shadow that had made me once
believe that she contained both rare and dense.

And there, Hyperion, I could sustain 142
the vision of your son, and saw Diöne
and Maia as they circled nearby him.

The temperate Jupiter appeared to me 145
between his father and his son; and I
saw clearly how they vary their positions.

And all the seven heavens showed to me 148
their magnitudes, their speeds, the distances
of each from each. The little threshing floor

that so incites our savagery was all— 151
from hills to river mouths—revealed to me
while I wheeled with eternal Gemini.

My eyes then turned again to the fair eyes. 154

e poi, quando mi fu grazia largita 118
d'entrar ne l'alta rota che vi gira,
la vostra regïon mi fu sortita.

A voi divotamente ora sospira 121
l'anima mia, per acquistar virtute
al passo forte che a sé la tira.

"Tu se' sì presso a l'ultima salute," 124
cominciò Bëatrice, "che tu dei
aver le luci tue chiare e acute;

e però, prima che tu più t'inlei, 127
rimira in giù, e vedi quanto mondo
sotto li piedi già esser ti fei;

sì che 'l tuo cor, quantunque può, giocondo 130
s'appresenti a la turba trïunfante
che lieta vien per questo etera tondo."

Col viso ritornai per tutte quante 133
le sette spere, e vidi questo globo
tal, ch'io sorrisi del suo vil sembiante;

e quel consiglio per migliore approbo 136
che l'ha per meno; e chi ad altro pensa
chiamar si puote veramente probo.

Vidi la figlia di Latona incensa 139
sanza quell' ombra che mi fu cagione
per che già la credetti rara e densa.

L'aspetto del tuo nato, Iperïone, 142
quivi sostenni, e vidi com' si move
circa e vicino a lui Maia e Dïone.

Quindi m'apparve il temperar di Giove 145
tra 'l padre e 'l figlio; e quindi mi fu chiaro
il varïar che fanno di lor dove;

e tutti e sette mi si dimostraro 148
quanto son grandi e quanto son veloci
e come sono in distante riparo.

L'aiuola che ci fa tanto feroci, 151
volgendom' io con li etterni Gemelli,
tutta m'apparve da' colli a le foci;

poscia rivolsi li occhi a li occhi belli. 154

# CANTO XXIII

As does the bird, among beloved branches,
when, through the night that hides things from us, she
has rested near the nest of her sweet fledglings

and, on an open branch, anticipates                                    4
the time when she can see their longed-for faces
and find the food with which to feed them—chore

that pleases her, however hard her labors—                              7
as she awaits the sun with warm affection,
steadfastly watching for the dawn to break:

so did my lady stand, erect, intent,                                   10
turned toward that part of heaven under which
the sun is given to less haste; so that,

as I saw her in longing and suspense,                                  13
I grew to be as one who, while he wants
what is not his, is satisfied with hope.

But time between one and the other *when*                              16
was brief—I mean the *when*s of waiting and
of seeing heaven grow more radiant.

And Beatrice said: "There you see the troops                           19
of the triumphant Christ—and all the fruits
ingathered from the turning of these spheres!"

It seemed to me her face was all aflame,                               22
and there was so much gladness in her eyes—
I am compelled to leave it undescribed.

Like Trivia—at the full moon in clear skies—                          25
smiling among the everlasting nymphs
who decorate all reaches of the sky,

I saw a sun above a thousand lamps;                                    28
it kindled all of them as does our sun
kindle the sights above us here on earth;

and through its living light the glowing Substance                     31
appeared to me with such intensity—
my vision lacked the power to sustain it.

*The Eighth Heaven: the Sphere of the Fixed Stars. Beatrice's*
*expectancy. The triumph of Christ. The smile of Beatrice. The*
*blessed in the radiance of Christ. Triumph and coronation of*
*Mary. The reascent of Christ and Mary to the Empyrean.*
*Hymn to Mary. St. Peter.*

Come l'augello, intra l'amate fronde,
posato al nido de' suoi dolci nati
la notte che le cose ci nasconde,

   che, per veder li aspetti disïati             4
e per trovar lo cibo onde li pasca,
in che gravi labor li sono aggrati,

   previene il tempo in su aperta frasca,           7
e con ardente affetto il sole aspetta,
fiso guardando pur che l'alba nasca;

   così la donna mïa stava eretta              10
e attenta, rivolta inver' la plaga
sotto la quale il sol mostra men fretta:

   sì che, veggendola io sospesa e vaga,         13
fecimi qual è quei che disïando
altro vorria, e sperando s'appaga.

   Ma poco fu tra uno e altro quando,          16
del mio attender, dico, e del vedere
lo ciel venir più e più rischiarando;

   e Bëatrice disse: "Ecco le schiere           19
del trïunfo di Cristo e tutto 'l frutto
ricolto del girar di queste spere!"

   Pariemi che 'l suo viso ardesse tutto,        22
e li occhi avea di letizia sì pieni,
che passarmen convien sanza costrutto.

   Quale ne' plenilunïi sereni               25
Trivïa ride tra le ninfe etterne
che dipingon lo ciel per tutti i seni,

   vid' i' sopra migliaia di lucerne            28
un sol che tutte quante l'accendea,
come fa 'l nostro le viste superne;

   e per la viva luce trasparea               31
la lucente sustanza tanto chiara
nel viso mio, che non la sostenea.

O Beatrice, sweet guide and dear! She said                 34
to me: "What overwhelms you is a Power
against which nothing can defend itself.

   This is the Wisdom and the Potency                 37
that opened roads between the earth and Heaven,
the paths for which desire had long since waited."

   Even as lightning breaking from a cloud,            40
expanding so that it cannot be pent,
against its nature, down to earth, descends,

   so did my mind, confronted by that feast,          43
expand; and it was carried past itself—
what it became, it cannot recollect.

   "Open your eyes and see what I now am;              46
the things you witnessed will have made you strong
enough to bear the power of my smile."

   I was as one who, waking from a dream               49
he has forgotten, tries in vain to bring
that vision back into his memory,

   when I heard what she offered me, deserving         52
of so much gratitude that it can never
be canceled from the book that tells the past.

   If all the tongues that Polyhymnia                  55
together with her sisters made most rich
with sweetest milk, should come now to assist

   my singing of the holy smile that lit              58
the holy face of Beatrice, the truth
would not be reached—not its one-thousandth part.

   And thus, in representing Paradise,                 61
the sacred poem has to leap across,
as does a man who finds his path cut off.

   But he who thinks upon the weighty theme,           64
and on the mortal shoulder bearing it,
will lay no blame if, burdened so, I tremble:

   this is no crossing for a little bark—              67
the sea that my audacious prow now cleaves—
nor for a helmsman who would spare himself.

   "Why are you so enraptured by my face               70
as to deny your eyes the sight of that
fair garden blossoming beneath Christ's rays?

   The Rose in which the Word of God became            73
flesh grows within that garden; there—the lilies
whose fragrance let men find the righteous way."

Oh Bëatrice, dolce guida e cara!                    34
Ella mi disse: "Quel che ti sobranza
è virtù da cui nulla si ripara.

   Quivi è la sapïenza e la possanza                37
ch'aprì le strade tra 'l cielo e la terra,
onde fu già sì lunga disïanza."

   Come foco di nube si diserra                     40
per dilatarsi sì che non vi cape,
e fuor di sua natura in giù s'atterra,

   la mente mia così, tra quelle dape               43
fatta più grande, di sé stessa uscìo,
e che si fesse rimembrar non sape.

   "Apri li occhi e riguarda qual son io;           46
tu hai vedute cose, che possente
se' fatto a sostener lo riso mio."

   Io era come quei che si risente                  49
di visïone oblita e che s'ingegna
indarno di ridurlasi a la mente,

   quand' io udi' questa proferta, degna            52
di tanto grato, che mai non si stingue
del libro che 'l preterito rassegna.

   Se mo sonasser tutte quelle lingue               55
che Polimnïa con le suore fero
del latte lor dolcissimo più pingue,

   per aiutarmi, al millesmo del vero               58
non si verria, cantando il santo riso
e quanto il santo aspetto facea mero;

   e così, figurando il paradiso,                   61
convien saltar lo sacrato poema,
come chi trova suo cammin riciso.

   Ma chi pensasse il ponderoso tema                64
e l'omero mortal che se ne carca,
nol biasmerebbe se sott' esso trema:

   non è pareggio da picciola barca                 67
quel che fendendo va l'ardita prora,
né da nocchier ch'a sé medesmo parca.

   "Perché la faccia mia sì t'innamora,             70
che tu non ti rivolgi al bel giardino
che sotto i raggi di Cristo s'infiora?

   Quivi è la rosa in che 'l verbo divino           73
carne si fece; quivi son li gigli
al cui odor si prese il buon cammino."

Thus Beatrice, and I—completely ready                                          76
to do what she might counsel—once again
took up the battle of my feeble brows.

Under a ray of sun that, limpid, streams                                       79
down from a broken cloud, my eyes have seen,
while shade was shielding them, a flowered meadow;

so I saw many troops of splendors here                                         82
lit from above by burning rays of light,
but where those rays began was not in sight.

O kindly Power that imprints them thus,                                        85
you rose on high to leave space for my eyes—
for where I was, they were too weak to see You!

The name of that fair flower which I always                                    88
invoke, at morning and at evening, drew
my mind completely to the greatest flame.

And when, on both my eye-lights, were depicted                                 91
the force and nature of the living star
that conquers heaven as it conquered earth,

descending through that sky there came a torch,                                94
forming a ring that seemed as if a crown:
wheeling around her—a revolving garland.

Whatever melody most sweetly sounds                                            97
on earth, and to itself most draws the soul,
would seem a cloud that, torn by lightning, thunders,

if likened to the music of that lyre                                           100
which sounded from the crown of that fair sapphire,
the brightest light that has ensapphired heaven.

"I am angelic love who wheel around                                            103
that high gladness inspired by the womb
that was the dwelling place of our Desire;

so shall I circle, Lady of Heaven, until                                       106
you, following your Son, have made that sphere
supreme, still more divine by entering it."

So did the circulating melody,                                                 109
sealing itself, conclude; and all the other
lights then resounded with the name of Mary.

The royal cloak of all the wheeling spheres                                    112
within the universe, the heaven most
intense, alive, most burning in the breath

of God and in His laws and ordinance,                                          115
was far above us at its inner shore,
so distant that it still lay out of sight

Così Beatrice; e io, che a' suoi consigli 76
tutto era pronto, ancora mi rendei
a la battaglia de' debili cigli.

Come a raggio di sol, che puro mei 79
per fratta nube, già prato di fiori
vider, coverti d'ombra, li occhi miei;

vid' io così più turbe di splendori, 82
folgorate di sù da raggi ardenti,
sanza veder principio di folgóri.

O benigna vertù che sì li 'mprenti, 85
sù t'essaltasti per largirmi loco
a li occhi lì che non t'eran possenti.

Il nome del bel fior ch'io sempre invoco 88
e mane e sera, tutto mi ristrinse
l'animo ad avvisar lo maggior foco;

e come ambo le luci mi dipinse 91
il quale e il quanto de la viva stella
che là sù vince come qua giù vinse,

per entro il cielo scese una facella, 94
formata in cerchio a guisa di corona,
e cinsela e girossi intorno ad ella.

Qualunque melodia più dolce suona 97
qua giù e più a sé l'anima tira,
parrebbe nube che squarciata tona,

comparata al sonar di quella lira 100
onde si coronava il bel zaffiro
del quale il ciel più chiaro s'inzaffira.

"Io sono amore angelico, che giro 103
l'alta letizia che spira del ventre
che fu albergo del nostro disiro;

e girerommi, donna del ciel, mentre 106
che seguirai tuo figlio, e farai dia
più la spera supprema perché li entre."

Così la circulata melodia 109
si sigillava, e tutti li altri lumi
facean sonare il nome di Maria.

Lo real manto di tutti i volumi 112
del mondo, che più ferve e più s'avviva
ne l'alito di Dio e nei costumi,

avea sopra di noi l'interna riva 115
tanto distante, che la sua parvenza,
là dov' io era, ancor non appariva:

76

79

82

85

88

91

94

97

100

103

106

109

112

115

CANTO XXIII 205

from that point where I was; and thus my eyes 118
possessed no power to follow that crowned flame,
which mounted upward, following her Son.

And like an infant who, when it has taken 121
its milk, extends its arms out to its mother,
its feeling kindling into outward flame,

each of those blessed splendors stretched its peak 124
upward, so that the deep affection each
possessed for Mary was made plain to me.

Then they remained within my sight, singing 127
*"Regina coeli"* with such tenderness
that my delight in that has never left me.

Oh, in those richest coffers, what abundance 130
is garnered up for those who, while below,
on earth, were faithful workers when they sowed!

Here do they live, delighting in the treasure 133
they earned with tears in Babylonian
exile, where they had no concern for gold.

Here, under the high Son of God and Mary, 136
together with the ancient and the new
councils, he triumphs in his victory—

he who is keeper of the keys of glory. 139

però non ebber li occhi miei potenza 118
di seguitar la coronata fiamma
che si levò appresso sua semenza.

    E come fantolin che 'nver' la mamma 121
tende le braccia, poi che 'l latte prese,
per l'animo che 'nfin di fuor s'infiamma;

    ciascun di quei candori in sù si stese 124
con la sua cima, sì che l'alto affetto
ch'elli avieno a Maria mi fu palese.

    Indi rimaser lì nel mio cospetto, 127
"Regina celi" cantando sì dolce,
che mai da me non si partì 'l diletto.

    Oh quanta è l'ubertà che si soffolce 130
in quelle arche ricchissime che fuoro
a seminar qua giù buone bobolce!

    Quivi si vive e gode del tesoro 133
ch s'acquistò piangendo ne lo essilio
di Babillòn, ove si lasciò l'oro.

    Quivi trïunfa, sotto l'alto Filio 136
di Dio e di Maria, di sua vittoria,
e con l'antico e col novo concilio,

      colui che tien le chiavi di tal gloria. 139

OVERLEAF:
*Christ Radiant*
*The Virgin*

# CANTO XXIV

"O fellowship that has been chosen for
the Blessed Lamb's great supper, where He feeds
you so as always to fulfill your need,

since by the grace of God, this man receives          4
foretaste of something fallen from your table
before death has assigned his time its limit,

direct your mind to his immense desire,          7
quench him somewhat: you who forever drink
from that Source which his thought and longing seek."

So Beatrice; and these delighted souls          10
formed companies of spheres around fixed poles,
flaming as they revolved, as comets glow.

And just as, in a clock's machinery,          13
to one who watches them, the wheels turn so
that, while the first wheel seems to rest, the last

wheel flies; so did those circling dancers—as          16
they danced to different measures, swift and slow—
make me a judge of what their riches were.

From that sphere which I noted as most precious,          19
I saw a fire come forth with so much gladness
that none it left behind had greater brightness;

and that sphere whirled three times round Beatrice          22
while singing so divine a song that my
imagination cannot shape it for me.

My pen leaps over it; I do not write:          25
our fantasy and, all the more so, speech
are far too gross for painting folds so deep.

"O you who pray to us with such devotion—          28
my holy sister—with your warm affection,
you have released me from that lovely sphere."

So, after he had stopped his motion, did          31
the blessed flame breathe forth unto my lady;
and what he said I have reported here.

Still the Eighth Heaven: the Sphere of the Fixed Stars. Beatrice's request to the spirits, and St. Peter's reply. Her asking of St. Peter to examine Dante on Faith. Dante's preparation and his examination. The approval and blessing of Dante by St. Peter.

"O sodalizio eletto a la gran cena
del benedetto Agnello, il qual vi ciba
sì, che la vostra voglia è sempre piena,

se per grazia di Dio questi preliba                    4
di quel che cade de la vostra mensa,
prima che morte tempo li prescriba,

ponete mente a l'affezione immensa                     7
e roratelo alquanto: voi bevete
sempre del fonte onde vien quel ch'ei pensa."

Così Beatrice; e quelle anime liete                   10
si fero spere sopra fissi poli,
fiammando, volte, a guisa di comete.

E come cerchi in tempra d'orïuoli                      13
si giran sì, che 'l primo a chi pon mente
quïeto pare, e l'ultimo che voli;

così quelle carole, differente-                        16
mente danzando, de la sua ricchezza
mi facieno stimar, veloci e lente.

Di quella ch'io notai di più carezza                   19
vid' ïo uscire un foco sì felice,
che nullo vi lasciò di più chiarezza;

e tre fïate intorno di Beatrice                        22
si volse con un canto tanto divo,
che la mia fantasia nol mi ridice.

Però salta la penna e non lo scrivo:                   25
chè l'imagine nostra a cotai pieghe,
non che 'l parlare, è troppo color vivo.

"O santa suora mia che sì ne prieghe                   28
divota, per lo tuo ardente affetto
da quella bella spera mi disleghe."

Poscia fermato, il foco benedetto                      31
a la mia donna dirizzò lo spiro,
che favellò così com' i' ho detto.

She answered: "O eternal light of that 34
great man to whom our Lord bequeathed the keys
of this astonishing gladness—the keys

He bore to earth—do test this man concerning 37
the faith by which you walked upon the sea;
ask him points light and grave, just as you please.

That he loves well and hopes well and has faith 40
is not concealed from you: you see that Place
where everything that happens is displayed.

But since this realm has gained its citizens 43
through the true faith, it rightly falls to him
to speak of faith, that he may glorify it."

Just as the bachelor candidate must arm 46
himself and does not speak until the master
submits the question for discussion—not

for settlement—so while she spoke I armed 49
myself with all my arguments, preparing
for such a questioner and such professing.

On hearing that light breathe, "Good Christian, speak, 52
show yourself clearly: what is faith?" I raised
my brow, then turned to Beatrice, whose glance

immediately signaled me to let 55
the waters of my inner source pour forth.
Then I: "So may the grace that grants to me

to make confession to the Chief Centurion 58
permit my thoughts to find their fit expression";
and followed, "Father, as the truthful pen

of your dear brother wrote—that brother who, 61
with you, set Rome upon the righteous road—
faith is the substance of the things we hope for

and is the evidence of things not seen; 64
and this I take to be its quiddity."
And then I heard: "You understand precisely,

if it is fully clear to you why he 67
has first placed faith among the substances
and then defines it as an evidence."

I next: "The deep things that on me bestow 70
their image here, are hid from sight below,
so that their being lies in faith alone,

and on that faith the highest hope is founded; 73
and thus it is that faith is called a substance.
And it is from this faith that we must reason,

Ed ella: "O luce etterna del gran viro                        34
a cui Nostro Segnor lasciò le chiavi,
ch'ei portò giù, di questo gaudio miro,

  tenta costui di punti lievi e gravi,                        37
come ti piace, intorno de la fede,
per la qual tu su per lo mare andavi.

  S'elli ama bene e bene spera e crede,                       40
non t'è occulto, perché 'l viso hai quivi
dov' ogne cosa dipinta si vede;

  ma perché questo regno ha fatto civi                        43
per la verace fede, a glorïarla,
di lei parlare è ben ch'a lui arrivi."

  Sì come il baccialier s'arma e non parla                    46
fin che 'l maestro la question propone,
per approvarla, non per terminarla,

  così m'armava io d'ogne ragione                             49
mentre ch'ella dicea, per esser presto
a tal querente e a tal professione.

  "Dì, buon Cristiano, fatti manifesto:                       52
fede che è?" Ond' io levai la fronte
in quella luce onde spirava questo;

  poi mi volsi a Beatrice, ed essa pronte                     55
sembianze femmi perch' ïo spandessi
l'acqua di fuor del mio interno fonte.

  "La Grazia che mi dà ch'io mi confessi,"                    58
comincia' io, "da l'alto primipilo,
faccia li miei concetti bene espressi."

  E seguitai: "Come 'l verace stilo                           61
ne scrisse, padre, del tuo caro frate
che mise teco Roma nel buon filo,

  fede è sustanza di cose sperate                             64
e argomento de le non parventi;
e questa pare a me sua quiditate."

  Allora udi': "Dirittamente senti,                           67
se bene intendi perché la ripuose
tra le sustanze, e poi tra li argomenti."

  E io appresso: "Le profonde cose                            70
che mi largiscon qui la lor parvenza,
a li occhi di là giù son sì ascose,

  che l'esser loro v'è in sola credenza,                      73
sopra la qual si fonda l'alta spene;
e però di sustanza prende intenza.

deducing what we can from syllogisms,                                    76
without our being able to see more:
thus faith is also called an evidence."

And then I heard: "If all one learns below                               79
as doctrine were so understood, there would
be no place for the sophist's cleverness."

This speech was breathed from that enkindled love.                       82
He added: "Now this coin is well-examined,
and now we know its alloy and its weight.

But tell me: do you have it in your purse?"                              85
And I: "Indeed I do—so bright and sound
that nothing in its stamp leads me to doubt."

Next, from the deep light gleaming there, I heard:                       88
"What is the origin of the dear gem
that comes to you, the gem on which all virtues

are founded?" I: "The Holy Ghost's abundant                              91
rain poured upon the parchments old and new;
that is the syllogism that has proved

with such persuasiveness that faith has truth—                           94
when set beside that argument, all other
demonstrations seem to me obtuse."

I heard: "The premises of old and new                                    97
impelling your conclusion—why do you
hold these to be the speech of God?" And I:

"The proof revealing truth to me relies                                  100
on acts that happened; for such miracles,
nature can heat no iron, beat no anvil."

"Say, who assures you that those works were real?"                       103
came the reply. "The very thing that needs
proof—no thing else—attests these works to you."

I said: "If without miracles the world                                   106
was turned to Christianity, that is
so great a miracle that all the rest

are not its hundredth part: for you were poor                            109
and hungry when you found the field and sowed
the good plant—once a vine and now a thorn."

This done, the high and holy court resounded                             112
throughout its spheres with *"Te Deum laudamus,"*
sung with the melody they use on high.

Then he who had examined me, that baron                                  115
who led me on from branch to branch so that
we now were drawing close to the last leaves,

E da questa credenza ci convene
silogizzar, sanz' avere altra vista:
però intenza d'argomento tene."

    Allora udi': "Se quantunque s'acquista     79
giù per dottrina, fosse così 'nteso,
non li avria loco ingegno di sofista."

    Così spirò di quello amore acceso;     82
indi soggiunse: "Assai bene è trascorsa
d'esta moneta già la lega e 'l peso;

    ma dimmi se tu l'hai ne la tua borsa."     85
Ond' io: "Sì ho, sì lucida e sì tonda,
che nel suo conio nulla mi s'inforsa."

    Appresso uscì de la luce profonda     88
che lì splendeva: "Questa cara gioia
sopra la quale ogne virtù si fonda,

    onde ti venne?" E io: "La larga ploia     91
de lo Spirito Santo, ch'è diffusa
in su le vecchie e 'n su le nuove cuoia,

    è silogismo che la m'ha conchiusa     94
acutamente sì, che 'nverso d'ella
ogne dimostrazion mi pare ottusa."

    Io udi' poi: "L'antica e la novella     97
proposizion che così ti conchiude,
perché l'hai tu per divina favella?"

    E io: "La prova che 'l ver mi dischiude,     100
son l'opere seguite, a che natura
non scalda ferro mai né batte incude."

    Risposto fummi: "Dì, chi t'assicura     103
che quell' opere fosser? Quel medesmo
che vuol provarsi, non altri, il ti giura."

    "Se 'l mondo si rivolse al cristianesmo,"     106
diss' io, "sanza miracoli, quest' uno
è tal, che li altri non sono il centesmo:

    ché tu intrasti povero e digiuno     109
in campo, a seminar la buona pianta
che fu già vite e ora è fatta pruno."

    Finito questo, l'alta corte santa     112
risonò per le spere un "Dio laudamo"
ne la melode che là sù si canta.

    E quel baron che sì di ramo in ramo,     115
essaminando, già tratto m'avea,
che a l'ultime fronde appressavamo,

began again: "That Grace which—lovingly— 118
directs your mind, until this point has taught
you how to find the seemly words for thought,

so that I do approve what you brought forth; 121
but now you must declare what you believe
and what gave you the faith that you receive."

"O holy father, soul who now can see 124
what you believed with such intensity
that, to His tomb, you outran younger feet,"

I then began, "you would have me tell plainly 127
the form of my unhesitating faith,
and also ask me to declare its source.

I answer: I believe in one God—sole, 130
eternal—He who, motionless, moves all
the heavens with His love and His desire;

for this belief I have not only proofs 133
both physical and metaphysical;
I also have the truth that here rains down

through Moses and the Prophets and the Psalms 136
and through the Gospels and through you who wrote
words given to you by the Holy Ghost.

And I believe in three Eternal Persons, 139
and these I do believe to be one essence,
so single and threefold as to allow

both *is* and *are*. Of this profound condition 142
of God that I have touched on, Gospel teaching
has often set the imprint on my mind.

This is the origin, this is the spark 145
that then extends into a vivid flame
and, like a star in heaven, glows in me."

Just as the lord who listens to his servant's 148
announcement, then, as soon as he is silent,
embraces him, both glad with the good news,

so did the apostolic light at whose 151
command I had replied, while blessing me
and singing, then encircle me three times:

the speech I spoke had brought him such delight. 154

ricominciò: "La Grazia, che donnea 118
con la tua mente, la bocca t'aperse
infino a qui come aprir si dovea,

sì ch'io approvo ciò che fuori emerse; 121
ma or convien espremer quel che credi,
e onde a la credenza tua s'offerse."

"O santo padre, e spirito che vedi 124
ciò che credesti sì, che tu vincesti
ver' lo sepulcro più giovani piedi,"

comincia' io, "tu vuo' ch'io manifesti 127
la forma qui del pronto creder mio,
e anche la cagion di lui chiedesti.

E io rispondo: Io credo in uno Dio 130
solo ed etterno, che tutto 'l ciel move,
non moto, con amore e con disio;

e a tal creder non ho io pur prove 133
fisice e metafisice, ma dalmi
anche la verità che quinci piove

per Moïsè, per profeti e per salmi, 136
per l'Evangelio e per voi che scriveste
poi che l'ardente Spirto vi fé almi;

e credo in tre persone etterne, e queste 139
credo una essenza sì una e sì trina,
che soffera congiunto 'sono' ed 'este.'

De la profonda condizion divina 142
ch'io tocco mo, la mente mi sigilla
più volte l'evangelica dottrina.

Quest' è 'l principio, quest' è la favilla 145
che si dilata in fiamma poi vivace,
e come stella in cielo in me scintilla."

Come 'l segnor ch'ascolta quel che i piace, 148
da indi abbraccia il servo, gratulando
per la novella, tosto ch'el si tace;

così, benedicendomi cantando, 151
tre volte cinse me, sì com' io tacqui,
l'appostolico lume al cui comando

io avea detto: sì nel dir li piacqui! 154

# CANTO XXV

If it should happen . . . If this sacred poem—
this work so shared by heaven and by earth
that it has made me lean through these long years—
    can ever overcome the cruelty               4
that bars me from the fair fold where I slept,
a lamb opposed to wolves that war on it,
    by then with other voice, with other fleece,     7
I shall return as poet and put on,
at my baptismal font, the laurel crown;
    for there I first found entry to that faith     10
which makes souls welcome unto God, and then,
for that faith, Peter garlanded my brow.
    Then did a light move toward us from that sphere     13
from which emerged the first—the dear, the rare—
of those whom Christ had left to be His vicars;
    and full of happiness, my lady said     16
to me: "Look, look—and see the baron whom,
below on earth, they visit in Galicia."
    As when a dove alights near its companion,     19
and each unto the other, murmuring
and circling, offers its affection, so
    did I see both those great and glorious     22
princes give greeting to each other, praising
the banquet that is offered them on high.
    But when their salutations were complete,     25
each stopped in silence *coram me,* and each
was so aflame, my vision felt defeat.
    Then Beatrice said, smiling: "Famous life     28
by whom the generosity of our
basilica has been described, do let
    matters of hope reecho at this height;     31
you can—for every time that Jesus favored
you three above the rest, you were the figure

*Still the Eighth Heaven: the Sphere of the Fixed Stars. Dante's hope to return to Florence, there to be crowned as poet. The appearance of St. James, who examines Dante on Hope. The appearance of St. John the Evangelist, who dismisses the false belief in his bodily assumption to Heaven. Dante's loss of sight.*

Se mai continga che 'l poema sacro
al quale ha posto mano e cielo e terra,
sì che m'ha fatto per molti anni macro,

vinca la crudeltà che fuor mi serra                4
del bello ovile ov' io dormi' agnello,
nimico ai lupi che li danno guerra;

con altra voce omai, con altro vello               7
ritornerò poeta, e in sul fonte
del mio battesmo prenderò 'l cappello;

però che ne la fede, che fa conte                  10
l'anime a Dio, quivi intra' io, e poi
Pietro per lei sì mi girò la fronte.

Indi si mosse un lume verso noi                    13
di quella spera ond' uscì la primizia
che lasciò Cristo d'i vicari suoi;

e la mia donna, piena di letizia,                  16
mi disse: "Mira, mira: ecco il barone
per cui là giù si vicita Galizia."

Sì come quando il colombo si pone                  19
presso al compagno, l'uno a l'altro pande,
girando e mormorando, l'affezione;

così vid' ïo l'un da l'altro grande                22
principe glorïoso essere accolto,
laudando il cibo che là sù li prande.

Ma poi che 'l gratular si fu assolto,              25
tacito *coram me* ciascun s'affisse,
ignito sì che vincëa 'l mio volto.

Ridendo allora Bëatrice disse:                     28
"Inclita vita per cui la larghezza
de la nostra basilica si scrisse,

fa risonar la spene in questa altezza:             31
tu sai, che tante fiate la figuri,
quante Iesù ai tre fé più carezza."

of hope." "Lift up your head, and be assured:     34
whatever comes here from the mortal world
has to be ripened in our radiance."

The second fire offered me this comfort;     37
at which my eyes were lifted to the mountains
whose weight of light before had kept me bent.

"Because our Emperor, out of His grace,     40
has willed that you, before your death, may face
His nobles in the inmost of His halls,

so that, when you have seen this court in truth,     43
hope—which, below, spurs love of the true good—
in you and others may be comforted,

do tell what hope is, tell how it has blossomed     46
within your mind, and from what source it came
to you"—so did the second flame continue.

And she, compassionate, who was the guide     49
who led my feathered wings to such high flight,
did thus anticipate my own reply:

"There is no child of the Church Militant     52
who has more hope than he has, as is written
within the Sun whose rays reach all our ranks:

thus it is granted him to come from Egypt     55
into Jerusalem that he have vision
of it, before his term of warring ends.

The other two points of your question, which     58
were not asked so that you may know, but that
he may report how much you prize this virtue,

I leave to him; he will not find them hard     61
or cause for arrogance; as you have asked,
let him reply, and God's grace help his task."

As a disciple answering his master,     64
prepared and willing in what he knows well,
that his proficiency may be revealed,

I said: "Hope is the certain expectation     67
of future glory; it is the result
of God's grace and of merit we have earned.

This light has come to me from many stars;     70
but he who first instilled it in my heart
was the chief singer of the Sovereign Guide.

'May those'—he says within his theody—     73
'who know Your name, put hope in You'; and if
one has my faith, can he not know God's name?

"Leva la testa e fa che t'assicuri:     34
ché ciò che vien qua sù del mortal mondo,
convien ch'ai nostri raggi si maturi."

Questo conforto del foco secondo     37
mi venne; ond' io leväi li occhi a' monti
che li 'ncurvaron pria col troppo pondo.

"Poi che per grazia vuol che tu t'affronti     40
lo nostro Imperadore, anzi la morte,
ne l'aula più secreta co' suoi conti,

sì che, veduto il ver di questa corte,     43
la spene, che là giù bene innamora,
in te e in altrui di ciò conforte,

dì quel ch'ell' è, dì come se ne 'nfiora     46
la mente tua, e dì onde a te venne."
Così seguì 'l secondo lume ancora.

E quella pïa che guidò le penne     49
de le mie ali a così alto volo,
a la risposta così mi prevenne:

"La Chiesa militante alcun figliuolo     52
non ha con più speranza, com' è scritto
nel Sol che raggia tutto nostro stuolo:

però li è conceduto che d'Egitto     55
vegna in Ierusalemme per vedere,
anzi che 'l militar li sia prescritto.

Li altri due punti, che non per sapere     58
son dimandati, ma perch' ei rapporti
quanto questa virtù t'è in piacere,

a lui lasc' io, ché non li saran forti     61
né di iattanza; ed elli a ciò risponda,
e la grazia di Dio ciò li comporti."

Come discente ch'a dottor seconda     64
pronto e libente in quel ch'elli è esperto,
perché la sua bontà si disasconda,

"Spene," diss' io, "è uno attender certo     67
de la gloria futura, il qual produce
grazia divina e precedente merto.

Da molte stelle mi vien questa luce;     70
ma quei la distillò nel mio cor pria
che fu sommo cantor del sommo duce.

'Sperino in te,' ne la sua tëodia     73
dice, 'color che sanno il nome tuo':
e chi nol sa, s'elli ha la fede mia?

And just as he instilled, you then instilled                          76
with your Epistle, so that I am full
and rain again your rain on other souls."
    While I was speaking, in the living heart         79
of that soul-flame there came a trembling flash,
sudden, repeated, just as lightning cracks.
    Then it breathed forth: "The love with which I still   82
burn for the virtue that was mine until
the palm and my departure from the field,
    would have me breathe again to you who take    85
such joy in hope; and I should welcome words
that tell what hope has promised unto you."
    And I: "The new and ancient Scriptures set     88
the mark for souls whom God befriends; for me,
that mark means what is promised us by hope.
    Isaiah says that all of the elect              91
shall wear a double garment in their land:
and their land is this sweet life of the blessed.
    And where your brother treats of those white robes,   94
he has—with words direct and evident—
made clear to us Isaiah's revelation."
    At first, as soon as I had finished speaking,   97
"*Sperent in te*" was heard above us, all
the circling garlands answering this call.
    And then, among those souls, one light became   100
so bright that, if the Crab had one such crystal,
winter would be a month of one long day.
    And as a happy maiden rises and                103
enters the dance to honor the new bride—
and not through vanity or other failing—
    so did I see that splendor, brightening,        106
approach those two flames dancing in a ring
to music suited to their burning love.
    And there it joined the singing and the circling,   109
on which my lady kept her eyes intent,
just like a bride, silent and motionless.
    "This soul is he who lay upon the breast        112
of Christ our Pelican, and he was asked
from on the Cross to serve in the great task."
    So spoke my lady; but her gaze was not          115
to be diverted from its steadfastness,
not after or before her words were said.

Tu mi stillasti, con lo stillar suo,         76
ne la pistola poi; sì ch'io son pieno,
e in altrui vostra pioggia repluo."

  Mentr' io diceva, dentro al vivo seno       79
di quello incendio tremolava un lampo
sùbito e spesso a guisa di baleno.

  Indi spirò: "L'amore ond' ïo avvampo      82
ancor ver' la virtù che mi seguette
infin la palma e a l'uscir del campo,

  vuol ch'io respiri a te che ti dilette        85
di lei; ed emmi a grato che tu diche
quello che la speranza ti 'mpromette."

  E io: "Le nove e le scritture antiche       88
pongon lo segno, ed esso lo mi addita,
de l'anime che Dio s'ha fatte amiche.

  Dice Isaia che ciascuna vestita          91
ne la sua terra fia di doppia vesta:
e la sua terra è questa dolce vita;

  e 'l tuo fratello assai vie più digesta,      94
là dove tratta de le bianche stole,
questa revelazion ci manifesta."

  E prima, appresso al fin d'este parole,     97
"Sperent in te" di sopr' a noi s'udì;
a che rispuoser tutte le carole.

  Poscia tra esse un lume si schiarì        100
sì che, se 'l Cancro avesse un tal cristallo,
l'inverno avrebbe un mese d'un sol dì.

  E come surge e va ed entra in ballo      103
vergine lieta, sol per fare onore
a la novizia, non per alcun fallo,

  così vid' io lo schiarato splendore       106
venire a' due che si volgieno a nota
qual conveniesi al loro ardente amore.

  Misesi lì nel canto e ne la rota;        109
e la mia donna in lor tenea l'aspetto,
pur come sposa tacita e immota.

  "Questi è colui che giacque sopra 'l petto   112
del nostro pellicano, e questi fue
di su la croce al grande officio eletto."

  La donna mia così; né però piùe        115
mosser la vista sua di stare attenta
poscia che prima le parole sue.

Even as he who squints and strains to see                    118
the sun somewhat eclipsed and, as he tries
to see, becomes sightless, just so did I
  in my attempt to watch the latest flame,                   121
until these words were said: "Why do you daze
yourself to see what here can have no place?
  On earth my body now is earth and shall                    124
be there together with the rest until
our number equals the eternal purpose.
  Only those two lights that ascended wear                   127
their double garment in this blessed cloister.
And carry this report back to your world."
  When he began to speak, the flaming circle                 130
had stopped its dance; so, too, its song had ceased—
that gentle mingling of their threefold breath—
  even as when, avoiding danger or                           133
simply to rest, the oars that strike the water,
together halt when rowers hear a whistle.
  Ah, how disturbed I was within my mind,                    136
when I turned round to look at Beatrice,
on finding that I could not see, though I
  was close to her, and in the world of gladness!           139

Qual è colui ch'adocchia e s'argomenta  118
di vedere eclissar lo sole un poco,
che, per veder, non vedente diventa;
   tal mi fec' ïo a quell' ultimo foco  121
mentre che detto fu: "Perché t'abbagli
per veder cosa che qui non ha loco?
   In terra è terra il mio corpo, e saragli  124
tanto con li altri, che 'l numero nostro
con l'etterno proposito s'agguagli.
   Con le due stole nel beato chiostro  127
son le due luci sole che saliro;
e questo apporterai nel mondo vostro."
   A questa voce l'infiammato giro  130
si quïetò con esso il dolce mischio
che si facea nel suon del trino spiro,
   sì come, per cessar fatica o rischio,  133
li remi, pria ne l'acqua ripercossi,
tutti si posano al sonar d'un fischio.
   Ahi quanto ne la mente mi commossi,  136
quando mi volsi per veder Beatrice,
per non poter veder, benché io fossi
   presso di lei, e nel mondo felice!  139

OVERLEAF:
*The Four Lights of Peter, James, John, and Adam*

# CANTO XXVI

While I, with blinded eyes, was apprehensive,
from that bright flame which had consumed my vision,
there breathed a voice that centered my attention,

saying: "Until you have retrieved the power          4
of sight, which you consumed in me, it would
be best to compensate by colloquy.

Then do begin; declare the aim on which             7
your soul is set—and be assured of this:
your vision, though confounded, is not dead,

because the woman who conducts you through          10
this godly region has, within her gaze,
that force the hand of Ananias had."

I said: "As pleases her, may solace—sooner           13
or later—reach these eyes, her gates when she
brought me the fire with which I always burn.

The good with which this court is satisfied          16
is Alpha and Omega of all writings
that Love has—loud or low—read out to me."

It was the very voice that had dispelled             19
the fear I felt at sudden dazzlement,
that now, with further words, made me concerned

to speak again. He said: "You certainly             22
must sift with a still finer sieve, must tell
who led your bow to aim at such a target."

And I: "By philosophic arguments                    25
and by authority whose source is here,
that love must be imprinted in me; for

the good, once it is understood as such,            28
enkindles love; and in accord with more
goodness comes greater love. And thus the mind

of anyone who can discern the truth                 31
on which this proof is founded must be moved
to love, more than it loves all else, that Essence

*Still the Eighth Heaven: the Sphere of the Fixed Stars. St.*
*John's examination of Dante on Charity or Love. Approbation*
*of Dante by the blessed and the restoration of his sight. Adam's*
*answers to Dante's four implicit questions.*

Mentr' io dubbiava per lo viso spento,
de la fulgida fiamma che lo spense
uscì un spiro che mi fece attento,

dicendo: "Intanto che tu ti risense                    4
de la vista che haï in me consunta,
ben è che ragionando la compense.

Comincia dunque; e dì ove s'appunta                    7
l'anima tua, e fa ragion che sia
la vista in te smarrita e non defunta:

perché la donna che per questa dia                     10
regïon ti conduce, ha ne lo sguardo
la virtù ch'ebbe la man d'Anania."

Io dissi: "Al suo piacere e tosto e tardo              13
vegna remedio a li occhi, che fuor porte
quand' ella entrò col foco ond' io sempr' ardo.

Lo ben che fa contenta questa corte,                   16
Alfa e O è di quanta scrittura
mi legge Amore o lievemente o forte."

Quella medesma voce che paura                          19
tolta m'avea del sùbito abbarbaglio,
di ragionare ancor mi mise in cura;

e disse: "Certo a più angusto vaglio                   22
ti conviene schiarar: dicer convienti
chi drizzò l'arco tuo a tal berzaglio."

E io: "Per filosofici argomenti                        25
e per autorità che quinci scende
cotale amor convien che in me si 'mprenti:

ché 'l bene, in quanto ben, come s'intende,            28
così accende amore, e tanto maggio
quanto più di bontate in sé comprende.

Dunque a l'essenza ov' è tanto avvantaggio,            31
che ciascun ben che fuor di lei si trova
altro non è ch'un lume di suo raggio,

which is preeminent (since any good                                         34
that lies outside of It is nothing but
a ray reflected from Its radiance).

My mind discerns this truth, made plain by him                              37
who demonstrates to me that the first love
of the eternal beings is their Maker.

The voice of the true Author states this, too,                              40
where He tells Moses, speaking of Himself:
'I shall show you all goodness.' You reveal

this, too, when you begin your high Evangel,                                43
which more than any other proclamation
cries out to earth the mystery of Heaven."

I heard: "Through human reasoning and through                               46
authorities according with it, you
conclude: your highest love is bent on God.

But tell me, too, if you feel other cords                                   49
draw you toward Him, so that you voice aloud
all of the teeth by which this love grips you."

The holy intent of Christ's Eagle was                                       52
not hidden; I indeed was made aware
of what he would most have my words declare.

Thus I began again: "My charity                                             55
results from all those things whose bite can bring
the heart to turn to God; the world's existence

and mine, the death that He sustained that I                                58
might live, and that which is the hope of all
believers, as it is my hope, together

with living knowledge I have spoken of—                                     61
these drew me from the sea of twisted love
and set me on the shore of the right love.

The leaves enleaving all the garden of                                      64
the Everlasting Gardener, I love
according to the good He gave to them."

As soon as I was still, a song most sweet                                   67
resounded through that heaven, and my lady
said with the others: "Holy, holy, holy!"

And just as a sharp light will startle us                                   70
from sleep because the spirit of eyesight
races to meet the brightness that proceeds

from layer to layer in the eye, and he                                      73
who wakens is confused by what he sees,
awaking suddenly, and knows no thing

più che in altra convien che si mova      34
la mente, amando, di ciascun che cerne
il vero in che si fonda questa prova.

   Tal vero a l'intelletto mïo sterne      37
colui che mi dimostra il primo amore
di tutte le sustanze sempiterne.

   Sternel la voce del verace autore,      40
che dice a Moïsè, di sé parlando:
'Io ti farò vedere ogne valore.'

   Sternilmi tu ancora, incominciando      43
l'alto preconio che grida l'arcano
di qui là giù sovra ogne altro bando."

   E io udi': "Per intelletto umano      46
e per autoritadi a lui concorde
d'i tuoi amori a Dio guarda il sovrano.

   Ma dì ancor se tu senti altre corde      49
tirarti verso lui, sì che tu suone
con quanti denti questo amor ti morde."

   Non fu latente la santa intenzione      52
de l'aguglia di Cristo, anzi m'accorsi
dove volea menar mia professione.

   Però ricominciai: "Tutti quei morsi      55
che posson far lo cor volgere a Dio,
a la mia caritate son concorsi:

   ché l'essere del mondo e l'esser mio,      58
la morte ch'el sostenne perch' io viva,
e quel che spera ogne fedel com' io,

   con la predetta conoscenza viva,      61
tratto m'hanno del mar de l'amor torto,
e del diritto m'han posto a la riva.

   Le fronde onde s'infronda tutto l'orto      64
de l'ortolano etterno, am' io cotanto
quanto da lui a lor di bene è porto."

   Sì com io tacqui, un dolcissimo canto      67
risonò per lo cielo, e la mia donna
dicea con li altri: "Santo, santo, santo!"

   E come a lume acuto si disonna      70
per lo spirto visivo che ricorre
a lo splendor che va di gonna in gonna,

   e lo svegliato ciò che vede aborre,      73
sì nescïa è la sùbita vigilia
fin che la stimativa non soccorre;

until his judgment helps him; even so          76
did Beatrice dispel, with her eyes' rays,
which shone more than a thousand miles, the chaff

from my eyes: I saw better than I had          79
before; and as if stupefied, I asked
about the fourth light that I saw among us.

My lady answered: "In those rays there gazes          82
with love for his Creator the first soul
ever created by the Primal Force."

As does a tree that bends its crown because          85
of winds that gust, and then springs up, raised by
its own sustaining power, so did I

while she was speaking. I, bewildered, then          88
restored to confidence by that desire
to speak with which I was inflamed, began:

"O fruit that was the only one to be          91
brought forth already ripe, o ancient father
to whom each bride is as a daughter and

daughter-in-law, devoutly as I can,          94
I do beseech you: speak with me. You see
my wish; to hear you sooner, I do not

declare it." And the primal soul—much as          97
an animal beneath a cover stirs,
so that its feelings are made evident

when what enfolds him follows all his movements—          100
showed me, through that which covered him, with what
rejoicing he was coming to delight me.

Then he breathed forth: "Though you do not declare          103
your wish, I can perceive it better than
you can perceive the things you hold as certain;

for I can see it in the Truthful Mirror          106
that perfectly reflects all else, while no
thing can reflect that Mirror perfectly.

You wish to hear how long it is since I          109
was placed by God in that high garden where
this lady readied you to climb a stair

so long, and just how long it pleased my eyes,          112
and the true cause of the great anger, and
what idiom I used and shaped. My son,

the cause of my long exile did not lie          115
within the act of tasting of the tree,
but solely in my trespass of the boundary.

così de li occhi miei ogne quisquilia     76
fugò Beatrice col raggio d'i suoi,
che rifulgea da più di mille milia:
    onde mei che dinanzi vidi poi;     79
e quasi stupefatto domandai
d'un quarto lume ch'io vidi tra noi.
    E la mia donna: "Dentro da quei rai     82
vagheggia il suo fattor l'anima prima
che la prima virtù creasse mai."
    Come la fronda che flette la cima     85
nel transito del vento, e poi si leva
per la propria virtù che la soblima,
    fec' io in tanto in quant' ella diceva,     88
stupendo, e poi mi rifece sicuro
un disio di parlare ond' ïo ardeva.
    E cominciai: "O pomo che maturo     91
solo prodotto fosti, o padre antico
a cui ciascuna sposa è figlia e nuro,
    divoto quanto posso a te supplìco     94
perché mi parli: tu vedi mia voglia,
e per udirti tosto non la dico."
    Talvolta un animal coverto broglia,     97
sì che l'affetto convien che si paia
per lo seguir che face a lui la 'nvoglia;
    e similmente l'anima primaia     100
mi facea trasparer per la coverta
quant' ella a compiacermi venìa gaia.
    Indi spirò: "Sanz' essermi proferta     103
da te, la voglia tua discerno meglio
che tu qualunque cosa t'è più certa;
    perch' io la veggio nel verace speglio     106
che fa di sé pareglio a l'altre cose,
e nulla face lui di sé pareglio.
    Tu vuogli udir quant' è che Dio mi puose     109
ne l'eccelso giardino, ove costei
a così lunga scala ti dispuose,
    e quanto fu diletto a li occhi miei,     112
e la propria cagion del gran disdegno,
e l'idïoma ch'usai e che fei.
    Or, figliuol mio, non il gustar del legno     115
fu per sé la cagion di tanto essilio,
ma solamente il trapassar del segno.

During four thousand three hundred and two            118
re-turnings of the sun, while I was in
that place from which your Lady sent you Virgil,

I longed for this assembly. While on earth,           121
I saw the sun return to all the lights
along its way, nine hundred thirty times.

The tongue I spoke was all extinct before            124
the men of Nimrod set their minds upon
the unaccomplishable task; for never

has any thing produced by human reason              127
been everlasting—following the heavens,
men seek the new, they shift their predilections.

That man should speak at all is nature's act,        130
but how you speak—in this tongue or in that—
she leaves to you and to your preference.

Before I was sent down to Hell's torments,          133
on earth, the Highest Good—from which derives
the joy that now enfolds me—was called *I*;

and then He was called *El*. Such change must be:    136
the ways that mortals take are as the leaves
upon a branch—one comes, another goes.

On that peak rising highest from the sea,            139
my life—first pure, then tainted—lasted from
the first hour to the hour that follows on

the sixth, when the sun shifts to a new quadrant.''  142

Quindi onde mosse tua donna Virgilio,      118
quattromilia trecento e due volumi
di sol desiderai questo concilio;
  e vidi lui tornare a tutt' i lumi      121
de la sua strada novecento trenta
fïate, mentre ch'ïo in terra fu'mi.
  La lingua ch'io parlai fu tutta spenta      124
innanzi che a l'ovra inconsummabile
fosse la gente di Nembròt attenta:
  ché nullo effetto mai razïonabile,      127
per lo piacere uman che rinovella
seguendo il cielo, sempre fu durabile.
  Opera naturale è ch'uom favella;      130
ma così o così, natura lascia
poi fare a voi secondo che v'abbella.
  Pria ch'i' scendessi a l'infernale ambascia,      133
*I* s'appellava in terra il sommo bene
onde vien la letizia che mi fascia;
  e *El* si chiamò poi: e ciò convene,      136
ché l'uso d'i mortali è come fronda
in ramo, che sen va e altra vene.
  Nel monte che si leva più da l'onda,      139
fu' io, con vita pura e disonesta,
da la prim' ora a quella che seconda,
  come 'l sol muta quadra, l'ora sesta."      142

# CANTO XXVII

"Unto the Father, Son, and Holy Ghost,
glory!"—all Paradise began, so that
the sweetness of the singing held me rapt.

What I saw seemed to me to be a smile      4
the universe had smiled; my rapture had
entered by way of hearing and of sight.

O joy! O gladness words can never speak!      7
O life perfected by both love and peace!
O richness so assured, that knows no longing!

Before my eyes, there stood, aflame, the four      10
torches, and that which had been first to come
began to glow with greater radiance,

and what its image then became was like      13
what Jupiter's would be if Mars and he
were birds and had exchanged their plumages.

After the Providence that there assigns      16
to every office its appointed time
had, to those holy choirs, on every side,

commanded silence, I then heard: "If I      19
change color, do not be amazed, for as
I speak, you will see change in all these flames.

He who on earth usurps my place, my place,      22
my place that in the sight of God's own Son
is vacant now, has made my burial ground

a sewer of blood, a sewer of stench, so that      25
the perverse one who fell from Heaven, here
above, can find contentment there below."

Then I saw all the heaven colored by      28
the hue that paints the clouds at morning and
at evening, with the sun confronting them.

And like a woman who, although secure      31
in her own honesty, will pale on even
hearing about another woman's failing,

*Still the Eighth Heaven: the Sphere of the Fixed Stars. The hymn of the blessed. St. Peter's condemnation of the popes and the corrupt Church. His urging of Dante to fulfill his mission on earth. Dante's earthward gaze. Ascent to the Ninth Heaven, the Primum Mobile. Its nature explained by Beatrice. Her discourse on the present straying of the world; her prophecy of its redemption.*

"Al Padre, al Figlio, a lo Spirito Santo,"
cominciò, "gloria!" tutto 'l paradiso,
sì che m'inebrïava il dolce canto.

    Ciò ch'io vedeva mi sembiava un riso           4
de l'universo; per che mia ebbrezza
intrava per l'udire e per lo viso.

    Oh gioia! oh ineffabile allegrezza!           7
oh vita intègra d'amore e di pace!
oh sanza brama sicura ricchezza!

    Dinanzi a li occhi miei le quattro face         10
stavano accese, e quella che pria venne
incominciò a farsi più vivace,

    e tal ne la sembianza sua divenne,          13
qual diverrebbe Iove, s'elli e Marte
fossero augelli e cambiassersi penne.

    La provedenza, che quivi comparte          16
vice e officio, nel beato coro
silenzio posto avea da ogne parte,

    quand' ïo udi': "Se io mi trascoloro,         19
non ti maravigliar, ché, dicend' io,
vedrai trascolorar tutti costoro.

    Quelli ch'usurpa in terra il luogo mio,        22
il luogo mio, il luogo mio che vaca
ne la presenza del Figliuol di Dio,

    fatt' ha del cimitero mio cloaca         25
del sangue e de la puzza; onde 'l perverso
che cadde di qua sù, là giù si placa."

    Di quel color che per lo sole avverso        28
nube dipigne da sera e da mane,
vid' ïo allora tutto 'l ciel cosperso.

    E come donna onesta che permane         31
di sé sicura, e per l'altrui fallanza,
pur ascoltando, timida si fane,

just so did Beatrice change in appearance;                              34
and I believe that such eclipse was in
the sky when He, the Highest Power, suffered.

Then his words followed with a voice so altered              37
from what it was before—even his likeness
did not display a greater change than that.

"The Bride of Christ was never nurtured by                    40
my blood, and blood of Linus and of Clitus,
to be employed in gaining greater riches;

but to acquire this life of joyousness,                            43
Sixtus and Pius, Urban and Calixtus,
after much lamentation, shed their blood.

We did not want one portion of Christ's people           46
to sit at the right side of our successors,
while, on the left, the other portion sat,

nor did we want the keys that were consigned             49
to me, to serve as an escutcheon on
a banner that waged war against the baptized;

nor did we want my form upon a seal                           52
for trafficking in lying privileges—
for which I often blush and flash with anger.

From here on high one sees rapacious wolves            55
clothed in the cloaks of shepherds. You, the vengeance
of God, oh, why do you still lie concealed?

The Gascons and the Cahorsines—they both              58
prepare to drink our blood: o good beginning,
to what a miserable end you fall!

But that high Providence which once preserved,         61
with Scipio, the glory of the world
for Rome, will soon bring help, as I conceive;

and you, my son, who through your mortal weight      64
will yet return below, speak plainly there,
and do not hide that which I do not hide."

As, when the horn of heaven's Goat abuts                   67
the sun, our sky flakes frozen vapors downward,
so did I see that ether there adorned;

for from that sphere, triumphant vapors now             70
were flaking up to the Empyrean—
returning after dwelling here with us.

My sight was following their semblances—                   73
until the space between us grew so great
as to deny my eyes all farther reach.

così Beatrice trasmutò sembianza;           34
e tale eclissi credo che 'n ciel fue
quando patì la supprema possanza.

    Poi procedetter le parole sue            37
con voce tanto da sé trasmutata,
che la sembianza non si mutò piùe:

    "Non fu la sposa di Cristo allevata        40
del sangue mio, di Lin, di quel di Cleto,
per essere ad acquisto d'oro usata;

    ma per acquisto d'esto viver lieto        43
e Sisto e Pïo e Calisto e Urbano
sparser lo sangue dopo molto fleto.

    Non fu nostra intenzion ch'a destra mano    46
d'i nostri successor parte sedesse,
parte da l'altra del popol cristiano;

    né che le chiavi che mi fuor concesse,       49
divenisser signaculo in vessillo
che contra battezzati combattesse;

    né ch'io fossi figura di sigillo          52
a privilegi venduti e mendaci,
ond' io sovente arrosso e disfavillo.

    In vesta di pastor lupi rapaci           55
si veggion di qua sù per tutti i paschi:
o difesa di Dio, perché pur giaci?

    Del sangue nostro Caorsini e Guaschi      58
s'apparecchian di bere: o buon principio,
a che vil fine convien che tu caschi!

    Ma l'alta provedenza, che con Scipio      61
difese a Roma la gloria del mondo,
soccorrà tosto, sì com' io concipio;

    e tu, figliuol, che per lo mortal pondo      64
ancor giù tornerai, apri la bocca,
e non asconder quel ch'io non ascondo.''

    Sì come di vapor gelati fiocca          67
in giuso l'aere nostro, quando 'l corno
de la capra del ciel col sol si tocca,

    in sù vid' io così l'etera addorno        70
farsi e fioccar di vapor trïunfanti
che fatto avien con noi quivi soggiorno.

    Lo viso mio seguiva i suoi sembianti,     73
e seguì fin che 'l mezzo, per lo molto,
li tolse il trapassar del più avanti.

At this, my lady, seeing me set free                              76
from gazing upward, told me: "Let your eyes
look down and see how far you have revolved."
    I saw that, from the time when I looked down     79
before, I had traversed all of the arc
of the first clime, from its midpoint to end,
    so that, beyond Cadiz, I saw Ulysses'              82
mad course and, to the east, could almost see
that shoreline where Europa was sweet burden.
    I should have seen more of this threshing floor    85
but for the motion of the sun beneath
my feet: it was a sign and more away.
    My mind, enraptured, always longing for            88
my lady gallantly, was burning more
than ever for my eyes' return to her;
    and if—by means of human flesh or portraits—       91
nature or art has fashioned lures to draw
the eye so as to grip the mind, all these
    would seem nothing if set beside the godly         94
beauty that shone upon me when I turned
to see the smiling face of Beatrice.
    The powers that her gaze now granted me            97
drew me out of the lovely nest of Leda
and thrust me into heaven's swiftest sphere.
    Its parts were all so equally alive                100
and excellent, that I cannot say which
place Beatrice selected for my entry.
    But she, who saw what my desire was—               103
her smile had so much gladness that within
her face there seemed to be God's joy—began:
    "The nature of the universe, which holds           106
the center still and moves all else around it,
begins here as if from its turning-post.
    This heaven has no other *where* than this:        109
the mind of God, in which are kindled both
the love that turns it and the force it rains.
    As in a circle, light and love enclose it,         112
as it surrounds the rest—and that enclosing,
only He who encloses understands.
    No other heaven measures this sphere's motion,     115
but it serves as the measure for the rest,
even as half and fifth determine ten;

Onde la donna, che mi vide assolto
de l'attendere in sù, mi disse: "Adima
il viso e guarda come tu se' vòlto."

Da l'ora ch'ïo avea guardato prima        79
i' vidi mosso me per tutto l'arco
che fa dal mezzo al fine il primo clima;

sì ch'io vedea di là da Gade il varco        82
folle d'Ulisse, e di qua presso il lito
nel qual si fece Europa dolce carco.

E più mi fora discoverto il sito        85
di questa aiuola; ma 'l sol procedea
sotto i mie' piedi un segno e più partito.

La mente innamorata, che donnea        88
con la mia donna sempre, di ridure
ad essa li occhi più che mai ardea;

e se natura o arte fé pasture        91
da pigliare occhi, per aver la mente,
in carne umana o ne le sue pitture,

tutte adunate, parrebber nïente        94
ver' lo piacer divin che mi refulse,
quando mi volsi al suo viso ridente.

E la virtù che lo sguardo m'indulse,        97
del bel nido di Leda mi divelse
e nel ciel velocissimo m'impulse.

Le parti sue vivissime ed eccelse        100
sì uniforme son, ch'i' non so dire
qual Bëatrice per loco mi scelse.

Ma ella, che vedëa 'l mio disire,        103
incominciò, ridendo tanto lieta,
che Dio parea nel suo volto gioire:

"La natura del mondo, che quïeta        106
il mezzo e tutto l'altro intorno move,
quinci comincia come da sua meta;

e questo cielo non ha altro dove        109
che la mente divina, in che s'accende
l'amor che 'l volge e la virtù ch'ei piove.

Luce e amor d'un cerchio lui comprende,        112
sì come questo li altri; e quel precinto
colui che 'l cinge solamente intende.

Non è suo moto per altro distinto,        115
ma li altri son mensurati da questo,
sì come diece da mezzo e da quinto;

and now it can be evident to you                          118
how time has roots within this vessel and,
within the other vessels, has its leaves.

O greediness, you who—within your depths—               121
cause mortals to sink so, that none is left
able to lift his eyes above your waves!

The will has a good blossoming in men;                   124
but then the never-ending downpours turn
the sound plums into rotten, empty skins.

For innocence and trust are to be found                  127
only in little children; then they flee
even before a full beard cloaks the cheeks.

One, for as long as he still lisps, will fast,           130
but when his tongue is free at last, he gorges,
devouring any food through any month;

and one, while he still lisps, will love and heed        133
his mother, but when he acquires speech
more fully, he will long to see her buried.

Just so, white skin turns black when it is struck        136
by direct light—the lovely daughter of
the one who brings us morning, leaves us evening.

That you not be amazed at what I say,                    139
consider this: on earth no king holds sway;
therefore, the family of humans strays.

But well before a thousand years have passed            142
(and January is unwintered by
day's hundredth part, which they neglect below),

this high sphere shall shine so, that Providence,       145
long waited for, will turn the sterns to where
the prows now are, so that the fleet runs straight;

and then fine fruit shall follow on the flower."        148

e come il tempo tegna in cotal testo 118
le sue radici e ne li altri le fronde,
omai a te può esser manifesto.

Oh cupidigia, che i mortali affonde 121
sì sotto te, che nessuno ha podere
di trarre li occhi fuor de le tue onde!

Ben fiorisce ne li uomini il volere; 124
ma la pioggia continüa converte
in bozzacchioni le sosine vere.

Fede e innocenza son reperte 127
solo ne' parvoletti; poi ciascuna
pria fugge che le guance sian coperte.

Tale, balbuzïendo ancor, digiuna, 130
che poi divora, con la lingua sciolta,
qualunque cibo per qualunque luna;

e tal, balbuzïendo, ama e ascolta 133
la madre sua, che, con loquela intera,
disïa poi di vederla sepolta.

Così si fa la pelle bianca nera 136
nel primo aspetto de la bella figlia
di quel ch'apporta mane e lascia sera.

Tu, perché non ti facci maraviglia, 139
pensa che 'n terra non è chi governi;
onde si svïa l'umana famiglia.

Ma prima che gennaio tutto si sverni 142
per la centesma ch'è là giù negletta,
raggeran sì questi cerchi superni,

che la fortuna che tanto s'aspetta, 145
le poppe volgerà u' son le prore,
sì che la classe correrà diretta;

e vero frutto verrà dopo 'l fiore." 148

OVERLEAF:
*Mediterranean*

# CANTO XXVIII

After the lady who imparadises
my mind disclosed the truth that is unlike
the present life of miserable mortals,

   then, just as one who sees a mirrored flame—      4
its double candle stands behind his back—
even before he thought of it or gazed

   directly at it, and he turns to gauge      7
if that glass tells the truth to him, and sees
that it accords, like voice and instrument,

   so—does my memory recall—I did      10
after I looked into the lovely eyes
of which Love made the noose that holds me tight.

   And when I turned and my own eyes were met      13
by what appears within that sphere whenever
one looks intently at its revolution,

   I saw a point that sent forth so acute      16
a light, that anyone who faced the force
with which it blazed would have to shut his eyes,

   and any star that, seen from earth, would seem      19
to be the smallest, set beside that point,
as star conjoined with star, would seem a moon.

   Around that point a ring of fire wheeled,      22
a ring perhaps as far from that point as
a halo from the star that colors it

   when mist that forms the halo is most thick.      25
It wheeled so quickly that it would outstrip
the motion that most swiftly girds the world.

   That ring was circled by a second ring,      28
the second by a third, third by a fourth,
fourth by a fifth, and fifth ring by a sixth.

   Beyond, the seventh ring, which followed, was      31
so wide that all of Juno's messenger
would be too narrow to contain that circle.

*The Ninth Heaven: the Primum Mobile. The nine luminous*
*circles of the angelic hierarchies. Their revolutions around a*
*Point. Beatrice's explanation. The celestial hierarchy. The correct*
*angelology of Dionysius and the mistake of St. Gregory.*

Poscia che 'ncontro a la vita presente
d'i miseri mortali aperse 'l vero
quella che 'mparadisa la mia mente,

come in lo specchio fiamma di doppiero     4
vede colui che se n'alluma retro,
prima che l'abbia in vista o in pensiero,

e sé rivolge per veder se 'l vetro     7
li dice il vero, e vede ch'el s'accorda
con esso come nota con suo metro;

così la mia memoria si ricorda     10
ch'io feci riguardando ne' belli occhi
onde a pigliarmi fece Amor la corda.

E com' io mi rivolsi e furon tocchi     13
li miei da ciò che pare in quel volume,
quandunque nel suo giro ben s'adocchi,

un punto vidi che raggiava lume     16
acuto sì, che 'l viso ch'elli affoca
chiuder conviensi per lo forte acume;

e quale stella per quinci più poca,     19
parrebbe luna, locata con esso
come stella con stella si collòca.

Forse cotanto quanto pare appresso     22
alo cigner la luce che 'l dipigne
quando 'l vapor che 'l porta più è spesso,

distante intorno al punto un cerchio d'igne     25
si girava sì ratto, ch'avria vinto
quel moto che più tosto il mondo cigne;

e questo era d'un altro circumcinto,     28
e quel dal terzo, e 'l terzo poi dal quarto,
dal quinto il quarto, e poi dal sesto il quinto.

Sopra seguiva il settimo sì sparto     31
già di larghezza, che 'l messo di Iuno
intero a contenerlo sarebbe arto.

The eighth and ninth were wider still; and each,                34
even as greater distance lay between
it and the first ring, moved with lesser speed;
    and, I believe, the ring with clearest flame        37
was that which lay least far from the pure spark
because it shares most deeply that point's truth.
    My lady, who saw my perplexity—                    40
I was in such suspense—said: "On that Point
depend the heavens and the whole of nature.
    Look at the circle that is nearest It,             43
and know: its revolutions are so swift
because of burning love that urges it."
    And I to her: "If earth and the nine spheres      46
were ordered like those rings, then I would be
content with what you have set out before me,
    but in the world of sense, what one can see        49
are spheres becoming ever more divine
as they are set more distant from the center.
    Thus, if my longing is to gain its end             52
in this amazing and angelic temple
that has, as boundaries, only love and light,
    then I still have to hear just how the model       55
and copy do not share in one same plan—
for by myself I think on this in vain."
    "You need not wonder if your fingers are           58
unable to undo that knot: no one
has tried, and so that knot is tightened, taut!"
    my lady said, and then continued: "If             61
you would be satisfied, take what I tell you—
and let your mind be sharp as I explain.
    The size of spheres of matter—large or small—     64
depends upon the power—more and less—
that spreads throughout their parts. More excellence
    yields greater blessedness; more blessedness       67
must comprehend a greater body when
that body's parts are equally complete.
    And thus this sphere, which sweeps along with it   70
the rest of all the universe, must be
the circle that loves most and knows the most,
    so that, if you but draw your measure round        73
the power within—and not the semblance of—
the angels that appear to you as circles,

Così l'ottavo e 'l nono; e ciascheduno     34
più tardo si movea, secondo ch'era
in numero distante più da l'uno;
    e quello avea la fiamma più sincera     37
cui men distava la favilla pura,
credo, però che più di lei s'invera.
    La donna mia, che mi vedëa in cura     40
forte sospeso, disse: "Da quel punto
depende il cielo e tutta la natura.
    Mira quel cerchio che più li è congiunto;     43
e sappi che 'l suo muovere è sì tosto
per l'affocato amore ond' elli è punto."
    E io a lei: "Se 'l mondo fosse posto     46
con l'ordine ch'io veggio in quelle rote,
sazio m'avrebbe ciò che m'è proposto;
    ma nel mondo sensibile si puote     49
veder le volte tanto più divine,
quant' elle son dal centro più remote.
    Onde, se 'l mio disir dee aver fine     52
in questo miro e angelico templo
che solo amore e luce ha per confine,
    udir convienmi ancor come l'essemplo     55
e l'essemplare non vanno d'un modo,
ché io per me indarno a ciò contemplo."
    "Se li tuoi diti non sono a tal nodo     58
sufficïenti, non è maraviglia:
tanto, per non tentare, è fatto sodo!"
    Così la donna mia; poi disse: "Piglia     61
quel ch'io ti dicerò, se vuo' saziarti;
e intorno da esso t'assottiglia.
    Li cerchi corporai sono ampi e arti     64
secondo il più e 'l men de la virtute
che si distende per tutte lor parti.
    Maggior bontà vuol far maggior salute;     67
maggior salute maggior corpo cape,
s'elli ha le parti igualmente compiute.
    Dunque costui che tutto quanto rape     70
l'altro universo seco, corrisponde
al cerchio che più ama e che più sape:
    per che, se tu a la virtù circonde     73
la tua misura, non a la parvenza
de le sustanze che t'appaion tonde,

you will discern a wonderful accord                                                76
between each sphere and its Intelligence:
greater accords with more, smaller with less."

    Just as the hemisphere of air remains                       79
splendid, serene, when from his gentler cheek
Boreas blows and clears the scoriae,

    dissolves the mist that had defaced the sky,                82
so that the heavens smile with loveliness
in all their regions; even so did I

    become after my lady had supplied                           85
her clear response to me, and—like a star
in heaven—truth was seen. And when her words

    were done, even as incandescent iron                        88
will shower sparks, so did those circles sparkle;
and each spark circled with its flaming ring

    sparks that were more in number than the sum                91
one reaches doubling in succession each
square of a chessboard—one to sixty-four.

    I heard "*Hosanna*" sung, from choir to choir               94
to that fixed Point which holds and always shall
hold them to where they have forever been.

    And she who saw my mind's perplexities                      97
said: "The first circles have displayed to you
the Seraphim and Cherubim. They follow

    the ties of love with such rapidity                         100
because they are as like the Point as creatures
can be, a power dependent on their vision.

    Those other loves that circle round them are                103
called Thrones of the divine aspect, because
they terminated the first group of three;

    and know that all delight to the degree                     106
to which their vision sees—more or less deeply—
that truth in which all intellects find rest.

    From this you see that blessedness depends                  109
upon the act of vision, not upon
the act of love—which is a consequence;

    the measure of their vision lies in merit,                  112
produced by grace and then by will to goodness:
and this is the progression, step by step.

    The second triad—blossoming in this                         115
eternal springtime that the nightly Ram
does not despoil—perpetually sings

tu vederai mirabil consequenza
di maggio a più e di minore a meno,
in ciascun cielo, a süa intelligenza."

Come rimane splendido e sereno                              79
l'emisperio de l'aere, quando soffia
Borea da quella guancia ond' è più leno,

per che si purga e risolve la roffia                        82
che pria turbava, sì che 'l ciel ne ride
con le bellezze d'ogne sua paroffia;

così fec'ïo, poi che mi provide                             85
la donna mia del suo risponder chiaro,
e come stella in cielo il ver si vide.

E poi che le parole sue restaro,                            88
non altrimenti ferro disfavilla
che bolle, come i cerchi sfavillaro.

L'incendio suo seguiva ogne scintilla;                      91
ed eran tante, che 'l numero loro
più che 'l doppiar de li scacchi s'inmilla.

Io sentiva osannar di coro in coro                          94
al punto fisso che li tiene a li *ubi*,
e terrà sempre, ne' quai sempre fuoro.

E quella che vedëa i pensier dubi                           97
ne la mia mente, disse: "I cerchi primi
t'hanno mostrato Serafi e Cherubi.

Così veloci seguono i suoi vimi,                            100
per somigliarsi al punto quanto ponno;
e posson quanto a veder son soblimi.

Quelli altri amori che 'ntorno li vonno,                    103
si chiaman Troni del divino aspetto,
per che 'l primo ternaro terminonno;

e dei saper che tutti hanno diletto                         106
quanto la sua veduta si profonda
nel vero in che si queta ogne intelletto.

Quinci si può veder come si fonda                           109
l'esser beato ne l'atto che vede,
non in quel ch'ama, che poscia seconda;

e del vedere è misura mercede,                              112
che grazia partorisce e buona voglia:
così di grado in grado si procede.

L'altro ternaro, che così germoglia                         115
in questa primavera sempiterna
che notturno Arïete non dispoglia,

'*Hosanna*' with three melodies that sound                    118
in the three ranks of bliss that form this triad;
within this hierarchy there are three

    kinds of divinities: first, the Dominions,            121
and then the Virtues; and the final order
contains the Powers. The two penultimate

    groups of rejoicing ones within the next            124
triad are wheeling Principalities
and the Archangels; last, the playful Angels.

    These orders all direct—ecstatically—               127
their eyes on high; and downward, they exert
such force that all are drawn and draw to God.

    And Dionysius, with much longing, set               130
himself to contemplate these orders: he
named and distinguished them just as I do.

    Though, later, Gregory disputed him,                133
when Gregory came here—when he could see
with opened eyes—he smiled at his mistake.

    You need not wonder if a mortal told                136
such secret truth on earth: it was disclosed
to him by one who saw it here above—

    both that and other truths about these circles."    139

perpetüalemente 'Osanna' sberna          118
con tre melode, che suonano in tree
ordini di letizia onde s'interna.

    In essa gerarcia son l'altre dee:        121
prima Dominazioni, e poi Virtudi;
l'ordine terzo di Podestadi èe.

    Poscia ne' due penultimi tripudi      124
Principati e Arcangeli si girano;
l'ultimo è tutto d'Angelici ludi.

    Questi ordini di sù tutti s'ammirano,    127
e di giù vincon sì, che verso Dio
tutti tirati sono e tutti tirano.

    E Dïonisio con tanto disio         130
a contemplar questi ordini si mise,
che li nomò e distinse com'io.

    Ma Gregorio da lui poi si divise;     133
onde, sì tosto come li occhi aperse
in questo ciel, di sé medesmo rise.

    E se tanto secreto ver proferse     136
mortale in terra, non voglio ch'ammiri:
ché chi 'l vide qua sù gliel discoperse

     con altro assai del ver di questi giri."  139

# CANTO XXIX

As long as both Latona's children take
(when, covered by the Ram and Scales, they make
their belt of the horizon at the same

moment) to pass from equilibrium—                          4
the zenith held in balance—to that state
where, changing hemispheres, each leaves that belt,

so long did Beatrice, a smile upon                         7
her face, keep silence, even as she gazed
intently at the Point that overwhelmed me.

Then she began: "I tell—not ask—what you                   10
now want to hear, for I have seen it there
where, in one point, all *whens* and *ubis* end.

Not to acquire new goodness for Himself—                   13
which cannot be—but that his splendor might,
as it shines back to Him, declare '*Subsisto*,'

in His eternity outside of time,                           16
beyond all other borders, as pleased Him,
Eternal Love opened into new loves.

Nor did he lie, before this, as if languid;               19
there was no *after*, no *before*—they were
not there until God moved upon these waters.

Then form and matter, either separately                    22
or in mixed state, emerged as flawless being,
as from a three-stringed bow, three arrows spring.

And as a ray shines into amber, crystal,                   25
or glass, so that there is no interval
between its coming and its lighting all,

so did the three—form, matter, and their union—           28
flash into being from the Lord with no
distinction in beginning: all at once.

Created with the substances were order                     31
and pattern; at the summit of the world
were those in whom pure act had been produced;

*Still the Ninth Heaven: the Primum Mobile. The silence of
Beatrice, then her discourse on creation and on rebel and faithful angels; her digressing diatribe against useless philosophizing
and preaching; and her conclusion, on the number of the angels.*

Quando ambedue li figli di Latona,
coperti del Montone e de la Libra,
fanno de l'orizzonte insieme zona,

quant' è dal punto che 'l cenìt inlibra          4
infin che l'uno e l'altro da quel cinto,
cambiando l'emisperio, si dilibra,

tanto, col volto di riso dipinto,                7
si tacque Bëatrice, riguardando
fiso nel punto che m'avëa vinto.

Poi cominciò: "Io dico, e non dimando,          10
quel che tu vuoli udir, perch' io l'ho visto
là 've s'appunta ogne *ubi* e ogne *quando*.

Non per aver a sé di bene acquisto,             13
ch'esser non può, ma perché suo splendore
potesse, risplendendo, dir 'Subsisto,'

in sua etternità di tempo fore,                 16
fuor d'ogne altro comprender, come i piacque,
s'aperse in nuovi amor l'etterno amore.

Né prima quasi torpente si giacque;             19
ché né prima né poscia procedette
lo discorrer di Dio sovra quest' acque.

Forma e materia, congiunte e purette,           22
usciro ad esser che non avia fallo,
come d'arco tricordo tre saette.

E come in vetro, in ambra o in cristallo        25
raggio resplende sì, che dal venire
a l'esser tutto non è intervallo,

così 'l triforme effetto del suo sire           28
ne l'esser suo raggiò insieme tutto
sanza distinzïone in essordire.

Concreato fu ordine e costrutto                 31
a le sustanze; e quelle furon cima
nel mondo in che puro atto fu produtto;

and pure potentiality possessed                              34
the lowest part; and in the middle, act
so joined potentiality that they
    never disjoin. For you, Jerome has written       37
that the creation of the angels came
long centuries before all else was made;
    but this, the truth I speak, is written by      40
scribes of the Holy Ghost—as you can find
if you look carefully—on many pages;
    and reason, too, can see in part this truth,    43
for it would not admit that those who move
the heavens could, for so long, be without
    their perfect task. Now you know where and when  46
and how these loving spirits were created:
with this, three flames of your desire are quenched.
    Then, sooner than it takes to count to twenty,   49
a portion of the angels violently
disturbed the lowest of your elements.
    The rest remained; and they, with such rejoicing, 52
began the office you can see, that they
never desert their circling contemplation.
    The fall had its beginning in the cursed         55
pride of the one you saw, held in constraint
by all of the world's weights. Those whom you see
    in Heaven here were modestly aware              58
that they were ready for intelligence
so vast, because of that Good which had made them:
    through this, their vision was exalted with     61
illuminating grace and with their merit,
so that their will is constant and intact.
    I would not have you doubt, but have you know    64
surely that there is merit in receiving
grace, measured by the longing to receive it.
    By now, if you have taken in my words,           67
you need no other aid to contemplate
much in regard to this consistory.
    But since on earth, throughout your schools, they teach 70
that it is in the nature of the angels
to understand, to recollect, to will,
    I shall say more, so that you may see clearly   73
the truth that, there below, has been confused
by teaching that is so ambiguous.

pura potenza tenne la parte ima;                34
nel mezzo strinse potenza con atto
tal vime, che già mai non si divima.

Ieronimo vi scrisse lungo tratto                37
di secoli de li angeli creati
anzi che l'altro mondo fosse fatto;

ma questo vero è scritto in molti lati          40
da li scrittor de lo Spirito Santo,
e tu te n'avvedrai se bene agguati;

e anche la ragione il vede alquanto,            43
che non concederebbe che ' motori
sanza sua perfezion fosser cotanto.

Or sai tu dove e quando questi amori            46
furon creati e come: sì che spenti
nel tuo disïo già son tre ardori.

Né giugneriesi, numerando, al venti            49
sì tosto, come de li angeli parte
turbò il suggetto d'i vostri alimenti.

L'altra rimase, e cominciò quest' arte          52
che tu discerni, con tanto diletto,
che mai da circüir non si diparte.

Principio del cader fu il maladetto             55
superbir di colui che tu vedesti
da tutti i pesi del mondo costretto.

Quelli che vedi qui furon modesti               58
a riconoscer sé da la bontate
che li avea fatti a tanto intender presti:

per che le viste lor furo essaltate             61
con grazia illuminante e con lor merto,
sì c'hanno ferma e piena volontate;

e non voglio che dubbi, ma sia certo,           64
che ricever la grazia è meritorio
secondo che l'affetto l'è aperto.

Omai dintorno a questo consistorio              67
puoi contemplare assai, se le parole
mie son ricolte, sanz' altro aiutorio.

Ma perché 'n terra per le vostre scole          70
si legge che l'angelica natura
è tal, che 'ntende e si ricorda e vole,

ancor dirò, perché tu veggi pura                73
la verità che là giù si confonde,
equivocando in sì fatta lettura.

These beings, since they first were gladdened by    76
the face of God, from which no thing is hidden,
have never turned their vision from that face,
    so that their sight is never intercepted    79
by a new object, and they have no need
to recollect an interrupted concept.
    So that, below, though not asleep, men dream,    82
speaking in good faith or in bad—the last,
however, merits greater blame and shame.
    Below, you do not follow one sole path    85
as you philosophize—your love of show
and thought of it so carry you astray!
    Yet even love of show is suffered here    88
with less disdain than the subordination
or the perversion of the Holy Scripture.
    There, they devote no thought to how much blood    91
it costs to sow it in the world, to how
pleasing is he who—humbly—holds it fast.
    Each one strives for display, elaborates    94
his own inventions; preachers speak at length
of these—meanwhile the Gospels do not speak.
    One says that, to prevent the sun from reaching    97
below, the moon—when Christ was crucified—
moved back along the zodiac, so as
    to interpose itself; who says so, lies—    100
for sunlight hid itself; not only Jews,
but Spaniards, Indians, too, saw that eclipse.
    Such fables, shouted through the year from pulpits—    103
some here, some there—outnumber even all
the Lapos and the Bindos Florence has;
    so that the wretched sheep, in ignorance,    106
return from pasture, having fed on wind—
but to be blind to harm does not excuse them.
    Christ did not say to his first company:    109
'Go, and preach idle stories to the world';
but he gave them the teaching that is truth,
    and truth alone was sounded when they spoke;    112
and thus, to battle to enkindle faith,
the Gospels served them as both shield and lance.
    But now men go to preach with jests and jeers,    115
and just as long as they can raise a laugh,
the cowl puffs up, and nothing more is asked.

Queste sustanze, poi che fur gioconde
de la faccia di Dio, non volser viso
da essa, da cui nulla si nasconde:
però non hanno vedere interciso                          79
da novo obietto, e però non bisogna
rememorar per concetto diviso;
sì che là giù, non dormendo, si sogna,                   82
credendo e non credendo dicer vero;
ma ne l'uno è più colpa e più vergogna.
Voi non andate giù per un sentiero                       85
filosofando: tanto vi trasporta
l'amor de l'apparenza e 'l suo pensiero!
E ancor questo qua sù si comporta                        88
con men disdegno che quando è posposta
la divina Scrittura o quando è torta.
Non vi si pensa quanto sangue costa                      91
seminarla nel mondo e quanto piace
chi umilmente con essa s'accosta.
Per apparer ciascun s'ingegna e face                     94
sue invenzioni; e quelle son trascorse
da' predicanti e 'l Vangelio si tace.
Un dice che la luna si ritorse                           97
ne la passion di Cristo e s'interpuose,
per che 'l lume del sol giù non si porse;
e mente, ché la luce si nascose                          100
da sé: però a li Spani e a l'Indi
come a' Giudei tale eclissi rispuose.
Non ha Fiorenza tanti Lapi e Bindi                       103
quante sì fatte favole per anno
in pergamo si gridan quinci e quindi:
sì che le pecorelle, che non sanno,                      106
tornan del pasco pasciute di vento,
e non le scusa non veder lo danno.
Non disse Cristo al suo primo convento:                  109
'Andate, e predicate al mondo ciance';
ma diede lor verace fondamento;
e quel tanto sonò ne le sue guance,                      112
sì ch'a pugnar per accender la fede
de l'Evangelio fero scudo e lance.
Ora si va con motti e con iscede                         115
a predicare, e pur che ben si rida,
gonfia il cappuccio e più non si richiede.

But such a bird nests in that cowl, that if                    118
the people saw it, they would recognize
as lies the pardons in which they confide—
    pardons through which the world's credulity          121
increases so, that people throng to every
indulgence backed by no authority;
    and this allows the Antonines to fatten              124
their pigs, and others, too, more piggish still,
who pay with counterfeit, illegal tender.
    But since we have digressed enough, turn back        127
your eyes now to the way that is direct;
our time is short—so, too, must be our path.
    The number of these angels is so great               130
that there has never been a mortal speech
or mortal thought that named a sum so steep;
    and if you look at that which is revealed            133
by Daniel, you will see that, while he mentions
thousands, he gives no number with precision.
    The First Light reaches them in ways as many        136
as are the angels to which It conjoins
Itself, as It illumines all of them;
    and this is why (because affection follows           139
the act of knowledge) the intensity
of love's sweetness appears unequally.
    By now you see the height, you see the breadth,      142
of the Eternal Goodness: It has made
so many mirrors, which divide Its light,
    but, as before, Its own Self still is One."          145

Ma tale uccel nel becchetto s'annida,                    118
che se 'l vulgo il vedesse, vederebbe
la perdonanza di ch'el si confida:
    per cui tanta stoltezza in terra crebbe,             121
che, sanza prova d'alcun testimonio,
ad ogne promession si correrebbe.
    Di questo ingrassa il porco sant' Antonio,           124
e altri assai che sono ancor più porci,
pagando di moneta sanza conio.
    Ma perché siam digressi assai, ritorci               127
li occhi oramai verso la dritta strada,
sì che la via col tempo si raccorci.
    Questa natura sì oltre s'ingrada                      130
in numero, che mai non fu loquela
né concetto mortal che tanto vada;
    e se tu guardi quel che si revela                    133
per Danïel, vedrai che 'n sue migliaia
determinato numero si cela.
    La prima luce, che tutta la raia,                    136
per tanti modi in essa si recepe,
quanti son li splendori a chi s'appaia.
    Onde, però che a l'atto che concepe                  139
segue l'affetto, d'amar la dolcezza
diversamente in essa ferve e tepe.
    Vedi l'eccelso omai e la larghezza                   142
de l'etterno valor, poscia che tanti
speculi fatti s'ha in che si spezza,
    uno manendo in sé come davanti."                     145

OVERLEAF:
*The Celestial Rose*

# CANTO XXX

Perhaps six thousand miles away from us,
the sixth hour burns, and now our world inclines
its shadow to an almost level bed,
    so that the span of heaven high above          4
begins to alter so, that some stars are
no longer to be seen from our deep earth;
    and as the brightest handmaid of the sun          7
advances, heaven shuts off, one by one,
its lights, until the loveliest is gone.
    So did the triumph that forever plays          10
around the Point that overcame me (Point
that seems enclosed by that which It encloses)
    fade gradually from my sight, so that          13
my seeing nothing else—and love—compelled
my eyes to turn again to Beatrice.
    If that which has been said of her so far          16
were all contained within a single praise,
it would be much too scant to serve me now.
    The loveliness I saw surpassed not only          19
our human measure—and I think that, surely,
only its Maker can enjoy it fully.
    I yield: I am defeated at this passage          22
more than a comic or a tragic poet
has ever been by a barrier in his theme;
    for like the sun that strikes the frailest eyes,          25
so does the memory of her sweet smile
deprive me of the use of my own mind.
    From that first day when, in this life, I saw          28
her face, until I had this vision, no
thing ever cut the sequence of my song,
    but now I must desist from this pursuit,          31
in verses, of her loveliness, just as
each artist who has reached his limit must.

*The departure of the spirits. The beauty of Beatrice. Arrival in*
*the Tenth Heaven, the Empyrean. The Celestial Rose. The seat*
*assigned to Henry VII. Beatrice's final words: her condem-*
*nation of Boniface VIII.*

Forse semilia miglia di lontano
ci ferve l'ora sesta, e questo mondo
china già l'ombra quasi al letto piano,

quando 'l mezzo del cielo, a noi profondo,      4
comincia a farsi tal, ch'alcuna stella
perde il parere infino a questo fondo;

e come vien la chiarissima ancella      7
del sol più oltre, così 'l ciel si chiude
di vista in vista infino a la più bella.

Non altrimenti il trïunfo che lude      10
sempre dintorno al punto che mi vinse,
parendo inchiuso da quel ch'elli 'nchiude,

a poco a poco al mio veder si stinse:      13
per che tornar con li occhi a Bëatrice
nulla vedere e amor mi costrinse.

Se quanto infino a qui di lei si dice      16
fosse conchiuso tutto in una loda,
poca sarebbe a fornir questa vice.

La bellezza ch'io vidi si trasmoda      19
non pur di là da noi, ma certo io credo
che solo il suo fattor tutta la goda.

Da questo passo vinto mi concedo      22
più che già mai da punto di suo tema
soprato fosse comico o tragedo:

ché, come sole in viso che più trema,      25
così lo rimembrar del dolce riso
la mente mia da me medesmo scema.

Dal primo giorno ch'i' vidi il suo viso      28
in questa vita, infino a questa vista,
non m'è il seguire al mio cantar preciso;

ma or convien che mio seguir desista      31
più dietro a sua bellezza, poetando,
come a l'ultimo suo ciascuno artista.

So she, in beauty (as I leave her to                           34
a herald that is greater than my trumpet,
which nears the end of its hard theme), with voice
    and bearing of a guide whose work is done,             37
began again: "From matter's largest sphere,
we now have reached the heaven of pure light,
    light of the intellect, light filled with love,            40
love of true good, love filled with happiness,
a happiness surpassing every sweetness.
    Here you will see both ranks of Paradise                43
and see one of them wearing that same aspect
which you will see again at Judgment Day."
    Like sudden lightning scattering the spirits            46
of sight so that the eye is then too weak
to act on other things it would perceive,
    such was the living light encircling me,                 49
leaving me so enveloped by its veil
of radiance that I could see no thing.
    "The Love that calms this heaven always welcomes    52
into Itself with such a salutation,
to make the candle ready for its flame."
    No sooner had these few words entered me             55
than I became aware that I was rising
beyond the power that was mine; and such
    new vision kindled me again, that even                  58
the purest light would not have been so bright
as to defeat my eyes, deny my sight;
    and I saw light that took a river's form—              61
light flashing, reddish-gold, between two banks
painted with wonderful spring flowerings.
    Out of that stream there issued living sparks,          64
which settled on the flowers on all sides,
like rubies set in gold; and then, as if
    intoxicated with the odors, they                         67
again plunged into the amazing flood:
as one spark sank, another spark emerged.
    "The high desire that now inflames, incites,           70
you to grasp mentally the things you see,
pleases me more as it swells more; but first,
    that you may satisfy your mighty thirst,                73
you must drink of these waters." So did she
who is the sun of my eyes speak to me.

Cotal qual io la lascio a maggior bando 34
che quel de la mia tuba, che deduce
l'ardüa sua matera terminando,

con atto e voce di spedito duce 37
ricominciò: "Noi siamo usciti fore
del maggior corpo al ciel ch'è pura luce:

luce intellettüal, piena d'amore; 40
amor di vero ben, pien di letizia;
letizia che trascende ogne dolzore.

Qui vederai l'una e l'altra milizia 43
di paradiso, e l'una in quelli aspetti
che tu vedrai a l'ultima giustizia."

Come sùbito lampo che discetti 46
li spiriti visivi, sì che priva
da l'atto l'occhio di più forti obietti,

così mi circunfulse luce viva, 49
e lasciommi fasciato di tal velo
del suo fulgor, che nulla m'appariva.

"Sempre l'amor che queta questo cielo 52
accoglie in sé con sì fatta salute,
per far disposto a sua fiamma il candelo."

Non fur più tosto dentro a me venute 55
queste parole brievi, ch'io compresi
me sormontar di sopr' a mia virtute;

e di novella vista mi raccesi 58
tale, che nulla luce è tanto mera,
che li occhi miei non si fosser difesi;

e vidi lume in forma di rivera 61
fulvido di fulgore, intra due rive
dipinte di mirabil primavera.

Di tal fiumana uscian faville vive, 64
e d'ogne parte si mettien ne' fiori,
quasi rubin che oro circunscrive;

poi, come inebrïate da li odori, 67
riprofondavan sé nel miro gurge,
e s'una intrava, un'altra n'uscia fori.

"L'alto disio che mo t'infiamma e urge, 70
d'aver notizia di ciò che tu vei,
tanto mi piace più quanto più turge;

ma di quest' acqua convien che tu bei 73
prima che tanta sete in te si sazi";
così mi disse il sol de li occhi miei.

She added this: "The river and the gems          76
of topaz entering and leaving, and
the grasses' laughter—these are shadowy
    prefaces of their truth; not that these things          79
are lacking in themselves; the defect lies
in you, whose sight is not yet that sublime."
    No infant who awakes long after his          82
usual hour would turn his face toward milk
as quickly as I hurried toward that stream;
    to make still finer mirrors of my eyes,          85
I bent down toward the waters which flow there
that we, in them, may find our betterment.
    But as my eyelids' eaves drank of that wave,          88
it seemed to me that it had changed its shape:
no longer straight, that flow now formed a round.
    Then, just as maskers, when they set aside          91
the borrowed likenesses in which they hide,
seem to be other than they were before,
    so were the flowers and the sparks transformed,          94
changing to such festivity before me
that I saw—clearly—both of Heaven's courts.
    O radiance of God, through which I saw          97
the noble triumph of the true realm, give
to me the power to speak of what I saw!
    Above, on high, there is a light that makes          100
apparent the Creator to the creature
whose only peace lies in his seeing Him.
    The shape which that light takes as it expands          103
is circular, and its circumference
would be too great a girdle for the sun.
    All that one sees of it derives from one          106
light-ray reflected from the summit of
the Primum Mobile, which from it draws
    power and life. And as a hill is mirrored          109
in waters at its base, as if to see
itself—when rich with grass and flowers—graced,
    so, in a thousand tiers that towered above          112
the light, encircling it, I saw, mirrored,
all of us who have won return above.
    And if the lowest rank ingathers such          115
vast light, then what must be the measure of
this Rose where it has reached its highest leaves!

Anche soggiunse: "Il fiume e li topazi 76
ch'entrano ed escono e 'l rider de l'erbe
son di lor vero umbriferi prefazi.

  Non che da sé sian queste cose acerbe; 79
ma è difetto da la parte tua,
che non hai viste ancor tanto superbe."

  Non è fantin che sì sùbito rua 82
col volto verso il latte, se si svegli
molto tardato da l'usanza sua,

  come fec' io, per far migliori spegli 85
ancor de li occhi, chinandomi a l'onda
che si deriva perché vi s'immegli;

  e sì come di lei bevve la gronda 88
de le palpebre mie, così mi parve
di sua lunghezza divenuta tonda.

  Poi, come gente stata sotto larve, 91
che pare altro che prima, se si sveste
la sembianza non süa in che disparve,

  così mi si cambiaro in maggior feste 94
li fiori e le faville, sì ch'io vidi
ambo le corti del ciel manifeste.

  O isplendor di Dio, per cu' io vidi 97
l'alto trïunfo del regno verace,
dammi virtù a dir com' ïo il vidi!

  Lume è là sù che visibile face 100
lo creatore a quella creatura
che solo in lui vedere ha la sua pace.

  E' si distende in circular figura, 103
in tanto che la sua circunferenza
sarebbe al sol troppo larga cintura.

  Fassi di raggio tutta sua parvenza 106
reflesso al sommo del mobile primo,
che prende quindi vivere e potenza.

  E come clivo in acqua di suo imo 109
si specchia, quasi per vedersi addorno,
quando è nel verde e ne' fioretti opimo,

  sì, soprastando al lume intorno intorno, 112
vidi specchiarsi in più di mille soglie
quanto di noi là sù fatto ha ritorno.

  E se l'infimo grado in sé raccoglie 115
sì grande lume, quanta è la larghezza
di questa rosa ne l'estreme foglie!

Within that breadth and height I did not find                    118
my vision gone astray, for it took in
that joy in all its quality and kind.

There, near and far do not subtract or add;                      121
for where God governs with no mediator,
no thing depends upon the laws of nature.

Into the yellow of the eternal Rose                              124
that slopes and stretches and diffuses fragrance
of praise unto the Sun of endless spring,

now Beatrice drew me as one who, though                          127
he would speak out, is silent. And she said:
"See how great is this council of white robes!

See how much space our city's circuit spans!                     130
See how our seated ranks are now so full
that little room is left for any more!

And in that seat on which your eyes are fixed                    133
because a crown already waits above it,
before you join this wedding feast, shall sit

the soul of noble Henry, he who is,                              136
on earth, to be imperial; he shall
come to set right your Italy—but when

she is unready. The blind greediness                            139
bewitching you, has made you like the child
who dies of hunger and drives off his nurse.

And in the holy forum such shall be                             142
your Prefect then, that either openly
or secretly he will not walk with Henry.

But God will not endure him long within                         145
the holy ministry: he shall be cast
down there, where Simon Magus pays; he shall

force the Anagnine deeper in his hole."                         148

La vista mia ne l'ampio e ne l'altezza                118
non si smarriva, ma tutto prendeva
il quanto e 'l quale di quella allegrezza.

  Presso e lontano, lì, né pon né leva:              121
ché dove Dio sanza mezzo governa,
la legge natural nulla rileva.

  Nel giallo de la rosa sempiterna,                  124
che si digrada e dilata e redole
odor di lode al sol che sempre verna,

  qual è colui che tace e dicer vole,                127
mi trasse Bëatrice, e disse: "Mira
quanto è 'l convento de le bianche stole!

  Vedi nostra città quant' ella gira;               130
vedi li nostri scanni sì ripieni,
che poca gente più ci si disira.

  E 'n quel gran seggio a che tu li occhi tieni      133
per la corona che già v'è sù posta,
prima che tu a queste nozze ceni,

  sederà l'alma, che fia giù agosta,                 136
de l'alto Arrigo, ch'a drizzare Italia
verrà in prima ch'ella sia disposta.

  La cieca cupidigia che v'ammalia                   139
simili fatti v'ha al fantolino
che muor per fame e caccia via la balia.

  E fia prefetto nel foro divino                     142
allora tal, che palese e coverto
non anderà con lui per un cammino.

  Ma poco poi sarà da Dio sofferto                   145
nel santo officio: ch'el sarà detruso
là dove Simon mago è per suo merto,

  e farà quel d'Alagna intrar più giuso."            148

# CANTO XXXI

So, in the shape of that white Rose, the holy
legion was shown to me—the host that Christ,
with His own blood, had taken as His bride.

The other host, which, flying, sees and sings     4
the glory of the One who draws its love,
and that goodness which granted it such glory,

just like a swarm of bees that, at one moment,     7
enters the flowers and, at another, turns
back to that labor which yields such sweet savor,

descended into that vast flower graced     10
with many petals, then again rose up
to the eternal dwelling of its love.

Their faces were all living flame; their wings     13
were gold; and for the rest, their white was so
intense, no snow can match the white they showed.

When they climbed down into that flowering Rose,     16
from rank to rank, they shared that peace and ardor
which they had gained, with wings that fanned their sides.

Nor did so vast a throng in flight, although     19
it interposed between the candid Rose
and light above, obstruct the sight or splendor,

because the light of God so penetrates     22
the universe according to the worth
of every part, that no thing can impede it.

This confident and joyous kingdom, thronged     25
with people of both new and ancient times,
turned all its sight and ardor to one mark.

O threefold Light that, in a single star     28
sparkling into their eyes, contents them so,
look down and see our tempest here below!

If the Barbarians, when they came from     31
a region that is covered every day
by Helice, who wheels with her loved son,

*The Tenth Heaven: the Empyrean. The Rose. Dante's amaze-*
*ment. The appearance of St. Bernard instead of Beatrice. Dante's*
*vision of—and prayer to—Beatrice. His response to St. Ber-*
*nard's urging him to contemplate the Rose and Mary. Mary's*
*delight in the festive angels.*

In forma dunque di candida rosa
mi si mostrava la milizia santa
che nel suo sangue Cristo fece sposa;

ma l'altra, che volando vede e canta       4
la gloria di colui che la 'nnamora
e la bontà che la fece cotanta,

sì come schiera d'ape che s'infiora       7
una fïata e una si ritorna
là dove suo laboro s'insapora,

nel gran fior discendeva che s'addorna       10
di tante foglie, e quindi risaliva
là dove 'l süo amor sempre soggiorna.

Le facce tutte avean di fiamma viva       13
e l'ali d'oro, e l'altro tanto bianco,
che nulla neve a quel termine arriva.

Quando scendean nel fior, di banco in banco       16
porgevan de la pace e de l'ardore
ch'elli acquistavan ventilando il fianco.

Né l'interporsi tra 'l disopra e 'l fiore       19
di tanta moltitudine volante
impediva la vista e lo splendore:

ché la luce divina è penetrante       22
per l'universo secondo ch'è degno,
sì che nulla le puote essere ostante.

Questo sicuro e gaudïoso regno,       25
frequente in gente antica e in novella,
viso e amore avea tutto ad un segno.

Oh trina luce che 'n unica stella       28
scintillando a lor vista, sì li appaga!
guarda qua giuso a la nostra procella!

Se i barbari, venendo da tal plaga       31
che ciascun giorno d'Elice si cuopra,
rotante col suo figlio ond' ella è vaga,

were, seeing Rome and her vast works, struck dumb    34
(when, of all mortal things, the Lateran
was the most eminent), then what amazement

    must have filled me when I to the divine    37
came from the human, to eternity
from time, and to a people just and sane

    from Florence came! And certainly, between    40
the wonder and the joy, it must have been
welcome to me to hear and speak nothing.

    And as a pilgrim, in the temple he    43
had vowed to reach, renews himself—he looks
and hopes he can describe what it was like—

    so did I journey through the living light,    46
guiding my eyes, from rank to rank, along
a path now up, now down, now circling round.

    There I saw faces given up to love—    49
graced with Another's light and their own smile—
and movements graced with every dignity.

    By now my gaze had taken in the whole    52
of Paradise—its form in general—
but without looking hard at any part;

    and I, my will rekindled, turning toward    55
my lady, was prepared to ask about
those matters that inclined my mind to doubt.

    Where I expected her, another answered:    58
I thought I should see Beatrice, and saw
an elder dressed like those who are in glory.

    His gracious gladness filled his eyes, suffused    61
his cheeks; his manner had that kindliness
which suits a tender father. "Where is she?"

    I asked him instantly. And he replied:    64
"That all your longings may be satisfied,
Beatrice urged me from my place. If you

    look up and to the circle that is third    67
from that rank which is highest, you will see
her on the throne her merits have assigned her."

    I, without answering, then looked on high    70
and saw that round her now a crown took shape
as she reflected the eternal rays.

    No mortal eye, not even one that plunged    73
into deep seas, would be so distant from
that region where the highest thunder forms,

veggendo Roma e l'ardüa sua opra,       34
stupefaciensi, quando Laterano
a le cose mortali andò di sopra;
   ïo, che al divino da l'umano,       37
a l'etterno dal tempo era venuto,
e di Fiorenza in popol giusto e sano,
   di che stupor dovea esser compiuto!       40
Certo tra esso e 'l gaudio mi facea
libito non udire e starmi muto.
   E quasi peregrin che si ricrea       43
nel tempio del suo voto riguardando,
e spera già ridir com' ello stea,
   su per la viva luce passeggiando,       46
menava ïo li occhi per li gradi,
mo sù, mo giù e mo recirculando.
   Vedëa visi a carità süadi,       49
d'altrui lume fregiati e di suo riso,
e atti ornati di tutte onestadi.
   La forma general di paradiso       52
già tutta mïo sguardo avea compresa,
in nulla parte ancor fermato fiso;
   e volgeami con voglia rïaccesa       55
per domandar la mia donna di cose
di che la mente mia era sospesa.
   Uno intendëa, e altro mi rispuose:       58
credea veder Beatrice e vidi un sene
vestito con le genti glorïose.
   Diffuso era per li occhi e per le gene       61
di benigna letizia, in atto pio
quale a tenero padre si convene.
   E "Ov' è ella?" sùbito diss' io.       64
Ond' elli: "A terminar lo tuo disiro
mosse Beatrice me del loco mio;
   e se riguardi sù nel terzo giro       67
dal sommo grado, tu la rivedrai
nel trono che suoi merti le sortiro."
   Sanza risponder, li occhi sù levai,       70
e vidi lei che si facea corona
reflettendo da sé li etterni rai.
   Da quella regïon che più sù tona       73
occhio mortale alcun tanto non dista,
qualunque in mare più giù s'abbandona,

as—there—my sight was far from Beatrice; 76
but distance was no hindrance, for her semblance
reached me—undimmed by any thing between.

"O lady, you in whom my hope gains strength, 79
you who, for my salvation, have allowed
your footsteps to be left in Hell, in all

the things that I have seen, I recognize 82
the grace and benefit that I, depending
upon your power and goodness, have received.

You drew me out from slavery to freedom 85
by all those paths, by all those means that were
within your power. Do, in me, preserve

your generosity, so that my soul, 88
which you have healed, when it is set loose from
my body, be a soul that you will welcome."

So did I pray. And she, however far 91
away she seemed, smiled, and she looked at me.
Then she turned back to the eternal fountain.

And he, the holy elder, said: "That you 94
may consummate your journey perfectly—
for this, both prayer and holy love have sent me

to help you—let your sight fly round this garden; 97
by gazing so, your vision will be made
more ready to ascend through God's own ray.

The Queen of Heaven, for whom I am all 100
aflame with love, will grant us every grace:
I am her faithful Bernard." Just as one

who, from Croatia perhaps, has come 103
to visit our Veronica—one whose
old hunger is not sated, who, as long

as it is shown, repeats these words in thought: 106
"O my Lord Jesus Christ, true God, was then
Your image like the image I see now?"—

such was I as I watched the living love 109
of him who, in this world, in contemplation,
tasted that peace. And he said: "Son of grace,

you will not come to know this joyous state 112
if your eyes only look down at the base;
but look upon the circles, look at those

that sit in a position more remote, 115
until you see upon her seat the Queen
to whom this realm is subject and devoted."

quanto lì da Beatrice la mia vista;
ma nulla mi facea, ché süa effige
non discendëa a me per mezzo mista.

"O donna in cui la mia speranza vige,          79
e che soffristi per la mia salute
in inferno lasciar le tue vestige,

di tante cose quant' i' ho vedute,          82
dal tuo podere e da la tua bontate
riconosco la grazia e la virtute.

Tu m'hai di servo tratto a libertate          85
per tutte quelle vie, per tutt' i modi
che di ciò fare avei la potestate.

La tua magnificenza in me custodi,          88
sì che l'anima mia, che fatt' hai sana,
piacente a te dal corpo si disnodi."

Così orai; e quella, sì lontana          91
come parea, sorrise e riguardommi;
poi si tornò a l'etterna fontana.

E 'l santo sene: "Acciò che tu assommi          94
perfettamente," disse, "il tuo cammino,
a che priego e amor santo mandommi,

vola con li occhi per questo giardino;          97
ché veder lui t'acconcerà lo sguardo
più al montar per lo raggio divino.

E la regina del cielo, ond' ïo ardo          100
tutto d'amor, ne farà ogne grazia,
però ch'i' sono il suo fedel Bernardo."

Qual è colui che forse di Croazia          103
viene a veder la Veronica nostra,
che per l'antica fame non sen sazia,

ma dice nel pensier, fin che si mostra:          106
"Segnor mio Iesù Cristo, Dio verace,
or fu sì fatta la sembianza vostra?";

tal era io mirando la vivace          109
carità di colui che 'n questo mondo,
contemplando, gustò di quella pace.

"Figliuol di grazia, quest' esser giocondo,"          112
cominciò elli, "non ti sarà noto,
tenendo li occhi pur qua giù al fondo;

ma guarda i cerchi infino al più remoto,          115
tanto che veggi seder la regina
cui questo regno è suddito e devoto."

I lifted up my eyes; and as, at morning,                    118
the eastern side of the horizon shows
more splendor than the side where the sun sets,

so, as if climbing with my eyes from valley                 121
to summit, I saw one part of the farthest
rank of the Rose more bright than all the rest.

And as, on earth, the point where we await                  124
the shaft that Phaethon had misguided glows
brightest, while to each side, the light shades off,

so did the peaceful oriflamme appear                        127
brightest at its midpoint, so did its flame,
on each side, taper off at equal pace.

I saw, around that midpoint, festive angels—                130
more than a thousand—with their wings outspread;
each was distinct in splendor and in skill.

And there I saw a loveliness that when                      133
it smiled at the angelic songs and games
made glad the eyes of all the other saints.

And even if my speech were rich as my                       136
imagination is, I should not try
to tell the very least of her delights.

Bernard—when he had seen my eyes intent,                    139
fixed on the object of his burning fervor—
turned his own eyes to her with such affection

that he made mine gaze still more ardently.                 142

Io levai li occhi; e come da mattina 118
la parte orïental de l'orizzonte
soverchia quella dove 'l sol declina,

    così, quasi di valle andando a monte 121
con li occhi, vidi parte ne lo stremo
vincer di lume tutta l'altra fronte.

    E come quivi ove s'aspetta il temo 124
che mal guidò Fetonte, più s'infiamma,
e quinci e quindi il lume si fa scemo,

    così quella pacifica oriafiamma 127
nel mezzo s'avvivava, e d'ogne parte
per igual modo allentava la fiamma;

    e a quel mezzo, con le penne sparte, 130
vid' io più di mille angeli festanti,
ciascun distinto di fulgore e d'arte.

    Vidi a lor giochi quivi e a lor canti 133
ridere una bellezza, che letizia
era ne li occhi a tutti li altri santi;

    e s'io avessi in dir tanta divizia 136
quanta ad imaginar, non ardirei
lo minimo tentar di sua delizia.

    Bernardo, come vide li occhi miei 139
nel caldo suo caler fissi e attenti,
li suoi con tanto affetto volse a lei,

    che ' miei di rimirar fé più ardenti. 142

OVERLEAF:
*Through Thought on Thought*

# CANTO XXXII

Though he had been absorbed in his delight,
that contemplator freely undertook
the task of teaching; and his holy words

began: "The wound that Mary closed and then          4
anointed was the wound that Eve—so lovely
at Mary's feet—had opened and had pierced.

Below her, in the seats of the third rank,           7
Rachel and Beatrice, as you see, sit.
Sarah, Rebecca, Judith, and the one

who was the great-grandmother of the singer          10
who, as he sorrowed for his sinfulness,
cried, '*Miserere mei*'—these you can see

from rank to rank as I, in moving through            13
the Rose, from petal unto petal, give
to each her name. And from the seventh rank,

just as they did within the ranks above,             16
the Hebrew women follow—ranging downward—
dividing all the tresses of the Rose.

They are the wall by which the sacred stairs         19
divide, depending on the view of Christ
with which their faith aligned. Upon one side,

there where the Rose is ripe, with all its petals,   22
are those whose faith was in the Christ to come;
and on the other side—that semicircle

whose space is broken up by vacant places—           25
sit those whose sight was set upon the Christ
who had already come. And just as on

this side, to serve as such a great partition,       28
there is the throne in glory of the Lady
of Heaven and the seats that range below it,

so, opposite, the seat of the great John—            31
who, always saintly, suffered both the desert
and martyrdom, and then two years of Hell—

*Still the Tenth Heaven: the Empyrean. The placement of the*
*blessed in the Rose. Predestination and the blessed infants.*
*Mary. The angel Gabriel. The great patricians of the Empyrean.*
*Bernard's urging of Dante to beseech Mary.*

Affetto al suo piacer, quel contemplante
libero officio di dottore assunse,
e cominciò queste parole sante:

"La piaga che Maria richiuse e unse,　　　　4
quella ch'è tanto bella da' suoi piedi
è colei che l'aperse e che la punse.

Ne l'ordine che fanno i terzi sedi,　　　　7
siede Rachel di sotto da costei
con Bëatrice, sì come tu vedi.

Sarra e Rebecca, Iudìt e colei　　　　10
che fu bisava al cantor che per doglia
del fallo disse 'Miserere mei,'

puoi tu veder così di soglia in soglia　　　　13
giù digradar, com' io ch'a proprio nome
vo per la rosa giù di foglia in foglia.

E dal settimo grado in giù, sì come　　　　16
infino ad esso, succedono Ebree,
dirimendo del fior tutte le chiome;

perché, secondo lo sguardo che fée　　　　19
la fede in Cristo, queste sono il muro
a che si parton le sacre scalee.

Da questa parte onde 'l fiore è maturo　　　　22
di tutte le sue foglie, sono assisi
quei che credettero in Cristo venturo;

da l'altra parte onde sono intercisi　　　　25
di vòti i semicirculi, si stanno
quei ch'a Cristo venuto ebber li visi.

E come quinci il glorïoso scanno　　　　28
de la donna del cielo e li altri scanni
di sotto lui cotanta cerna fanno,

così di contra quel del gran Giovanni,　　　　31
che sempre santo 'l diserto e 'l martiro
sofferse, e poi l'inferno da due anni;

serves to divide; below him sit, assigned      34
to this partition, Francis, Benedict,
and Augustine, and others, rank on rank,

down to this center of the Rose. Now see      37
how deep is God's foresight: both aspects of
the faith shall fill this garden equally.

And know that there, below the transverse row      40
that cuts across the two divisions, sit
souls who are there for merits not their own,

but—with certain conditions—others' merits;      43
for all of these are souls who left their bodies
before they had the power of true choice.

Indeed, you may perceive this by yourself—      46
their faces, childlike voices, are enough,
if you look well at them and hear them sing.

But now you doubt and, doubting, do not speak;      49
yet I shall loose that knot; I can release
you from the bonds of subtle reasoning.

Within the ample breadth of this domain,      52
no point can find its place by chance, just as
there is no place for sorrow, thirst, or hunger;

whatever you may see has been ordained      55
by everlasting law, so that the fit
of ring and finger here must be exact;

and thus these souls who have, precociously,      58
reached the true life do not, among themselves,
find places high or low without some cause.

The King through whom this kingdom finds content      61
in so much love and so much joyousness
that no desire would dare to ask for more,

creating every mind in His glad sight,      64
bestows His grace diversely, at His pleasure—
and here the fact alone must be enough.

And this is clearly and expressly noted      67
for you in Holy Scripture, in those twins
who, in their mother's womb, were moved to anger.

Thus, it is just for the celestial light      70
to grace their heads with a becoming crown,
according to the color of their hair.

Without, then, any merit in their works,      73
these infants are assigned to different ranks—
proclivity at birth, the only difference.

e sotto lui così cerner sortiro                                    34
Francesco, Benedetto e Augustino
e altri fin qua giù di giro in giro.

    Or mira l'alto proveder divino:                                37
ché l'uno e l'altro aspetto de la fede
igualmente empierà questo giardino.

    E sappi che dal grado in giù che fiede                         40
a mezzo il tratto le due discrezioni,
per nullo proprio merito si siede,

    ma per l'altrui, con certe condizioni:                         43
ché tutti questi son spiriti asciolti
prima ch'avesser vere elezïoni.

    Ben te ne puoi accorger per li volti                           46
e anche per le voci püerili,
se tu li guardi bene e se li ascolti.

    Or dubbi tu e dubitando sili;                                  49
ma io discioglierò 'l forte legame
in che ti stringon li pensier sottili.

    Dentro a l'ampiezza di questo reame                            52
casüal punto non puote aver sito,
se non come tristizia o sete o fame:

    ché per etterna legge è stabilito                              55
quantunque vedi, sì che giustamente
ci si risponde da l'anello al dito;

    e però questa festinata gente                                  58
a vera vita non è *sine causa*
intra sé qui più e meno eccellente.

    Lo rege per cui questo regno pausa                             61
in tanto amore e in tanto diletto,
che nulla volontà è di più ausa,

    le menti tutte nel suo lieto aspetto                           64
creando, a suo piacer di grazia dota
diversamente; e qui basti l'effetto.

    E ciò espresso e chiaro vi si nota                             67
ne la Scrittura santa in quei gemelli
che ne la madre ebber l'ira commota.

    Però, secondo il color d'i capelli,                            70
di cotal grazia l'altissimo lume
degnamente convien che s'incappelli.

    Dunque, sanza mercé di lor costume,                            73
locati son per gradi differenti,
sol differendo nel primiero acume.

    In early centuries, their parents' faith     76
alone, and their own innocence, sufficed
for the salvation of the children; when
    those early times had reached completion, then    79
each male child had to find, through circumcision,
the power needed by his innocent
    member; but then the age of grace arrived,    82
and without perfect baptism in Christ,
such innocence was kept below, in Limbo.
    Look now upon the face that is most like    85
the face of Christ, for only through its brightness
can you prepare your vision to see Him."
    I saw such joy rain down upon her, joy    88
carried by holy intellects created
to fly at such a height, that all which I
    had seen before did not transfix me with    91
amazement so intense, nor show to me
a semblance that was so akin to God.
    And the angelic love who had descended    94
earlier, now spread his wings before her,
singing "*Ave Maria, gratïa plena.*"
    On every side, the blessed court replied,    97
singing responses to his godly song,
so that each spirit there grew more serene.
    "O holy father—who, for me, endure    100
your being here below, leaving the sweet
place where eternal lot assigns your seat—
    who is that angel who with such delight    ·103
looks into our Queen's eyes—he who is so
enraptured that he seems to be a flame?"
    So, once again, I called upon the teaching    106
of him who drew from Mary beauty, as
the morning star draws beauty from the sun.
    And he to me: "All of the gallantry    109
and confidence that there can be in angel
or blessed soul are found in him, and we
    would have it so, for it was he who carried    112
the palm below to Mary, when God's Son
wanted to bear our flesh as His own burden.
    But follow with your eyes even as I    115
proceed to speak, and note the great patricians
of this most just and merciful empire.

Bastavasi ne' secoli recenti
con l'innocenza, per aver salute,
solamente la fede d'i parenti;

poi che le prime etadi fuor compiute,  79
convenne ai maschi a l'innocenti penne
per circuncidere acquistar virtute;

ma poi che 'l tempo de la grazia venne,  82
sanza battesmo perfetto di Cristo
tale innocenza là giù si ritenne.

Riguarda omai ne la faccia che a Cristo  85
più si somiglia, ché la sua chiarezza
sola ti può disporre a veder Cristo."

Io vidi sopra lei tanta allegrezza  88
piover, portata ne le menti sante
create a trasvolar per quella altezza,

che quantunque io avea visto davante,  91
di tanta ammirazion non mi sospese,
né mi mostrò di Dio tanto sembiante;

e quello amor che primo lì discese,  94
cantando "Ave, Maria, gratïa plena,"
dinanzi a lei le sue ali distese.

Rispuose a la divina cantilena  97
da tutte parti la beata corte,
sì ch'ogne vista sen fé più serena.

"O santo padre, che per me comporte  100
l'esser qua giù, lasciando il dolce loco
nel qual tu siedi per etterna sorte,

qual è quell' angel che con tanto gioco  103
guarda ne li occhi la nostra regina,
innamorato sì che par di foco?"

Così ricorsi ancora a la dottrina  106
di colui ch'abbelliva di Maria,
come del sole stella mattutina.

Ed elli a me: "Baldezza e leggiadria  109
quant' esser puote in angelo e in alma,
tutta è in lui; e sì volem che sia,

perch' elli è quelli che portò la palma  112
giuso a Maria, quando 'l Figliuol di Dio
carcar si volse de la nostra salma.

Ma vieni omai con li occhi sì com' io  115
andrò parlando, e nota i gran patrici
di questo imperio giustissimo e pio.

Those two who, there above, are seated, most 118
happy to be so near the Empress, may
be likened to the two roots of this Rose:
the one who, on her left, sits closest, is 121
the father whose presumptuous tasting
caused humankind to taste such bitterness;
and on the right, you see that ancient father 124
of Holy Church, into whose care the keys
of this fair flower were consigned by Christ.
And he who saw, before he died, all of 127
the troubled era of the lovely Bride—
whom lance and nails had won—sits at his side;
and at the side of Adam sits that guide 130
under whose rule the people, thankless, fickle,
and stubborn, lived on manna. Facing Peter,
Anna is seated, so content to see 133
her daughter that, as Anna sings hosannas,
she does not move her eyes. And opposite
the greatest father of a family, 136
Lucia sits, she who urged on your lady
when you bent your brows downward, to your ruin.
But time, which brings you sleep, takes flight, and now 139
we shall stop here—even as a good tailor
who cuts the garment as his cloth allows—
and turn our vision to the Primal Love, 142
that, gazing at Him, you may penetrate—
as far as that can be—His radiance.
But lest you now fall back when, even as 145
you move your wings, you think that you advance,
imploring grace, through prayer you must beseech
grace from that one who has the power to help you; 148
and do you follow me with your affection—
so may my words and your heart share one way."
And he began this holy supplication: 151

Quei due che seggon là sù più felici 118
per esser propinquissimi ad Agusta,
son d'esta rosa quasi due radici:
   colui che da sinistra le s'aggiusta 121
è 'l padre per lo cui ardito gusto
l'umana specie tanto amaro gusta;
   dal destro vedi quel padre vetusto 124
di Santa Chiesa a cui Cristo le chiavi
raccomandò di questo fior venusto.
   E quei che vide tutti i tempi gravi, 127
pria che morisse, de la bella sposa
che s'acquistò con la lancia e coi clavi,
   siede lungh' esso, e lungo l'altro posa 130
quel duca sotto cui visse di manna
la gente ingrata, mobile e retrosa.
   Di contr' a Pietro vedi sedere Anna, 133
tanto contenta di mirar sua figlia,
che non move occhio per cantare osanna;
   e contro al maggior padre di famiglia 136
siede Lucia, che mosse la tua donna
quando chinavi, a rovinar, le ciglia.
   Ma perché 'l tempo fugge che t'assonna, 139
qui farem punto, come buon sartore
che com' elli ha del panno fa la gonna;
   e drizzeremo li occhi al primo amore, 142
sì che, guardando verso lui, penètri
quant' è possibil per lo suo fulgore.
   Veramente, ne forse tu t'arretri 145
movendo l'ali tue, credendo oltrarti,
orando grazia conven che s'impetri
   grazia da quella che puote aiutarti; 148
e tu mi seguirai con l'affezione,
sì che dal dicer mio lo cor non parti."
   E cominciò questa santa orazione: 151

# CANTO XXXIII

"Virgin mother, daughter of your Son,
more humble and sublime than any creature,
fixed goal decreed from all eternity,
    you are the one who gave to human nature     4
so much nobility that its Creator
did not disdain His being made its creature.
    That love whose warmth allowed this flower to bloom   7
within the everlasting peace—was love
rekindled in your womb; for us above,
    you are the noonday torch of charity,     10
and there below, on earth, among the mortals,
you are a living spring of hope. Lady,
    you are so high, you can so intercede,     13
that he who would have grace but does not seek
your aid, may long to fly but has no wings.
    Your loving-kindness does not only answer     16
the one who asks, but it is often ready
to answer freely long before the asking.
    In you compassion is, in you is pity,     19
in you is generosity, in you
is every goodness found in any creature.
    This man—who from the deepest hollow in     22
the universe, up to this height, has seen
the lives of spirits, one by one—now pleads
    with you, through grace, to grant him so much virtue   25
that he may lift his vision higher still—
may lift it toward the ultimate salvation.
    And I, who never burned for my own vision     28
more than I burn for his, do offer you
all of my prayers—and pray that they may not
    fall short—that, with your prayers, you may disperse   31
all of the clouds of his mortality
so that the Highest Joy be his to see.

*Still the Tenth Heaven: the Empyrean. Prayer of St. Bernard to*
*the Virgin. Her acknowledgment of his prayer. Dante sees the*
*Eternal Light. The three circles of the Trinity. The mystery of*
*the Incarnation. The flashing light that fulfills Dante's vision.*
*His desire and will at one with Love.*

"Vergine Madre, figlia del tuo figlio,
umile e alta più che creatura,
termine fisso d'etterno consiglio,

tu se' colei che l'umana natura                                  4
nobilitasti sì, che 'l suo fattore
non disdegnò di farsi sua fattura.

Nel ventre tuo si raccese l'amore,                               7
per lo cui caldo ne l'etterna pace
così è germinato questo fiore.

Qui se' a noi meridïana face                                     10
di caritate, e giuso, intra ' mortali,
se' di speranza fontana vivace.

Donna, se' tanto grande e tanto vali,                            13
che qual vuol grazia e a te non ricorre,
sua disïanza vuol volar sanz' ali.

La tua benignità non pur soccorre                                16
a chi domanda, ma molte fïate
liberamente al dimandar precorre.

In te misericordia, in te pietate,                               19
in te magnificenza, in te s'aduna
quantunque in creatura è di bontate.

Or questi, che da l'infima lacuna                                22
de l'universo infin qui ha vedute
le vite spiritali ad una ad una,

supplica a te, per grazia, di virtute                            25
tanto, che possa con li occhi levarsi
più alto verso l'ultima salute.

E io, che mai per mio veder non arsi                             28
più ch'i' fo per lo suo, tutti miei preghi
ti porgo, e priego che non sieno scarsi,

perché tu ogne nube li disleghi                                  31
di sua mortalità co' prieghi tuoi,
sì che 'l sommo piacer li si dispieghi.

This, too, o Queen, who can do what you would,            34
I ask of you: that after such a vision,
his sentiments preserve their perseverance.

    May your protection curb his mortal passions.      37
See Beatrice—how many saints with her!
They join my prayers! They clasp their hands to you!"

    The eyes that are revered and loved by God,      40
now fixed upon the supplicant, showed us
how welcome such devotions are to her;

    then her eyes turned to the Eternal Light—      43
there, do not think that any creature's eye
can find its way as clearly as her sight.

    And I, who now was nearing Him who is      46
the end of all desires, as I ought,
lifted my longing to its ardent limit.

    Bernard was signaling—he smiled—to me      49
to turn my eyes on high; but I already
was doing what he wanted me to do,

    because my sight, becoming pure, was able      52
to penetrate the ray of Light more deeply—
that Light, sublime, which in Itself is true.

    From that point on, what I could see was greater      55
than speech can show: at such a sight, it fails—
and memory fails when faced with such excess.

    As one who sees within a dream, and, later,      58
the passion that had been imprinted stays,
but nothing of the rest returns to mind,

    such am I, for my vision almost fades      61
completely, yet it still distills within
my heart the sweetness that was born of it.

    So is the snow, beneath the sun, unsealed;      64
and so, on the light leaves, beneath the wind,
the oracles the Sibyl wrote were lost.

    O Highest Light, You, raised so far above      67
the minds of mortals, to my memory
give back something of Your epiphany,

    and make my tongue so powerful that I      70
may leave to people of the future one
gleam of the glory that is Yours, for by

    returning somewhat to my memory      73
and echoing awhile within these lines,
Your victory will be more understood.

Ancor ti priego, regina, che puoi       34
ciò che tu vuoli, che conservi sani,
dopo tanto veder, li affetti suoi.

  Vinca tua guardia i movimenti umani:       37
vedi Beatrice con quanti beati
per li miei prieghi ti chiudon le mani!''

  Li occhi da Dio diletti e venerati,       40
fissi ne l'orator, ne dimostraro
quanto i devoti prieghi le son grati;

  indi a l'etterno lume s'addrizzaro,       43
nel qual non si dee creder che s'invii
per creatura l'occhio tanto chiaro.

  E io ch'al fine di tutt' i disii       46
appropinquava, sì com' io dovea,
l'ardor del desiderio in me finii.

  Bernardo m'accennava, e sorridea,       49
perch' io guardassi suso; ma io era
già per me stesso tal qual ei volea:

  ché la mia vista, venendo sincera,       52
e più e più intrava per lo raggio
de l'alta luce che da sé è vera.

  Da quinci innanzi il mio veder fu maggio       55
che 'l parlar mostra, ch'a tal vista cede,
e cede la memoria a tanto oltraggio.

  Qual è colüi che sognando vede,       58
che dopo 'l sogno la passione impressa
rimane, e l'altro a la mente non riede,

  cotal son io, ché quasi tutta cessa       61
mia visïone, e ancor mi distilla
nel core il dolce che nacque da essa.

  Così la neve al sol si disigilla;       64
così al vento ne le foglie levi
si perdea la sentenza di Sibilla.

  O somma luce che tanto ti levi       67
da' concetti mortali, a la mia mente
ripresta un poco di quel che parevi,

  e fa la lingua mia tanto possente,       70
ch'una favilla sol de la tua gloria
possa lasciare a la futura gente;

  ché, per tornare alquanto a mia memoria       73
e per sonare un poco in questi versi,
più si conceperà di tua vittoria.

The living ray that I endured was so                                76
acute that I believe I should have gone
astray had my eyes turned away from it.

I can recall that I, because of this,                               79
was bolder in sustaining it until
my vision reached the Infinite Goodness.

O grace abounding, through which I presumed                         82
to set my eyes on the Eternal Light
so long that I spent all my sight on it!

In its profundity I saw—ingathered                                  85
and bound by love into one single volume—
what, in the universe, seems separate, scattered:

substances, accidents, and dispositions                            88
as if conjoined—in such a way that what
I tell is only rudimentary.

I think I saw the universal shape                                   91
which that knot takes; for, speaking this, I feel
a joy that is more ample. That one moment

brings more forgetfulness to me than twenty-                        94
five centuries have brought to the endeavor
that startled Neptune with the Argo's shadow!

So was my mind—completely rapt, intent,                             97
steadfast, and motionless—gazing; and it
grew ever more enkindled as it watched.

Whoever sees that Light is soon made such                          100
that it would be impossible for him
to set that Light aside for other sight;

because the good, the object of the will,                          103
is fully gathered in that Light; outside
that Light, what there is perfect is defective.

What little I recall is to be told,                                106
from this point on, in words more weak than those
of one whose infant tongue still bathes at the breast.

And not because more than one simple semblance                     109
was in the Living Light at which I gazed—
for It is always what It was before—

but through my sight, which as I gazed grew stronger,              112
that sole appearance, even as I altered,
seemed to be changing. In the deep and bright

essence of that exalted Light, three circles                       115
appeared to me; they had three different colors,
but all of them were of the same dimension;

Io credo, per l'acume ch'io soffersi
del vivo raggio, ch'i' sarei smarrito,
se li occhi miei da lui fossero aversi.

   E' mi ricorda ch'io fui più ardito         79
per questo a sostener, tanto ch'i' giunsi
l'aspetto mio col valore infinito.

   Oh abbondante grazia ond' io presunsi    82
ficcar lo viso per la luce etterna,
tanto che la veduta vi consunsi!

   Nel suo profondo vidi che s'interna,      85
legato con amore in un volume,
ciò che per l'universo si squaderna:

   sustanze e accidenti e lor costume       88
quasi conflati insieme, per tal modo
che ciò ch'i' dico è un semplice lume.

   La forma universal di questo nodo       91
credo ch'i' vidi, perché più di largo,
dicendo questo, mi sento ch'i' godo.

   Un punto solo m'è maggior letargo      94
che venticinque secoli a la 'mpresa
che fé Nettuno ammirar l'ombra d' Argo.

   Così la mente mia, tutta sospesa,        97
mirava fissa, immobile e attenta,
e sempre di mirar faceasi accesa.

   A quella luce cotal si diventa,         100
che volgersi da lei per altro aspetto
è impossibil che mai si consenta;

   però che 'l ben, ch'è del volere obietto,  103
tutto s'accoglie in lei, e fuor di quella
è defettivo ciò ch'è lì perfetto.

   Omai sarà più corta mia favella,       106
pur a quel ch'io ricordo, che d'un fante
che bagni ancor la lingua a la mammella.

   Non perché più ch'un semplice sembiante  109
fosse nel vivo lume ch'io mirava,
che tal è sempre qual s'era davante;

   ma per la vista che s'avvalorava      112
in me guardando, una sola parvenza,
mutandom' io, a me si travagliava.

   Ne la profonda e chiara sussistenza    115
de l'alto lume parvermi tre giri
di tre colori e d'una contenenza;

one circle seemed reflected by the second,          118
as rainbow is by rainbow, and the third
seemed fire breathed equally by those two circles.

    How incomplete is speech, how weak, when set          121
against my thought! And this, to what I saw
is such—to call it little is too much.

    Eternal Light, You only dwell within          124
Yourself, and only You know You; Self-knowing,
Self-known, You love and smile upon Yourself!

    That circle—which, begotten so, appeared          127
in You as light reflected—when my eyes
had watched it with attention for some time,

    within itself and colored like itself,          130
to me seemed painted with our effigy,
so that my sight was set on it completely.

    As the geometer intently seeks          133
to square the circle, but he cannot reach,
through thought on thought, the principle he needs,

    so I searched that strange sight: I wished to see          136
the way in which our human effigy
suited the circle and found place in it—

    and my own wings were far too weak for that.          139
But then my mind was struck by light that flashed
and, with this light, received what it had asked.

    Here force failed my high fantasy; but my          142
desire and will were moved already—like
a wheel revolving uniformly—by

    the Love that moves the sun and the other stars.          145

e l'un da l'altro come iri da iri
parea reflesso, e 'l terzo parea foco
che quinci e quindi igualmente si spiri.

Oh quanto è corto il dire e come fioco          121
al mio concetto! e questo, a quel ch'i' vidi,
è tanto, che non basta a dicer "poco."

O luce etterna che sola in te sidi,          124
sola t'intendi, e da te intelletta
e intendente te ami e arridi!

Quella circulazion che sì concetta          127
pareva in te come lume reflesso,
da li occhi miei alquanto circunspetta,

dentro da sé, del suo colore stesso,          130
mi parve pinta de la nostra effige:
per che 'l mio viso in lei tutto era messo.

Qual è 'l geomètra che tutto s'affige          133
per misurar lo cerchio, e non ritrova,
pensando, quel principio ond' elli indige,

tal era io a quella vista nova:          136
veder voleva come si convenne
l'imago al cerchio e come vi s'indova;

ma non eran da ciò le proprie penne:          139
se non che la mia mente fu percossa
da un fulgore in che sua voglia venne.

A l'alta fantasia qui mancò possa;          142
ma già volgeva il mio disio e 'l *velle*,
sì come rota ch'igualmente è mossa,

l'amor che move il sole e l'altre stelle.          145

# A NOTE ON THE DRAWINGS FOR THE CALIFORNIA DANTE

The *Paradiso* drawings began on December 13, 1983, and were completed on January 15, 1984. I began the *Purgatorio* drawings on June 18, 1981, and they were completed on August 4 of that same summer. The majority of the *Inferno* drawings were produced in July of 1979. This rapidity of execution is significant. As I noted in the afterword to *Inferno*, it produces a sense of dance and a sense of expediency. The drawings are, as Dante is, quick and laconic.

When I approached the *Inferno* in 1979, I was filled with much apprehension and some fear in the face of my predecessors. For me, the company of Botticelli and Blake, Baskin and Lebrun was awe-striking. By June 1981, when I illustrated *Purgatorio*, those early apprehensions had given way to calm, and a sense of ease. I was able to begin the *Paradiso* suite in December 1983 with a sense of confidence. The five ensuing years had nourished growth and maturity, had broadened my understanding and self-assurance, had made me more willing to venture and to risk failure. Thus, spontaneity is the first premise of my illustration scheme for *The Divine Comedy*.

The second scheme is the progression from complexity to simplicity. To that end we see a transition from the painfully scratchy and detailed drawings of *Inferno*, through the simpler, darker, and more fluid drawings of *Purgatorio*, toward the abstract drawings of *Paradiso*. Further, if one looks carefully at the California Dante, one will notice that *Inferno* often has several drawings to the page. Those crowded images are finally resolved to single images that face single images. The resolution in *Inferno* thus becomes the standard for *Purgatorio*. There, the single drawings are further resolved to a diptych form (The Triumphal Chariot of Beatrice). One drawing for two pages then becomes the standard for *Paradiso*—each opening save the very first has been conceived as a diptych.

The third premise of my illustration scheme is tonal progression. The drawings for *Inferno* are distinctly high-key; the drawings for *Purgatorio* are in the middle registers, while the drawings for *Paradiso* are distinctly low-key. They go from a pale Hell to a dark Paradise—the opposite of what is expected. There are two reasons for this.

First, the torment of the Holocaust has influenced the tonality of post-World War II illustrators of *Inferno*. That horror has been reflected in dark and brooding tones—rightfully so. However, I see the gas seeping through shower nozzles with the lights on. I hear incandescent screams of mothers. I see the blinding light of the fires of furnaces whose gaping maws ate the corpses of murdered Jews. It seems fitting to me, then, that lightness, not darkness, is the proper graphic response to the Holocaust, vis-à-vis *Inferno*. If that assumption be true, then darkness befits *Paradiso*; the great and profound quiet of dark contrasting the frightening, complex cacophony and pain of light.

Second, Paradise is full of brilliant lights that punctuate darkness: spirit-flames, the sun, the Celestial Rose. Graphically, light can be represented only by the whiteness of the paper, and then only when it is surrounded by darks. To these ends, I had to rethink my medium.

Whereas the drawings for *Inferno* and *Purgatorio* were conceived of as positive drawings (the pen and brush make black lines that are reproduced as black lines, black always equaling black, white always equaling white), the *Paradiso* drawings, in keeping with the ideas stated earlier, were conceived of as negative drawings. For the sake of coherency and unity, the *Paradiso* drawings would, of course, have to be executed in the same manner as those for *Inferno* and *Purgatorio*, using the same media, the same tools, the same paper, with the same (or an accelerated) degree of spontaneity.

Once photographed, however, the printing plates could easily be made from the photographic negatives rather than from positive prints. Black could be white, white could be black. And thus the drawings were done—invisible gestures of clear water, urgently dashed upon the paper, mingled with thick black ink—spontaneous and for the most part uncontrolled.

In most instances the abstraction of these drawings was provoking, sufficient, and correct: The Sun, The Never-Ending Light, The Celestial Rose, Through Thought on Thought. In others, a hint of subject seemed wanted and necessary. Pencil drawings and calligraphic emblems were developed as overlays to the negatives: The Pool of Light, Beatrice, The First Star, The Resurrection, The Evocation of Florence, The Saints, Jesus, Mary, and The Eye of the Eagle. The final printing plates were made by overlaying positive film from the pencil drawings with the negative film of the wash drawings.

I am, of course, aware that Dante does not pretend to see human lineaments in those spirit-flames he sees before he reaches the Empyrean. I have opted for license. These subjects are, I think, appropriately introduced by a medium heretofore unseen in the *Commedia* drawings—the graphite pencil.

It is interesting to note that the only drawing in the *Paradiso* suite that was executed *and* reproduced in the positive mode is the Crucifixion. As a result, it and the portrait of Dante are the only drawings from this suite that exist as they are seen here.

*West Hatfield, Massachusetts*                    Barry Moser
*June, 1984*

ALLEN MANDELBAUM's verse volumes are: *Chelmaxioms: The Maxims, Axioms, Maxioms of Chelm*; *Leaves of Absence*; *A Lied of Letterpress*; *Journeyman*; and the forthcoming *The Savantasse of Montparnasse*. In addition to *The Aeneid of Virgil: A Verse Translation*, a University of California Press volume for which he won a National Book Award, and the *Inferno, Purgatorio,* and *Paradiso* volumes of the California Dante, his verse translations/editions include: *Life of a Man* by Giuseppe Ungaretti; *Selected Writings of Salvatore Quasimodo*; *Selected Poems of Giuseppe Ungaretti*; and the forthcoming *Mediterranean: Selected Poems of Eugenio Montale*. The general title of his selected verse translations will be *Targuman*, with the first three volumes devoted to modern Italian, Latin, and medieval Hebrew poetry, respectively. A recipient of the Order of Merit from the Republic of Italy, Mr. Mandelbaum was in the Society of Fellows at Harvard University, a Rockefeller Fellow in Humanities, and a Fulbright Research Scholar in Italy. On leaves away from the Graduate Center of the City University of New York, where he is Professor of English and Comparative Literature, he has been Hurst Professor at Washington University in St. Louis, Honors Professor of Humanities at the University of Houston, Distinguished Professor of Humanities at the University of Colorado at Boulder, and Distinguished Visiting Scholar at Purdue University.

Born in Chattanooga in 1940, BARRY MOSER was educated at Auburn University, the University of Tennessee at Chattanooga, and the University of Massachusetts, where he did his graduate studies. His work as illustrator, designer, and printer, which includes the books of Pennyroyal Press, is represented in numerous collections, museums, and libraries in the United States and abroad, among them, the British Museum, the Library of Congress, the New York Public Library, the National Library of Australia, the London College of Printing, the Houghton Library at Harvard University, the Beinecke Library at Yale University, and the Firestone Library at Princeton University. Mr. Moser's illustrated books form a list of over sixty titles, including the Arion Press *Moby Dick*, the University of California Press edition of this translation of *The Divine Comedy*, and the Limited Editions Club of New York edition of Homer's *Odyssey*. The recent Pennyroyal *Alice's Adventures in Wonderland* was awarded the American Book Award for design/pictorial. An associate of the National Academy of Design, Mr. Moser frequently lectures and acts as visiting artist at universities and institutions across the country.

This volume of *The California Dante* was designed by Barry Moser and Czeslaw Jan Grycz. The typeface, Monotype Dante, was designed in 1957 by the late Giovanni Mardersteig and first used by him at the Officina Bodoni, Verona. The type was set by Michael and Winifred Bixler, Skaneateles, New York. The paper is Mohawk Superfine, manufactured by the Mohawk Paper Mills, Cohoes, New York. The illustrations were reproduced by the three-dot process under the supervision of Rudy Heinz and were printed with the text by the Southeastern Printing Company, Stuart, Florida.